'The Change Catalyst *is essential reading for CEOs and leaders of change. A how-to guide for accomplishing one of the most critical assignments in business – the successful instigation of sustainable change. Campbell not only explains what we should be doing, but more importantly, why and how.'*

—Martin Davis, CEO Kames Capital

'It's a rare business book where you feel like the author is sitting with you having a conversation and guiding you. Campbell gives us the ability to identify the distractions that kill most change initiatives and bring to the surface those things that truly matter. He will restore your faith that positive and lasting change is possible.'

—Sean Russo, MD Noah's Rule; Ex Rothschild
Board Member & MD Rothschild Treasury

'From the start to the end I was captivated by Campbell's easy-to-read, natural writing style. The book contains innumerable moments of insight and his nuggets of reality are spot on. He reminds us of what we need to stay focused on to really make change happen.'

—Carlos Sabugueiro, CEO ME & Africa, Copart;
Ex CEO Zurich Hong Kong & Middle East

'The Change Catalyst *is the most accessible, entertaining and insightful book on the subject I have read in many a year. Campbell possesses the rare ability to simplify complex subjects, and with his own inimitable style and humour, he gives the reader the confidence and insight they will need to achieve what most fail to deliver – successful and sustainable change.'*

—David Pitman, Global Finance Partner, Boston Consulting Group

'If you want your next change or strategy to be the 1 in 8 that succeeds; buy this book.'

—Alastair Conway, CEO James Hay Partnership

THE CHANGE CATALYST

CATALYST

SECRETS TO SUCCESSFUL
AND SUSTAINABLE BUSINESS CHANGE

CAMPBELL MACPHERSON

Library of Congress Cataloging-in-Publication Data to come

A catalogue record for this book is available from the British Library.

ISBN 978-1-119-38626-1 (pbk)
ISBN 978-1-119-38627-8 (ebk)
ISBN 978-1-119-38621-6 (ebk)

Cover Design: Wiley
Cover Image: © Simon Booth/Shutterstock

Set in 10/14.5 pt PalatinoLTStd by Thomson Digital, Noida, India
Printed in Great Britain by TJ International Ltd, Padstow, Cornwall, UK

'I am personally convinced that one person can be a change catalyst, a "transformer" in any situation, any organization. Such an individual is yeast that can leaven an entire loaf. It requires vision, initiative, patience, respect, persistence, courage and faith to be a transforming leader.'

Stephen Covey (1932–2012)

American educator, businessman,
keynote speaker and
author of one of the most successful
business books of all time;
The 7 Habits of Highly Effective People.

CONTENTS

ACKNOWLEDGEMENTS

'Why don't I write a book?' I thought. How hard could it be? I suppose this is how all new ventures begin – with the triumph of optimism over experience. But I must admit, it has been one of the most rewarding experiences of my life. Even the times spent staring at a blank screen while the cursor flashed contemptuously at me, silently deriding the presumptuousness of the entire enterprise. Luckily, the times when the words gushed forth, overwhelming my pedestrian typing skills to be honest, were far more frequent and uplifting. The whole process forced me into a very healthy period of contemplation; to re-assess all of the tools and approaches I have used over the years to help organisations change; to better understand why change fails and how people and companies can be helped to achieve successful and sustainable change.

I would first like to thank all of the people within the many organisations that I have worked with, for and occasionally against over the last quarter of a century. The leaders, managers, employees, consultants, mentors and coaches that have helped hone my understanding of the business of change. Without them, there would be no book.

I completely underestimated the effort required in proof-reading and editing. So my deep gratitude goes out to my darling wife, Jane, a great friend, Katherine Mathers, and my incredible daughter, Emily, for their tireless and thorough efforts in reading and re-reading the earliest drafts, spotting a myriad of grammatical errors, spelling mistakes and gaps in content. Thanks also to my sublime son, Charlie, who may not actually have contributed even remotely to the exercise but nevertheless excelled in his role as chief cheerleader.

However, the proof-reader of the year award must go to Carlos Sabugueiro, a wonderful friend and highly impressive CEO who, as luck would have it, was holed up with the flu in a hotel on a business trip to the US and therefore managed to read the entire manuscript over his three-day period of internment. His detailed notes were invaluable.

Thank you to the subjects of my three key case studies – Michael Gould of Anaplan, Tim Wallace of iPipeline and Michael Sheargold of The Real Estate Results Network – each of whom has not only built highly successful businesses, but has also been a catalyst for change for an entire industry. Each of them has my utmost admiration and respect as leaders, as people and for what they have achieved. Thank you for your generous time and support.

Thanks also to soon-to-be-retiring agent, Arthur Goodhart, who convinced me to start with a chapter on the inevitability of change and balance the first two key chapters. Thanks also to the fabulous Fiona Petheram who helped me review the Wiley contract.

And of course, a special thanks to the highly professional, organised and thorough team at Wiley. To Pete Gaughan of the Content Enablement team in San Francisco; Tessa Allen, Senior Production Editor in Chichester; copy-editor, Helen Heyes; Publishing Assistant, Chloe Satchell-Cobbett; and most of all, Senior Commissioning Editor, Annie Knight. Annie, thank you for your belief in the project from the outset and the enthusiasm and determination with which you championed the book and steered it so successfully through commissioning and publication. Wiley was the publisher I had always hoped would publish the book. Thank you for turning this dream into a reality.

Thanks also to James Poole, MD of the Gordon Poole Speakers' Bureau, who recommended the book proposal to Wiley in the first place. I am proud to be part of James's stable of speakers and authors.

Finally, a very special thank you to my gorgeous wife and life-long partner, Jane. You are, and always will be, the best thing that has ever happened to me. Life with a self-acclaimed Change Catalyst is rarely smooth or predictable, but it is also never dull! Janey, you are the island of sanity in my sea of change.

Thank you.

Campbell

ABOUT THE AUTHOR

 **Campbell Macpherson** has been enabling or- ganisations to instigate successful and sustain- able change for more than 25 years across the UK, Europe, US, Australia, Asia and the Mid- dle East – as an adviser, consultant, executive, Board member and in-house change leader.

Campbell believes passionately in the power of clarity and aligning people to deliver, as your people are the only ones who can deliver your strategy. What drives him is a burning desire to make a positive differ- ence to the way that organisations work, and the impact they have on their customers, employees and shareholders.

The organisations he has worked with to date include one of the world's largest Sovereign Wealth Funds, International Financial Data Systems, Aviva, Friends Life, James Hay, Cofunds, iPipeline, Centaur Media, GoCompare, International Personal Finance, BP, Zurich, Capital Radio, Telewest, Misys, BBC, Lazard, British Airways, National Mutual and the Singapore Convention Centre.

He was a Senior Adviser to one of the largest Sovereign Funds in the Middle East.

He was Strategy Director of Zurich Global Life Emerging Markets, covering Asia, the Middle East, LatAm and Central and Eastern Europe.

He was the award-winning HR Director of Sesame, the UK's largest IFA Network, having been drafted in by its parent company, Misys, to forge one company out of the five they had acquired.

He was a founder executive and Marketing Director of Virgin Wines.

He was eBusiness Director of the AMP Group covering Pearl, Virgin Direct, Henderson, Cogent and NPI. He founded a multimedia business in the 1990s and was a Senior Manager in the Change Management division of Andersen Consulting. He also flew jets (poorly) in the RAAF.

He is a strategic change adviser for many dozens of organisations via his consultancy Change & Strategy International Ltd (www .changeandstrategy.com). He has a Physics degree from Melbourne University.

Campbell lives in Oxfordshire, UK, and is married with two adult children. He divides his time between the UK, Australia and wherever his clients need him to be.

www.campbellmacpherson.co.uk

INTRODUCTION

88% of change initiatives fail.

According to a 2016 Bain & Company survey of 250 large companies,[1] only 12% of change projects achieve or exceed their projected outcomes. A further 38% produce less than half of their expected results. The final 50% 'settle for a significant dilution of results'. In other words, seven out of eight change initiatives fail.

A similar proportion of mergers and acquisitions fail. A comparable proportion of corporate strategies fail. A similar number of large IT projects fail.

While there may be some debate about the percentages, Bain isn't the only consultancy to arrive at a similar conclusion. A 2008 McKinseys survey estimated that two-thirds of change projects fail. John Kotter, in his seminal book, *Leading Change* (1996), estimated the number to be around 70%.

Several studies by several consultancies over several decades have all deduced that change is so difficult to achieve, and so fraught with obstacles, that organisations usually end up abandoning change programmes altogether or settling for significantly watered-down outcomes; wasting vast sums of money doing the former and foregoing opportunities for increased revenue, profit and shareholder value doing the latter.

Only one in eight change initiatives deliver the results they set out to achieve. Why?

There are many reasons and they are all intertwined. But from my many decades of experience assisting organisations large and small to instigate change, I have come to the conclusion that the reasons why change projects, programmes or initiatives fail can be grouped into ten key categories. This top ten is detailed in Part One of the book.

The key reason that infuses every other is the fact we humans don't like change. When it comes to change, especially in the workplace, we have an innate desire to cling on to the status quo. We find change extraordinarily difficult, even when it is good change. We fear that the new world may not be any better than today. We fear that accepting change will be tantamount to being blamed for the way we currently work. We fear that we may try and fail.

Therefore, we need help; we need someone to help take the fear away. To be encouraged to change, we need both the 'carrot' of a better tomorrow and the 'stick' of negative consequences if we stay with the status quo. Sometimes we require a 'burning platform'[2] to force us to take the leap into a new world; other times the motivation needs to be far more subtle, but it must be just as compelling.

However, rational motivation alone is not sufficient; we humans need to be motivated *emotionally* if we are to embrace any sort of change. Our pride, our ego, our sense of self-worth, our heart, our gut; these are the areas that need to be motivated if we are to proceed successfully down a new path. When it comes to engaging people in change, logic alone is simply not enough... and rarely do change programmes expend anywhere near enough time or energy providing a positive emotional reason to embrace the new world or addressing the emotional barriers to change.

You need look no further than the disastrous campaign to Remain in the EU by the then Prime Minister, David Cameron, and Chancellor, George Osborne, during last year's UK referendum. These two highly intelligent men and their teams of advisers completely ignored the fact that it is our emotions that drive our decision-making. They tried to convince people to vote 'Remain' through a mixture of logic, statistics and fear. They also completely lacked empathy, failing to understand that, for a large proportion of Britons, the 'platform' was already ablaze – too many voters felt they had nothing to lose by voting to leave the EU. These voters had been left behind by globalisation and the free movement of people across the EU and had spent eight long years reaching into their own pockets to pay for the failure of the global banking system in 2008. They needed a positive emotional reason to vote for the status quo – and none was forthcoming. Another school-boy error from the Remain camp was complacency (a common cancer that scuppers many change initiatives, as we discuss later in the book). Cameron and Co. didn't seriously consider that the UK voters would actually vote to leave – either because they honestly didn't understand what life was like for a large proportion of their constituents or they simply assumed that 'fear of the unknown' would win the day. Either way, their complacency was palpable.

In direct contrast, the 'Leave' camp, spearheaded by the opportunistic Boris Johnson, appealed directly to the emotions of many millions of voters with a brilliant slogan ('Vote Leave, Take Control'), a catchy 'Brexit' name and, most important of all, the promise of a better tomorrow outside the EU. It worked. The UK voted to leave the European Union by 52% to 48%.[3] A key reason for the win is that the Leave campaign spoke directly to voters' emotions. They acknowledged that people were already unhappy with the status quo and fearful for their future livelihoods and the future of their communities if things kept heading in the current direction. The Leave campaign also spoke directly to a significant proportion of the population's latent fear of foreigners but, more powerfully, it spoke to people's pride in their country. Boris Johnson and Co. gave the electorate the belief that Britain could stand on its own; they appealed to the nationalistic emotion that, to borrow Donald Trump's superficial but nevertheless catchy slogan, Britain could be 'Great' again.

Donald Trump made none of Cameron's mistakes. He may have made plenty of others during his divisive and yet ultimately successful election campaign, but unlike Cameron he did not suffer from complacency, he was long on emotion and he knew that a significant proportion of the population was crying out for change – any change. Trump voters could be divided into three camps: 'The Tribals' who always vote Republican and didn't have to waste one moment thinking about it. Every political party has them. 'The ABHs' (Anyone But Hillary) who loathe and distrust anything Clinton. This is a surprisingly populous group. The third group was 'The Victims'; the victims of globalisation. Like their British counterparts, these Americans have been left behind by globalisation and felt that they literally had nothing to lose. They had been continually ignored for decades by political elites of all persuasions and were ready to vote for almost anyone that they hoped could help them – as long as their surname wasn't Clinton or Bush. Hence an outsider, anti-politician has become the 45th President of the United States.

The intensity of this desire for change – any change – was so strong that the fact that Trump was not one of the political establishment outweighed all of his negatives. The fact he was a billionaire that manufactured his products in cheap-labour countries overseas rather than American factories didn't matter. The fact his Atlantic City gambling business filed for bankruptcy twice, with $1.8bn in debt[4] the first time and $500m the second time around was of no consequence. His refusal to publish his tax return was dismissed as irrelevant. The fact he showed himself to be a vengeful bully was seen as him being tough. His misogyny was ignored. His pledge to build a wall across the Mexican border and to stop Muslims coming into the country wasn't seen as racist and islamophobic; it was seen as protecting American lives and American jobs. Denying the science of climate change was not seen as pro-ignorance and profoundly dangerous for future generations of humans and countless other species of life on this planet; it was seen as anti-elitist and pro-industry.

The desire for change was that strong. And only Donald Trump and Bernie Sanders recognised it.

But back to the world of business… a 2004 study of some 50 000 employees by the US-based Corporate Executive Council showed that, when it comes to engaging employees, emotional commitment is four times more powerful than rational commitment. Four times. To convince people to change we have to appeal to their emotions.

In business, as in life, there is a 'right' reason and a 'real' reason for just about everything. This is especially pertinent when it comes to change. The 'right' reason for the change will be the one that is widely communicated. But lurking in the shadows will almost always be a 'real' reason that is not made public. When it comes to finding your people's emotional triggers, you will need to unearth the 'real' reasons behind their resistance and the 'real' things that will genuinely motivate them. This book has been designed to help you do precisely that.

The book starts with Part Zero: a discussion of the inevitability of change – highlighting some of the incredible changes we have already managed to cope with and previewing just a little of the tsunami of change that will soon be crashing down upon us.

The rest of the book is then divided into four parts.

Part One explores why 88% of change initiatives fail. If we are to have any chance of improving these odds, we must fully understand why seven out of eight change initiatives do not deliver. Another reason for starting with what could be considered to be a negative viewpoint is that we learn far more from our failures than we do from our successes.

Part Two switches into proactive mode and answers the key question on every Change Leader's lips: *'How can I ensure that my change initiative is the one in eight that succeeds?'*

The short answer to this question is: appoint a Change Catalyst – someone who is obsessed with the delivery of the outcomes the company requires, in a manner that is in tune with your corporate culture.

A Change Catalyst is different from a Project Manager. In fact, the roles are complementary. A Change Catalyst's strength lies in his/her focus on outcomes. A Project Manager's strength lies in his/her focus on process. You need both. The Change Catalyst is the yin to the Project Manager's yang. A Change Catalyst is a business person – senior enough to command the respect, confidence and total support of the leadership. A good Change Catalyst is completely aligned with the interests of the shareholders.

My advice is: find this person, trust this person and, most importantly of all, give them all the 'air cover' they need to deliver.

Your Change Catalyst will be your secret weapon to deliver any change initiative, big or small. He or she will be the special ingredient to enable your organisation not only to set a powerful strategy but also to execute it; to transform that key area of your business that is vital to your future success; to help your people embrace change, own it and deliver it.

The life of a Change Catalyst can be a rollercoaster of a ride, with ups preceding downs and wins preceding losses at a frightening pace. But it is certainly never dull. It requires passion, enthusiasm, self-motivation and an optimistic, 'can do' attitude. Emotional intelligence and empathy are mandatory, as the Change Catalyst will need to help people embrace new ways of doing things and this cannot be done without a good understanding of how and why they currently work – and what genuinely motivates them. But the most important trait in any Change Catalyst is a burning desire to make a difference; to improve the way the organisation works; to give the organisation and the people within it a better future.

Your Change Catalyst will ensure that the other nine ingredients for successful change are also present – complete clarity regarding what we are trying to achieve and why; a detailed understanding of the implications of the change; a laser-like focus on the outcomes; a change process that includes a 'pause for reflection'; clear governance and thorough planning; genuine engagement and communications; finding the emotional triggers; a strong, committed, aligned and unwavering leadership team; and the development of a change-ready culture. Part Two dedicates a chapter to each one.

Part Three of the book discusses the thorny issue of culture change, which I liken to 'teaching people to walk in the rain'.

In this section, we also explore the relatively new concept of 'Cultural Intelligence', the challenges of instigating change in a different culture, and the importance of starting any cultural transformation by understanding the way your organisation currently works – and why and how the culture has evolved.

Part Four is where we get down to the business of planning and implementing sustainable change.

Every successful change starts with strategy, which is why the first three chapters of Part Four are dedicated to setting a Vision, Mission and/or Purpose, understanding values and exploring what a good strategy looks like. We also discuss strategy execution, as even the most expensive and innovative strategy is a complete waste of time unless it can be executed. And the execution of your strategy will depend upon your greatest asset – your people. So we also explore how to design an organisation capable of delivering (and how Organisation Design is so much more than structure), how to overcome corporate complacency, what good leadership looks like, building extraordinary leadership teams and managing and developing your people. Change is personal.

Then we explore some pertinent case studies of three real-life Change Catalysts, an example of successful change and an example of spectacular failure, quite literally on a global scale. We round the section off with The Change Toolbox, which contains the main tools, models and methodologies that I have found most useful over the years. I hope you will, too.

We end our exploration with a concise summary of the entire book.

Many dozens of anecdotes and examples from organisations around the world are sprinkled liberally throughout the following pages; stories of outrageous success, of soul-searching failure and innumerable shades of grey in between. Some of the company names have been anonymised for reasons of confidentiality, but every single case study and anecdote contained in these pages, however difficult to believe a few of them may be, is wonderfully genuine.

Change is inevitable. Successful change isn't.

With the approaches outlined in this book and the appointment of a Change Catalyst, you will be able to help your people embrace the future and ensure that your next strategy, M&A or change initiative will be among the one in eight that enjoys outrageous success.

Campbell Macpherson

Notes

1. 'The What, Who and How of Delivering Results,' published February 2016.
2. A phrase coined by change consultant and author, Daryl Connor, in 1998 as he watched a news report about people jumping from a burning oil rig in the North Sea.
3. It is interesting to note that 28% of registered voters failed to vote in the UK referendum. 17.4m voted to leave, 16.1m voted to Remain and 12.9m registered voters failed to vote. The UK is now in the process of exiting the EU because of the wishes of just 38% of registered voters.
4. 'The Truth About the Rise and Fall of Donald Trump's Atlantic City Empire,' Dan McQuade, 16 August, 2015. http://www.phillymag.com/news/2015/08/16/donald-trump-atlantic-city-empire/

Part Zero

Change is Inevitable

'Change is inevitable; change is constant.'

Benjamin Disraeli[1]

Disraeli's statement is correct, but incomplete. Yes, change is inevitable. It is a fact of life that individuals, organisations and nations alike have no choice but to deal with. Those who are able to acknowledge this fact and cope with change will survive. Those who are able to seek out change and actively embrace it will thrive. And yes, change is constant in the sense that it is always present. But to complete Disraeli's statement we need to add one further critical observation – the pace of change is accelerating.

The myriad of changes our societies have undergone in the last 100 years is quite staggering. The breadth of changes that we have embraced over the last 50 years is even more impressive. The amount of change we have all adapted to in the last 20 years is quite incredible. The changes we will all have to face in the next 20 years may just blow our minds.

As individuals and as leaders, we will need to be ready.

Live long . . . and prosper?

Due to advances in clean water, nutrition, antibiotics and disease eradication during the last century, average worldwide life expectancy has sky-rocketed. Up until the 20th century, worldwide average human life expectancy had been remarkably consistent throughout the millennia of our species' existence. As recently as 1900, humans lived, on average, a mere 31 years, according to the World Health Organisation. Today, the worldwide average life expectancy is 71.4 – and this ranges from 83 in Hong Kong, Japan, Singapore, Italy and Switzerland to 49–50 in Sierra Leone, Lesotho, the Central African Republic, Swaziland and the Ivory Coast. Average life expectancy is now above 80 in the vast majority of Western countries (the US trails its peers slightly at 78.9).[2] The proportion of Americans who reach the age of 65 has tripled since 1900, from 30% to 90%.[3] Five per cent of British males now live to 96 (98 for females).[4]

But it pays to be rich. In 2016, *The New Yorker* reported that the richest 1% of American men live 15 years longer, on average, than the poorest 1% – and that the gap appears to be growing. The Brookings Institute reported that the life expectancy gap between rich and poor for people born in 1920 was just five years. For people born just 20 years later in 1940, the gap had grown to 12 years.[5] For those born in 1960 and later . . . ? The gap is surely only widening further; after all, it is well known that poor people have poorer diets, and future advances in medical science will almost inevitably favour the wealthy.

Our expanding life expectancies are already playing havoc with pension companies, many of which are now severely under-funded and desperately searching for higher and higher investment returns – not easy to come by in the low-interest-rate, low-growth world in which we currently find ourselves. I know of one pension company that has been increasing investment in life insurance companies as a hedge of sorts – with the dubious assumption that life insurers will be more profitable as people live longer.

Famine used to be the biggest killer of humans for many thousands of years. Throughout the vast majority of human existence, droughts, floods and crop diseases have been death sentences for entire communities. Without the ability to move food from one community to another when famine struck, people simply starved to death – in their millions. Today, the only time we hear of significant numbers of people dying of starvation is if they have been caught in an isolated, local war zone and aid was unable to get to them in time. We may not have eradicated malnutrition; we may not have eradicated poverty; but, generally speaking, humans don't die from famine any more. In fact, it is quite the opposite. Three times as many humans die from over-eating than from malnutrition.[6]

It is the same with disease. The 14th century's bubonic plague killed a quarter of the population of Europe. Four out of every ten English people succumbed to this horrible disease. A visit to the churchyards of countless English towns makes this terrifying statistic all too real. Entire extended families were extinguished. Villages were laid waste. But it wasn't until Europeans started to travel that the carnage really began, as they innocently exported their European bacteria and viruses to the rest of the world – with disastrous consequences. Smallpox, carried to South and Central America by the Spanish Armadas in the 16th century, decimated communities and nations. The English exported the likes of influenza, tuberculosis, syphilis, typhoid and smallpox to the Pacific, eventually killing the vast majority of the Hawaiian population and having a similar devastating effect on other island nations. Only 100 years ago, Spanish Flu infected a third of the world's population, killing between 50 and 100 million people.

But the ravaging of human societies by disease appears to be a thing of the past, thanks to immunisation, antibiotics and the fact that the world is far better organised. Around the turn of the 20th century, 200 children out of every 1000 died before they were five. Today that figure, in the West at least, is less than three.[7] We have had outbreaks of new and dangerous diseases – AIDS, Bird Flu, SARS, MERS, Ebola – but each one has been contained. Smallpox has been eradicated. Malaria may be next.

As a species, we now live long enough to die from heart disease and cancer.

But that too may be about to change.

Solving death

A relatively simple way to increase human life expectancy even further would be to wean the West off its addiction to sugar. More people die today from diabetes and sugar-fuelled cancers than those who are killed by war, crime, terrorism or suicide.[8] As Yuval Noah Harari phrased it in his excellent book *Homo Deus* (2016), 'sugar is now more dangerous than gunpowder'. Will the sugar-dependent food and drink manufacturers come to be regarded as pariahs in the same way as the tobacco industry has? Will the likes of McDonalds, Coca-Cola, Pepsi, Kelloggs and Nestlé face bans on advertising their products to children? Will they find themselves in court facing charges of knowingly fuelling obesity, diabetes and cancer? It may sound far-fetched, but the parallels between the arguments put forward by today's processed food industry and those espoused by yesterday's tobacco industry are frighteningly similar.[9]

But while removing excess sugar from our diets (and decreasing our consumption of meat[10]) will almost certainly increase life expectancy further, such increases will only be incremental.

For a quantum leap in human lifespans we will need to turn to the mysterious world of biotechnology and genetic medicine. Revolutionary advances in these fields look set to push the limits of human life expectancy well beyond its current level. Several pundits are now proclaiming that the human race may indeed be standing on the cusp of near-immortality.

The ability to grow your own organs in a lab is no longer the realm of science fiction. Artificial hearts and lungs have been a reality for some time. In the future, will artificial organs be used as temporary stop-gaps while the labs grow them for you using your own stem cells? Genetic medicine and immunotherapy will provide solutions for your own body's immune system to fight cancer without the need for the horrible intrusion of chemotherapy. This has already begun. 'Checkpoint inhibitor' drugs are being developed to free immune cells to fight cancer, and immune cells are being genetically modified to kill cancer cells. Stem cell research is being used to improve the efficacy of the latter treatment and may even enable us to change the way our cells operate; revitalising old cells and dramatically slowing down the ageing process – perhaps one day even stopping it altogether.

Has the first person who could live to 200 already been born?

But will many of these treatments be affordable to the average human? Imagine the disruption to social order if only the wealthy could afford to lengthen their lives in such a manner: a handful of Haves living for centuries surrounded by a multitude of Have-Nots living for decades.

But assuming the new treatments were affordable for everyone, imagine the number of different careers one could enjoy in such a long lifespan! Imagine the impact on demographics, insurance, pensions and youth unemployment if we didn't 'retire' until we were 200 or older. Imagine the mayhem as eight generations sit down to Christmas dinner.

Imagine the over-population of the planet that would inevitably ensue.

Science fiction or science fact? In 2013, Google launched a company called Calico,[11] of which *Time* magazine asked, 'Can Google solve death?'[12] Calico's stated mission is: 'To harness advanced technologies to increase our understanding of the biology that controls lifespan. We will use that knowledge to devise interventions that enable people to lead longer and healthier lives.'

Could death become a technical problem that needs solving rather than a biological certainty?

Gaia strikes back

Climate change will inevitably become one of the world's biggest challenges, exacerbated by the election of a small, but increasing, number of Western politicians who are climate science sceptics or deniers. And yet the science is clear. As the latest Intergovernmental Panel on Climate Change Synthesis Report (2014) points out:

1. 'Warming of the climate system is unequivocal, and since the 1950s, many of the observed changes are unprecedented. The atmosphere and ocean have warmed, the amounts of snow and ice have diminished, and sea levels have risen.' Observed surface temperature has increased by about 0.65 °C ± 0.1 °C since 1950.

2. 'Greenhouse gases' such as carbon dioxide, nitrous oxide and methane have been proven to have warming effects on the atmosphere and the ocean, hence the name.

3. Man-made greenhouse gas emissions are now higher than ever – annual emissions are around ten times what they were in 1900. In fact, they are at levels that 'are unprecedented in at least the last 800 000 years. Their effects are *extremely likely* to have been the dominant cause of the observed warming since the mid-20th century.'

4. 'Continued emission gases will cause further warming and long-lasting changes in all components of the climate system, increasing the likelihood of severe, pervasive and irreversible impacts for people and ecosystems.'

5. 'Surface temperature is projected to rise over the 21st century under all assessed emission scenarios (up to 5 degrees by 2100 depending upon the scenario). It is very likely that heat waves will occur

more often and last longer, and that extreme precipitation events will become more intense and frequent in many regions. The ocean will continue to warm and acidify, and global mean sea level to rise (between 0.3m and 1m by 2100 depending upon the scenario).'

Precisely how global warming will play out we don't know. Will it be as dramatic as a new Ice Age or will it 'only' result in rising sea levels, more frequent La Niña/El Niño super-cycles, more severe hurricanes and cyclones, more droughts and increased flooding?

Bluepeace

Will the pollution of our oceans continue? At least 8 million, and perhaps as much as 12 million, tons of plastic enter the ocean every year, according to a report published in *Science* magazine. This staggering figure may even be an underestimate as the calculations were limited to plastic coming from communities located within 31 miles of a coastline. This is likely to be a significant omission, as Europe's Danube River alone releases approximately 1700 tons of plastic into the sea every year.[13] In a one-day clean-up of beaches around the world in 2014, International Coastal Cleanup volunteers collected more than 5500 metric tons of rubbish, including more than two million cigarette butts and hundreds of thousands of food wrappers, drink bottles, bottle caps, drinking straws and plastic bags.

Large patches of the Great Barrier Reef are dying due to warmer ocean temperatures and increased acidification of the ocean from coastal run-off.

The end of the Oil Age

'The Stone Age came to an end not because we had a lack of stones, and the Oil Age will come to an end not because we have a lack of oil.'[14] The Oil Age will end when oil is no longer an expensive commodity; once long-term supply significantly exceeds long-term demand. It appears that this day may be arriving much sooner than we thought.

A little more than 100 years ago, no one knew what to do with this strange, flammable, treacle-like substance that lay buried beneath the ground. The conversion of the automobile engine to gasoline solved that problem and the world has been oil-mad ever since. Winston Churchill's conversion of the Royal Navy's fleet from coal to oil and the defeat of the Ottoman Empire in WWI resulted in a redrawing of the Middle East to protect Britain's newly found reliance on the 'black gold'. The imposition of a puppet dictator in Iran and the deal that Rockefeller's Standard Oil did with the Saudis completed the recipe for much of the turmoil in that region ever since.

Right up until the middle of 2014, the oil producers' cartel, OPEC, was firmly in control. Their influence seemed to have diminished once US shale oil reached such a peak that America realised it may not have to rely on the Middle East for oil any more. Oil was $115 a barrel in June of 2014. By January of 2016 it had dropped to $25 a barrel, and it has fluctuated between $30 and $55 ever since. Oil-producing countries are now desperately trying to transform their economies, which will, in turn, alter the economic and political landscape of the Middle East, central Asia and Latin America. The Saudi government has slashed wages, imposed taxes and has desperately formulated an ambitious plan to try to wean its economy off oil. Will it work? Either way, the consequences will be dramatic.

The USA has already started to distance itself from the region. If they don't need the oil, why do they need the hassle? As Russia and Iran move in to fill the political vacuum . . . perhaps a low oil price will be even more destabilising to the Middle East than a high oil price.

Water will be the new wealth

So, while oil may become plentiful and cheap, water is likely to become scarce and, until we work out how to manufacture it efficiently and at scale through the fusion of hydrogen and oxygen, the most highly valuable commodity of all. Future wars are unlikely to be waged covertly over oil; they are likely to be waged overtly over water.

The auto industry changes gears

It was only a hundred or so years ago that the horse-drawn carriage was in the early stages of being replaced by the automobile. By the end of the 20th century, the pollution from cars had begun to rival the 19th century pollution from coal. In the first 17 years of the 21st century, electric trains, electric buses, dramatic decreases in car emissions and increases in fuel efficiency, plus the arrival of hybrid and electric cars, have started to make a significant difference. In what seems like no time, driverless cars have moved from the pages of geeky science fiction magazines and onto our roads. It may take less than a decade for our city streets to be bumper-to-bumper with electric cars and no drivers.

The distinction between the auto industry and the tech industry is blurring rapidly.

Pocket super-computers

Thomas Watson, the founder of IBM, famously said in 1943 that 'I think there is a world market for maybe five computers.' Today, billions of us carry around more computing power in our phones than Tom Watson could ever dream of. The processor in your iPhone is more than 30 000 times faster than the computers that NASA used to put men on the moon in 1969. It is far more powerful than IBM's 'Deep Blue' super-computer that beat world champion Garry Kasparov in 1997.

It was not even 25 years ago that the Internet tiptoed out of the US military and was introduced to the world. In the mid-1990s, a few geeks then decided to put information online. The rest of us had no idea why. The Internet today is the backbone of just about everything. Very few companies would survive without it. Many of the world's largest companies only exist because of it. In 2015, the performance of just four companies was equivalent to the entire gains of the S&P 500 – Facebook, Amazon, Netflix and Google. These upstarts have disrupted entire industries: Netflix (along with Amazon Prime and Apple TV) has destroyed Blockbuster and an entire video industry; Amazon has changed the entire landscape of retailing across the Western world as all but the best prime-location shopping malls and department stores now struggle to be commercially viable; Facebook and Google have changed the world of advertising forever. Google is changing the entire world.

The democratisation of entertainment

A hundred years ago, we recited poetry around a piano. Fifty years ago, we watched tiny, grainy black-and-white television and considered it to be a miracle. Today, our ultra-high-definition televisions cover entire walls with surround sound that assaults our eardrums. We can pause live action and, even if we live to be 300, we will not have enough time to watch even a fraction of the content that is available to view. Today, anyone can be a broadcaster thanks to YouTube. The latest generation hardly watches television any more.

Fifty years ago, if we wanted to film family events, we did so using expensive film cameras and displayed them on grainy reel-to-reel projectors. Today, we either use the HD video camera on our phone or the even better one strapped to our heads/bikes/surfboard/drone.

My kids are 21 and 19. They have never experienced life without mobile phones. They have seen VHS cassettes replaced by DVDs and then disappear altogether. You want to watch a film? Stream it. They have never seen a cassette tape. They haven't bought songs for years. They pay for access to Apple Music or Spotify. As Guy Hands[15] would surely attest, the music industry has changed forever.

Instantaneous communication

A hundred years ago, one communicated through beautifully crafted letters. Fifty years ago, the telegram could be used for urgent, brief messages, but it was outrageously expensive and charged by the word.

Twenty-five years ago, facsimiles could be delivered anywhere in the world cheaply in just a few seconds. Today, we just use email or messaging apps. Electronic signatures have replaced the need to sign bits of paper. Fax machines have gone the way of the VHS player and the land line.

Thirty years ago, teenagers would hog the family phone for hours on end, and making an international call was eye-wateringly expensive. Today, everyone has a mobile phone and telecommunications companies throw in national calls for free to entice teenagers to subscribe – a service they neither value nor use as they rarely talk to one another! They don't call. They message. They WhatsApp. They Instagram. Their parents make cheap international calls or Skype for free.

The rise of the machines

Artificial intelligence still has a long way to go, but the arrival of machines that can learn and adapt was definitely heralded last year when Google's 'Deep Mind' program beat the Go world champion – a game notorious for its complexity and the number of possible moves. It is a game that requires intuition and a deep understanding of patterns rather than pure logic.

In his book, *The Singularity is Near*,[16] Ray Kurzweil, futurist, a director of engineering at Google and winner of the 1999 US National Medal of Technology and Innovation, predicted that, by 2029, 'the manufacturing, agriculture, and transportation sectors of the economy will be almost entirely automated'. It is reported that Kurzweil has made 147 predictions since 1990 – with an alleged 86% accuracy record. 2029 is only 12 years away and the process of removing humans from factories has already begun. Enhanced robotics has already started to clear factory floors of its few remaining humans, and with a massive dose of irony, China is leading the way.

At the heart of the still-new Chinese economic miracle were factories full to the rafters with cheap workers. This is changing swiftly, as the headline in the December 2015 *MIT Technology Review* declared, 'China Wants to Replace Millions of Workers with Robots'. Six months later, the *FT* gave us a snapshot of 'China's Robot Revolution' in the form of just one of many thousands of Chinese companies, a sink manufacturer called Ying Ao that makes 1500 sinks a day bound for European kitchens. The owner had to pay his staff $1200 a month, twice the average rate of pay in the rest of the Guangdong Province, due to the parlous state of his factory. So, he decided to leap-frog his local competitors with robotics. Nine robots now do the work of 140 ex-employees. 'These machines are cheaper, more precise and more reliable than people,' the owner, Chen, told the *FT*. 'I've never had a whole batch ruined by robots. I look forward to replacing more humans in future,' he added, with a wry smile (wrote the *FT* journalist).

Chen's competitors are following suit in response to Chinese President Xi Jinping's 2014 call for a 'robot revolution' that would transform first China, and then the world. If a $600 per month worker can be replaced by robots, what hope is there for the equivalent worker in the West who is currently paid five times that, or an Australian worker who was being paid up to ten times that when he/she was working in the recently defunct Australian automobile manufacturing industry?

Will this decimate the fledgling Chinese middle class before it has had a chance to really develop? One could argue that this is happening at precisely the wrong time for Chinese society, as the leaders of the world's most populous country try desperately to rebalance their economy from its current reliance on the manufacturing and exporting of products to a more balanced mix that includes domestic consumption and services. This alone is such a massive change that some Western economists doubt that such a rebalancing act is even possible. And that is before they start replacing hundreds of millions of potential consumers with robots.

Mind the gap

Will both income inequality and wealth inequality increase even further from their current parlous state? (Refer to the 'Globalisation' Case Study in Chapter 34 for more detail.) In 1965, the CEO-to-worker compensation ratio in the US was 20:1. Today, it is 300:1.[17] Wealth inequality is worse, with the top 1% possessing 40% of the US's wealth, according to President Obama's 2014 State of the Union address.

The widening gap between the Haves and the Have-Nots, further exacerbated by the response of Western leaders to the Great Recession of 2008, has already triggered political reaction in the West. Bernie Sanders's anti-Wall Street message attracted so many millions of voters in the Democrat primaries that Hillary Clinton was forced to include several of his policies within her manifesto. The most left-wing Labour leader in half a century has been elected, twice, to lead the British Labour Party. Like Sanders, Jeremy Corbyn has energised younger and older voters alike. The British Labour Party is now the biggest political party in Europe by numbers of members. In addition, 17 million British people voted to leave

Europe, feeling they had nothing to lose. Sixty-three million Americans elected President Trump for the same reason.

Will the widening wealth and income gaps trigger an increase in civil disorder? The way that police forces around the world are arming themselves, one would assume so. The widening gap between Haves and Have-Nots should raise serious questions about the way that Capitalism is both led and governed.

Political change . . . for the better?

Politically, the European Union is (finally, surely) bound to undergo fundamental change, triggered by the aftermath of the UK's departure from the club. Logic dictates that the EU will not be able to carry on indefinitely in its half-pregnant form and must either become the 'United States of Europe' with full fiscal union and one set of Eurobonds backed by one central bank, or it will shatter into its pre-2002 myriad of national currencies – returning to the day when it was predominantly a trading block. The former will require northern countries to underwrite the debts of southern nations. The latter will require the writing-off of a large proportion of several southern nations' debts and probably the dissolution of much of the European parliament. Either way, it isn't going to be pretty.

It appears as though the world is becoming a more dangerous place, fuelled and, perhaps to a large degree, caused by a 24/7 media with an increasing abrogation of responsibility for the effect of their sensationalistic reporting.

Western politics appears to be becoming more insular with every passing news bulletin, due to a combination of factors including the ill-considered implications of globalisation and an apparent rise in militant religious fundamentalism. An increasing number of politicians are deepening the latent divisions within our society; feeding on and fuelling people's in-built tribal fears and xenophobia. This is threatening to roll back economic progress, international cooperation, humanitarian aid, trade and open borders.

Trump

Sixty-three million Americans voted for change last November. Republicans now have control of the White House, the House of Representatives and the Senate. They have at least two years (until the next mid-term Congressional elections) within which to make sweeping changes with little or no opposition. I am writing this the week after the election and it seems the world can rightly expect:

- A reduction in US corporate tax rates to encourage companies to invest and make it less attractive for US multinationals to stash cash in overseas subsidiaries.

- A one-time amnesty/very low windfall tax to encourage US multi-nationals to repatriate money into the US.

- An increase in training and assistance for displaced workers – one would hope.

- A right-wing US Supreme Court for decades to come.

- A routing out of undocumented immigrant workers across the US.

- A replacement of Obamacare.

- Increased investment in US infrastructure.

- Immigration restrictions – the US Treasury may advise the new President that the cost of building a physical wall along the Mexican border will be prohibitive, but this was such a core election promise it may still proceed. We should at least expect a virtual one.

- An increase in protectionism, the winding back of NAFTA and the cessation of the Trans-Atlantic Trade and Investment Partnership and the TPP. The latter would benefit China, which was excluded from the Trans-Pacific Partnership.

- The labelling of China as a 'currency manipulator' is interesting because (a) it isn't, (b) it doesn't meet the official criteria for such a label and (c) it would not make one iota of difference anyway.

- Will Trump's vow to place a tariff on goods made in China ('something like 45%') get through the Republican-controlled houses of Congress? Most Republicans are pro-free trade as it is good for business. Trade tariffs only make imports more expensive for voters/consumers. No one wins a trade war.

- US allies leant on either to put more of their budgets into defence (and encouraged to use this to buy more American-made weaponry I assume) and/or to pay for the cost of US bases on their soil.

- An emboldened Russia and a weakened NATO.

- A relationship between Putin and Trump that should be fascinating to watch. Two larger-than-life, impetuous, proud, hothead chauvinists with nukes; what could possibly go wrong?

- An increase in US military spending. More troops, more weapons, more aircraft, more warships.

- A strengthening of the relationship with Israel, perhaps even an increase in military 'aid' – moves unlikely to decrease tensions in the region.

- A further cooling of the relationship between the US and its Middle East Muslim allies. The driving reason our countries were in the Middle East in the first place was our need for oil. With the advent of shale and fracking, the US's dependency on Arabian oil seems to have evaporated. So, why does it need to be embroiled in senseless Middle Eastern conflicts any longer? As long as a Trump-led America doesn't mind Russia and Iran asserting more influence over the region, it could leave the entire region alone to sort itself out.

However, the US needs a market for its enormous defence industry. Will it willingly leave the entire Arab arms market open for its Russian, French, British and Chinese competitors? I doubt the lobbyists in Washington would allow that to happen.

- A renegotiation of the Iran nuclear deal – fraught with unintended consequences.

Sixty-three million Americans voted for change. The change will affect us all.

Don't build it; print it

New applications for the miracle of 3D printing are being discovered daily. In August of 2016, the world's first fully functional 3D printed house was inaugurated in Dubai by His Highness Sheikh Mohammad Bin Rashid Al Maktoum, Vice-President and Prime Minister of the UAE and Ruler of Dubai. This technology has the potential to streamline manufacturing and design processes across a plethora of industries, reduce costs and create a slew of new jobs in disciplines that we are yet even to categorise properly. In doing this, 3D printing will render a larger slew of existing manufacturing jobs superfluous to requirements.

Enter the entrepreneur

In terms of our careers, the 'job for life' days are long gone. Thirty years ago, your CV needed to show stability; the fewer employers the better. Today, that would signify a lack of drive and/or talent. The US Bureau of Labor Statistics has been conducting a study to better assess US workers' job stability over time, interviewing 10 000 individuals, first surveyed in 1979, when group members were between 14 and 22 years old. So far, members of the group have held 10.8 jobs, on average, between ages 18 and 42.

Home working is predicted to rise – given the advent of the Internet and cloud computing. The impact of this on local communities will be positive, but perhaps negative on commercial real estate.

The future will see more part-time work, more contract work. Even more of us will be self-employed. A senior partner in one of the world's largest global consultancies told me that he could see the number of full-time employees in his firm shrinking by two-thirds or even more over time. 'A core group of employees employing large numbers of contractors as required' is the model he envisioned.

Change: just embrace it

And I have really only scratched the surface with all of the above. The future is shaping up to be like nothing that our species, our planet or our organisations have ever experienced. The way we work, the way our organisations work, the way our governments work will all change – and the changes will be dramatic.

So, as individuals and as leaders we have a simple choice:

1. **We can be ostriches** – shove our heads deep into the sand and pretend that change isn't going to happen. Or worse, convince ourselves that we can do nothing about it. Then, when the change comes, we – and our people – can then bask in our glorious victimhood; or . . .

2. **We can be lionesses** (male lions are just lazy) – meet the challenge, embrace the future, find the opportunities, help our people to embrace the new changes, fight to make the future a better place and do our very best to reap the rewards of the new world.

My money is on the lioness.

But before we can channel our inner lionesses, we must first fully appreciate what we are up against. We need to understand why successful change is so difficult to instigate.

We need to understand why 88% of change initiatives fail.

Notes

1. Benjamin Disraeli, 1st Earl of Beaconsfield, KG, PC, FRS (1804–1881) was a British politician and writer who twice served as Prime Minister.
2. 'UN World Population Prospects 2015', United Nations Department of Economic and Social Affairs.
3. 'A Profile of Older Americans' (2012), US Department of Health & Human Services.
4. *The Independent*, 3 May 2016 using figures from the Human Mortality Database.
5. 'What Growing Life Expectancy Gaps Mean for the Promise of Social Security', Barry P. Bosworth, Gary Burtless and Kan Zhang. Brookings Institution report, Friday, 12 February, 2016.
6. 'Obesity Killing Three Times as Many As Malnutrition', *The Telegraph*, 13 December 2012.
7. https://ourworldindata.org/child-mortality/
8. 'Global Health Observatory Data 2012', World Health Organisation via *Homo Deus*.
9. Two brilliant movies I recommend on the subject are *Fed Up* from the US and *That Sugar Film* from Australia.
10. Another excellent film on this subject is *Forks over Knives*, which explores how an organic, vegetarian diet can reverse diabetes and even shrink certain cancerous tumours.
11. www.calicolabs.com
12. *Time* magazine front cover, 30 September 2013.
13. www.nrdc.org
14. Former Saudi Oil Minister Sheik Ahmed Zaki Yamani in an interview for *The Telegraph* in 2000. In the same interview, he also said, 'Thirty years from now there will be a huge amount of oil – and no buyers. Oil will be left in the ground.'
15. Founder and chairman of Terra Firma, a UK-based Venture Capital firm which purchased EMI in 2007 for a massive £4.2bn. Citibank took the company over

in 2011 to try to recover some of the £2.5bn in loans it had made to finance the deal. Terra Firma lost its £1.75bn stake in EMI when Citi finally took over.

16. Kurtzweil, R. (2006) *The Singularity is Near*, Penguin Books.

17. Courtesy of an Economic Policy Unit Report by Alyssa Davis and Lawrence Mishel, 12 June, 2014.

Part One

Why 88% of Change Initiatives Fail

After several decades of instigating change in many dozens of organisations of all sizes – as a consultant, as an adviser and as an in-house change leader – I have come to the conclusion that there are ten main reasons why the vast majority of change initiatives fail:

1. People don't like change

2. Lack of clarity regarding what we are trying to achieve and why

3. The implications are not fully understood

4. Obsession with process over outcomes

5. Inertia

6. The project is set up to fail

7. Poor communications and disingenuous stakeholder engagement

8. We forget that emotions trump logic every time

9. A change-averse culture

10. Leadership doesn't stay the course.

All of the above are intertwined. We humans seem to be hard-wired to resist change, which means that every change initiative starts with an inherent handicap. On top of this, change leaders can be unclear about what they are aiming to achieve and why – a cast-iron guarantee that the change programme is unlikely to deliver. 'Implications' are often overlooked. Outcomes are often overshadowed by process. The power of inertia is such that it is difficult enough getting a change programme off the ground let alone diverting it when it starts to go off-track. Accountability can be unclear or the governance structure inappropriate. Communications can be far too superficial, stakeholder management can be a 'tick-the-box' exercise and we forget that people need to be motivated *emotionally* to embrace change. Sometimes, an organisation's culture can work against the adoption of new ways of working. Then, to top it all off, leadership commitment can wane, often as implementation begins.

Let us address each one of the above points in a little more detail.

Chapter 1

People
Don't Like Change

*'The world hates change, yet it is the only thing
that has brought progress.'*
Charles Kettering[1]

Source: https://www.torbenrick.eu/blog/change-management/change-management-comic-strips/

The over-riding conundrum that change leaders must continually confront is that we humans simply do not want to change.

And yet we have to.

Companies certainly have to change constantly – or there is a very real danger that they will cease to exist. Does anyone remember Netscape and its once-dominant Navigator web browser that Microsoft saw off with Internet Explorer 20 years ago?

Why change fails:

People don't like change

Lack of clarity

Implications unknown

Process over outcomes

Inertia

Set up to fail

Poor communications

Emotions trump logic

A change-averse culture

Ineffective leadership

Or PanAm, once the world's premier international airline? Polaroid? Circuit City? Borders? Blockbuster? Enron, Eastern Airlines, TWA, MCI Worldcom, Compaq, Woolworths (both the US and UK varieties), Standard Oil, Bear Stearns, Lehman Brothers, Arthur Andersen, General Foods, HMV, Kodak, Game, Clinton Cards, Jessops, Comet, Zavvi (nee Virgin Megastore), Ansett Airlines, British Leyland, Rover, NPI, Telewest, Northern Rock, RBS, BHS[2]... an infinitesimally small selection of the brands and companies that either no longer exist or are shadows of their former selves.

Corporate history is indeed littered with now defunct organisations which, once they truly recognised the reality of the situation and the seriousness of the dangers lurking ahead, were unable to change their business model in time. Complacency is the cancer that has killed many a corporation. But, as Hayden Christensen explained brilliantly in his book *The Innovator's Dilemma*,[3] complacency is a trap that befalls a significant number of market leaders. It is inordinately difficult to instigate change when things are going well.

One company that has been able to change with the times is the perennial Microsoft, still one of the top five companies in the US. It has had its fair share of flops (Zune, Windows ME, Vista, Windows Messenger, IE6, Windows Mobile...) but this small list of fumbles pales into insignificance beside the gigantic successes of MS-DOS, Windows XP, MS Office, X-Box, *et al.*

One of Bill Gates's most impressive accomplishments was the way in which he fundamentally changed the direction of the entire company in the mid-1990s. The arrival of Netscape alerted the world to the fact that the all-powerful Microsoft had missed the biggest development in computing since the PC itself – the Internet. As soon as Bill Gates recognised that he and his mighty company had been caught napping, he set about transforming Microsoft to be completely focused on the web.

The technological transformation (supported by aggressive marketing techniques that, in turn, almost brought Microsoft down) ensured that Windows and Internet Explorer were swiftly cemented as the world's de facto standards. Microsoft emerged even more powerful and more dominant than before. The clarity of vision and the determination to execute the change was one of the most impressive and successful major change initiatives that the business world has ever witnessed.

Of course, companies cannot change unless individuals do. Corporate change is the culmination of a myriad of personal changes. As individuals, we too must change continually. We need to learn, grow, adapt and improve. If we don't, the best outcome is that we will stagnate. More often than not, we will be left behind. If you are in any doubt about this, just ask any of the many millions of lower-skilled workers in the West who have been left jobless and hopeless by globalisation (an ideal case study of exceedingly poor change management on a global scale which we discuss in Chapter 34).

We humans don't like change. Why?

From my experience, fear is the main reason why people resist change: fear of failure, fear of the unknown and fear of being blamed for not changing earlier. Another strong obstacle to change is what I call 'the comfort of victimhood'. Perceiving one's self as a victim is both seductive and destructive – and it is very common.

Sometimes, the long-term gains simply don't seem to be worth the short-term pain. The last major change resistor is a lack of support – we need help to change but it is nowhere to be found, so we give up at the first hurdle.

If you want your people to embrace a new way of working, these are the demons you will need to help them confront. And it doesn't matter where they sit in your organisation – in the Board room or on the shop floor – the demons are the same for everybody.

#1 reason why people resist change: fear of failure

'Failure seldom stops you. What stops you is the fear of failure.'

Jack Lemmon[4]

Fear of failure is an extremely strong source of resistance.

Why we resist change:

Fear of failure
Fear of the unknown
Fear of blame
Victimhood
Incredible upside
Lack of assistance

We know that we need to change; we may even genuinely believe that the new world (if it arrives as promised) will be better than today. But then we pick up a damned business book and find that the odds of success are 8:1 against!

Fear of failure is a recognised condition – 'atychiphobia'.

According to that repository of sometimes dubious wisdom, Wikipedia:

'Those with atychiphobia create a direct link between the possibility of failure and competition; and in an inherently competitive society, they find that it is best to avoid the problem altogether. The person more strongly motivated to avoid failure, rather than to achieve success, tends to be more unrealistic in aspiration.

Because the modern society places so much emphasis on perfection in every aspect of life, a person with atychiphobia will often not risk trying until perfection is assured. They draw their value as an individual from their success relative to societal standards. This dynamic is most readily observed in the classroom setting, where students are forced to compete for a limited number of rewards, most often the scarcity of good grades. A restricted supply of rewards pushes student aspirations for grades and other forms of recognition beyond the capabilities of many children, with the result that they are unable to keep pace with these inappropriate goals. Such circumstances tend to force a fateful decision for countless youngsters. The child may reason, unwittingly and without recognition of the consequences, that if they cannot be sure of succeeding, then at least they can try to protect a sense of dignity by avoiding failure. In essence, the atychiphobe seeks to avoid, at whatever cost, the same experience he or she may have endured that triggered such a potent and irrational fear of failure.

Symptoms of atychiphobia can be real – shortness of breath, irregular heartbeat, diarrhea, stomach disorders, feelings of dread,... They manifest themselves when one is confronted with the possibility of failure, such as when they are asked to perform a task at which they believe they cannot be 100% successful. The individual may suffer from a breakdown, and if left unchecked, these symptoms will continue to worsen. A drop in self-confidence and loss of motivation are likely to occur, which can lead to depression. As a result, it is common to avoid situations where this confrontation may occur. However, it is this avoidance that impairs the sufferer's freedom as opportunities are lost in all aspects of life such as career and family. In addition, the inability to overcome this anxiety is, in itself, a form of failure. Achievement-oriented individuals learn... to strive for excellence, maintain optimistic expectations, and not to be readily discouraged by failure. Conversely, individuals who consistently fear failure... set goals that are too high or too low and become easily discouraged by obstacles.'

Fear of failure can stop us doing the things that we need to do to be successful – and it is not the exclusive realm of those formally diagnosed with atychiphobia.

Tennyson claimed that 'Tis better to have loved and lost than never to have loved at all.' But have you ever had your heart broken? It is horrible! *If you don't try, you can't fail. It is better to be a victim of circumstance beyond your control than a failure.* This is pure nonsense of course, but it is most compelling and the sentiments are very common and all too real.

Fear of failure is why most people don't quit their job and buy that bar in the Bahamas. Fear of failure is what keeps people in a job they hate. Fear of failure may even, weirdly, be the reason why we don't change our diet when we know we should. It is certainly why sensible executives will run a mile rather than take on accountability for large IT transformation projects.

Fear of failure also manifests itself as a fear of not being competent in the new world – fear that it requires experience that I don't have; new skills that I don't have.

As change leaders, we need to recognise this as a genuine – and common – barrier to change. Not only do we need to be on the lookout for it but we also need to prepare the ground beforehand; removing, or at least reducing, the consequences of failure. Knowing that only 12% of change projects succeed, only a committed gambler or madman would take on those odds without some sort of safety net. When it comes to change, focusing on the outcomes is paramount but there also need to be points for genuinely trying – and no recriminations if the results don't quite live up to expectations.

Otherwise, no one will ever try to change anything again.

#2 reason why people resist change: fear of the unknown

> 'The oldest and strongest emotion of mankind is fear, and the oldest and strongest kind of fear is fear of the unknown.'
>
> H. P. Lovecraft[5]

Why we resist change:

Fear of failure
Fear of the unknown
Fear of blame
Victimhood
Incredible upside
Lack of assistance

Fear of the unknown may not be a formal 'phobia' *per se* nor does it have a recognisable Latin translation (and *metus rerum ignotarum*' doesn't exactly roll off the tongue) but it is all too real. It often manifests itself as fear of the future – whether the future is tomorrow, the next year, the next ten years or the hereafter. Some psychologists use an anagram to describe the phenomenon – False Evidence Appearing Real. Being fearful of the future can cause people to anticipate bad things ahead and exaggerate both their likelihood and their importance.

As Rosabeth Kanter, Professor at Harvard Business School, said in the September 2012 *Harvard Business Review*, 'People will often prefer to remain mired in misery than to head toward the unknown'.[6]

It is a proven fact that people are far more anxious when they think something bad *might* occur than when they know something bad *will* occur. Just one example of this phenomenon is an experiment run by Maastricht University in the Netherlands, where they gave subjects a series of 20 electric shocks. Some subjects knew they would receive an intense shock every time. Others knew they would receive 17 mild shocks and 3 intense shocks, but they didn't know when the intense shocks would come. Those in the second camp were much more anxious

– sweating profusely and with faster heart rates – than those in the first group. Fear of the unknown – uncertainty about the future – is a genuine and tangible fear.

Sometimes fear of the unknown shows up in the form of its uglier cousin, xenophobia: the fear of anything foreign or, as the *Oxford English Dictionary* defines it, 'deep-rooted, irrational hatred towards foreigners'. Donald Trump's election promises to build a wall to keep Mexicans out and to stop Muslims coming to the US both feed on the xenophobic fears of many millions of US citizens. By tapping into the UK's xenophobic seam, the United Kingdom Independence Party, UKIP, 'won' the 2014 European Parliamentary elections and is now the largest UK political party in the European Parliament. The party went on to attract a massive four million votes in the 2015 UK parliamentary election. And, of course, the number one reason given for voting for 'Brexit' during the 2016 UK Referendum was to 'take back control' of the UK's borders.

Xenophobia may be 'deplorable', but it is real – and understandable. It cannot be solved with name-calling or shaming. In fact, that sort of approach will only deepen the resolve of the xenophobes – as Hillary Clinton discovered during last year's Presidential election. After describing half of Trump's supporters as a 'basket of deplorables' for being racist, xenophobic, homophobic and Islamophobic, Trump's followers were seen sporting 'I am a Deplorable' T-shirts at his rally the next day. Insulting people doesn't change their minds.[7]

The only way to combat the fear of the unknown and xenophobia is through a combination of empathy and communication. The Remain politicians displayed zero empathy with the voters on the issue of Brexit and a large proportion of the people who voted to secure the UK's borders didn't understand how the UK benefits from the free movement of people across the EU.

As change leaders, we can confront these genuine fears by first acknowledging that they are genuine, then working to make the unknown known and finally making sure we give our people a sense of safety.

We need to paint a credible picture of what the future will look like. Notice I said 'credible'. A Nirvana-esque view of the future won't convince anyone. Your people know that the new world will have cons as well as pros, so treat them like adults and clearly articulate both sides of the story. We also need to make the journey 'safe', to give them a sense that the path ahead is achievable and not so threatening.

We must treat their concerns with the respect they deserve and provide them the opportunity to vent their fears, understand the facts and genuinely believe that the future will be worth the effort they will have to expend to change.

#3 reason why people resist change: fear of blame

'Liberty means responsibility.
That is why most men dread it.'
George Bernard Shaw[8]

The fear of being blamed for not having changed earlier is also a strong source of resistance.

Why we resist change:

Fear of failure
Fear of the unknown
Fear of blame
Victimhood
Incredible upside
Lack of assistance

Nobody wants to be told, either directly or indirectly, that they are doing a bad job – or could have been doing a better job. Not only is this an understandable blow to the ego, but the fear of negative consequences is very real. The implications of having someone else uncover the fact that you may have slipped into complacency can be drastic. Rarely does this situation end well for the person involved.

Even accepting the need to review how things are done currently can imply an admission that we may not be doing things correctly; that there might be a better way. It has genuine blame attached. Why didn't we see the challenges? Why weren't we looking for improvement opportunities ourselves? When did we get so complacent?

Pointing out that the organisation lacks a clearly articulated strategy and a measurable set of objectives can beg the question of how long this has been going on and why no one has done anything about it before now.

Pointing out that the employee survey, of which the leadership is mightily proud, has significant shortcomings and there are far better options available can be met with fierce resistance from the person who manages the survey as well as the executive who is ultimately accountable for it.

Fear of blame is one of the reasons why consultants are universally feared and loathed. They descend on an organisation, armed with MBAs, sharp suits, case studies and 'proven methodologies', and the first thing they seek to do is create a 'burning platform' – via a 'current state analysis' that uncovers all the things the employees are doing poorly, the gaps in the organisation's strategy and precisely where the company falls down compared to its peer group.

Even if this is what the CEO wanted the consultants to do, the very act of conducting this 'current state analysis' creates barriers to change all over the company.

I have been guilty of this many times. For some reason, I have thought that providing the leadership with a long list of gaps and a perfectly articulated list of improvement suggestions would illicit thunderous applause, their grateful thanks and an energetic willingness to address all of the improvement opportunities by starting at the top of the list and working their way down – for the betterment of the organisation. But, strangely enough, that has rarely been the reaction. Sometimes I have forgotten the fact that, no matter how senior they may be, I am dealing with humans with all-too-human fears and drivers.

The truth (especially a consultant's cold, clinical, independent version of the truth) can hurt for the simple reason that when it comes to change, the truth often arrives accompanied by the shadowy figure of blame.

As change leaders, we have to work tirelessly to try and ensure that blame is removed from the equation as much as possible. If people genuinely believe that there will be an amnesty on blame, they will be much more open to reviewing things from a new perspective and much more receptive to new ideas.

The Practice of Shining Light

Here is a fascinating little tale of how Buddhist monks confront the whole vexed subject of accepting accountability, giving feedback and improving performance.

In the Thai Buddhist Monastery of Plum Village, each monk is asked to 'shine a light of their mindfulness on a situation'.[9]

At least once a year, every monk kneels down before his brothers and asks them to shine a light on him, meaning to tell him how they see him, to express themselves concerning his body, his feelings, his perceptions, his strengths and weaknesses. His brothers come together to provide him with the advice he needs. After having received the recommendations of his brothers, the monk prostrates deeply before them three times in thanks, and in the days that follow, he tries to practise in the light of their recommendations.

This kind of love letter from your Sangha (the Buddhist monastic community) can help you see clearly what you should and should not do; and you can do the same thing with your family, your parents or your partner. You have a need for illumination and the other person does, too. So you can say to them, 'My dear one, you must help me. I have my strengths and weaknesses, and I want you to help me to see them more clearly. I have within me positive seeds, such as hope, understanding, compassion and joy, and I try to water them every day. I would like you to recognise the presence of these seeds in me and to try to water them several times a day, too. That will be a pleasure for me, and if I blossom like a flower, that will be a pleasure for you, too.

For my part, I promise you that I will do my best to recognise and water the positive seeds in you, and I appreciate them a lot. Every time the seeds manifest, I am very happy, because at such times you are wonderful. You are so full of love and joy that I vow to water these seeds in you every day. I see as well that there are seeds of suffering in you, and I will make every effort not to water these. In that way, I will not make you suffer either.'

Imagine executive teams performing such a ritual; prostrating themselves in front of their peers who then provide them with blunt and honest feedback without insult or retribution. All those elephants in all those rooms would simply disappear. Executives would learn how to seek feedback, how to receive it and how to give it constructively, knowing that their turn to receive it was coming soon.

The clarity that would result; the improvements in the way things were done; the enhanced collaboration (once the shock of all this honesty had receded)...

Anyway, back to the real world.

#4 reason why people resist change: the comfort of victimhood

'If it's never our fault, we can't take responsibility for it. If we can't take responsibility for it, we'll always be its victim.'

Richard Bach[10]

Why don't fat people just lose weight? Why don't abused women just leave their violent husbands? Why don't people who have lost their jobs simply retrain and do something else?

Why we resist change:

Fear of failure

Fear of the unknown

Fear of blame

Victimhood

Incredible upside

Lack of assistance

Because it is not that simple.

One part of the response is that being a victim can be a source of comfort. It is false, cold comfort, but comfort nonetheless.

We all know people who are perennial victims. They are in a crummy job, they have been made redundant, they have 'big bones' or 'fat genes', their boss doesn't understand them, their friends get all the breaks, their parents didn't love/educate/discipline them sufficiently... life has dealt them a bad hand.

Victimhood can be seductive for the simple reason that it places the blame squarely onto someone or something else – your boss, the company, the system, the government, the EU, your parents, your genetics, your teachers... but it doesn't really. Victimhood is a self-induced con trick. It can become both a self-fulfilling prophecy and a downward spiral. The more we think of ourselves as a victim, the less we rate ourselves and therefore the less competent we actually become.

Many of us have found ourselves in this position from time to time. The only way out of this black hole is to recognise that you are thinking of yourself as a victim and then try to reassert some control – or at least influence – over events.

When we are in victim mode, we fool ourselves into thinking that someone else is solely responsible for our current predicament. We do not accept any of the responsibility. Let's be honest, accepting accountability for failure is tough. Acknowledging that maybe we played a small role in how events unfolded and maybe we can learn from the experience demands a degree of self-awareness that can be highly uncomfortable and is most uncommon.

When we are in victim mode, we like to search for something or someone else to blame – even when things are beyond our control. Of course, what we should be doing is summed up beautifully by Reinhold Niebuhr's wonderful 'Serenity Prayer' in which he asks to be granted *'the serenity to accept the things I cannot change, courage to change the things I can, and wisdom to know the difference.'*[11]

But perhaps worst of all, when we are in victim mode we can also fool ourselves into thinking that someone else is responsible for our future, too; that someone or something is preventing us from action. This is very dangerous – for the last thing we are, even when the chips are down, is powerless.

When instigating organisational change, we need to be fully aware that many of the people affected will descend into victim mode. They won't want to but they won't be able to help themselves. As change leaders, we need to help them clamber out of this pit – for their own sake and for the good of the organisation.

We have to help them to take ownership.

The 'Victim' Triangle

Sometimes victimhood can be a little more complex.

In 1968, Stephen Karpman, MD invented what he called 'The Drama Triangle'[12] to map 'transactions' in conflicted or drama-intense relationship situations. Sports coaches and psychologists alike have found it to be an extremely handy tool for helping teams succeed and helping individuals to pull themselves out of anxiety or depression. Many psychologists refer to it as The 'Victim' Triangle, as, no matter where a person starts out on the triangle, they all become a victim of one form or another.

It is a fascinating concept and device that can be used to help people (a) look at a situation objectively, (b) realise they are caught in a no-win situation, (c) understand the role they are playing in the drama and (d) do something about it.

Karpman defined three roles in the conflict: Persecutor (P), Rescuer (R) and Victim (V) and referred to them as the three aspects, or faces, of a relationship (or 'drama'). The roles and relationships are explained as follows.

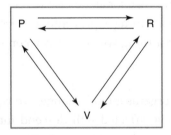

Source: Karpman, S. (1968) Fairy tales and script drama analysis. *Transactional Analysis Bulletin,* 7(26), 39–43.

The Victim in the relationship feels oppressed, helpless, hopeless, powerless, ashamed and seems unable to make decisions or solve problems. The Victim will often seek out a Persecutor. He/she will certainly look for a Rescuer to save the day – who will only serve to perpetuate the Victim's negative feelings.

The Rescuer revels in the role of 'he/she who rescues'. The rescuer's surface-level motive to boost their self-esteem by resolving the problem (and they may go to great efforts in doing so) often hides a deeper motive *not* to succeed – in order to prolong the satisfaction of being the Rescuer. They tend to keep the Victim dependent, thus giving the Victim permission to fail, feel sorry for themselves and constantly need rescuing. While the Rescuer's 'right' reason is to help the victim, their 'real' reason is often to avoid their own problems – disguised as concern for the Victim's needs.

The Persecutor within this little ménage à trois will be a combination of controlling, blaming, critical, oppressive, angry, authoritative, rigid and superior. They are also completely self-unaware; in complete denial about their blaming tactics. When it is pointed out to them, they may even argue that attack is warranted.

Participants tend to have a 'default' setting, naturally taking on the role of Victim, Rescuer or Persecutor whenever they enter into drama triangles. But even though participants each have a role with which they most identify, once on the triangle, participants can rotate through all the positions at different stages of the conflict.

Often, a drama triangle arises when a person takes on the role of Victim or Persecutor. This person then feels the need to enlist other players in the conflict. A Rescuer is often encouraged to enter the situation. These enlisted players take on roles of their own that are not static. As circumstances play out, people can change roles, sometimes frequently, in reaction to a different set of events; for example, the Victim might turn on the Rescuer and the Rescuer might switch to Persecutor in response.

As Karpman explained, the motivations for each participant and the reason the dysfunctional situation endures is that each gets their unspoken (and frequently unconscious) psychological wishes/needs met in a manner they feel to be justified, without having to acknowledge the broader dysfunctional situation. Each participant is focused on their own version of events rather than standing back and looking at what is actually going on.

Any character in this triangle can, at times, appear to be a plaintive Victim, or can switch into the role of Persecutor providing it is 'accidental', and then apologise for it.

Escaping the vicious triangle

Several escape routes have been identified – all based around helping the participants to re-frame the roles. One particularly innovative solution published by Acey Choy in the January 1990 edition of the *Transactional Analysis* journal[13] was entitled 'The Winner's Triangle'. It recommends that anyone feeling like a Victim should redefine themselves as 'vulnerable'; that anyone cast as a Persecutor should redefine themselves as 'assertive'; and anyone recruited to be a Rescuer should define their approach as 'caring'. A Victim is encouraged to accept their vulnerability as something rational. A Persecutor should be encouraged to understand and admit responsibility for their behaviour – and never to punish. A Rescuer should be encouraged to show concern and be caring, but not over-reach and problem solve for others, especially if nobody has asked for it.

Another, arguably better, solution, is called 'The Power of TED (The Empowerment Dynamic)'. Published in 2009, this approach focuses on the Victim. It recommends that the Victim adopts the alternative role of 'Creator', views the Persecutor as a 'Challenger' and enlists a 'Coach' instead of a Rescuer. I like this approach because it puts the soon-to-be-ex Victim in the driver's seat. It implicitly gives them control.

In this solution, a 'Creator' (nee 'Victim') is someone who is outcome-oriented as opposed to problem-oriented.

A 'Challenger' (nee 'Persecutor') is a person or situation that forces the Creator to clarify their needs, and focus on resolving the difference between current reality and the envisioned goal or outcome by taking incremental steps toward the outcomes they are trying to achieve.

A Coach (nee 'Rescuer') is a person who asks questions that are intended to help the individual to make informed choices. The key difference between a Rescuer and a Coach is that the Coach sees the Creator as capable of making choices and of solving their own problems.

So... be a Creator, see Persecutors as Challengers and look for a Coach. It is good advice whether you find yourself in a triangle or not.

People trapped in The Victim Triangle first need to accept they are in one. Then they need to acknowledge the roles they have been playing, the harm they are doing to themselves and the other participants and the dysfunctional effect of the entire situation. Next they need to adopt an escape strategy. Finally, they have to implement it. No one can do all of this alone. To emerge successfully from a Victim Triangle requires assistance from an external party – a manager, an occupational psychologist... or a Change Catalyst.

#5 reason why people resist change: the long-term gains don't seem to be worth the short-term pain

'The power of accurate observation is commonly called cynicism by those who have not got it.'

George Bernard Shaw

Why we resist change:

Fear of failure

Fear of the unknown

Fear of blame

Victimhood

Incredible upside

Lack of assistance

This change barrier isn't so much fear of the unknown; it is complete and utter cynicism regarding the forecast benefits of the change. It is a belief issue. It is a trust issue.

'I simply do not believe that the future will be better than the present. You well-paid leaders and over-paid consultants (or should that be the other way around?) may think your numbers add up and your new business model makes sense – but I don't believe you. I question your numbers, your assumptions, your assertions, your conclusions and the motivation behind the whole thing.'

Addressing this barrier to change requires effective communication and genuine stakeholder engagement at all levels of the organisation.

The great thing about this particular barrier is that it is at least partly based on analysis and logic (albeit with a heavy dose of cynicism) – and therefore can be addressed to some degree with analysis and logic. In fact, identifying the likely analytical cynics ahead of time and engaging them in the change process – especially the production of the business case – is the best way to reduce this change barrier.

But be careful. Rational arguments are likely to mask other irrational barriers to change – and, as we will cover in later chapters, the irrational barriers are more powerful, harder to identify and more difficult to address.

#6 reason why people resist change: we need help but it is nowhere to be found, so we give up at the first hurdle

'I asked for help, which is the hardest thing in the world.'
Marcia Wallace[14]

Our internal resistance to change is strong. If we want our people to change, we will need to help them confront the change demons: the fear of blame, the fear of failure, the comfort of victimhood, the fear of the unknown and the fear that the long-term gains don't seem to be worth the short-term pain.

> **Why we resist change:**
>
> Fear of failure
> Fear of the unknown
> Fear of blame
> Victimhood
> Incredible upside
> *Lack of assistance*

A further challenge is that rarely will people ask for help; they will just give up when it isn't forthcoming.

As change leaders, we must remember that all change, even good change, by definition means a loss of something. Even if you experience a net gain, a loss of some kind is always involved; it is a *net* gain. For example, when someone is promoted, they may receive more pay, a bigger office, more prestige; but they may also be stepping out of their comfort zone. The fear of having reached their 'Peter Plateau'[15] may be strong.

Change inevitably means taking a risk and will always involve a loss of some kind, large or small. If you want your people to embrace a change, it would help them to understand this. It would also help them to know you understand it too.

One of the many ways we went about trying to help people face change at Sesame (once the UK's largest IFA Network with 1000 employees and a turnover of £400m) was a 'Coping with Change' course. We designed a one-day course for every single person in the company that was designed purely to help them personally cope with change.

It explained the 'change curve' model and the different emotional states that we all go through when confronted with change. The model was first introduced by Swiss psychiatrist Elisabeth Kübler-Ross in her 1969 book *On Death and Dying*.

It discussed the barriers to change; the fact that change is a common part of life and illustrated the technology, social and workplace changes that everyone in the class had witnessed without blinking. The course tried to make change as normal as possible. It gave people 'permission' to be wary of change but, more importantly, the mechanisms for coping with it.

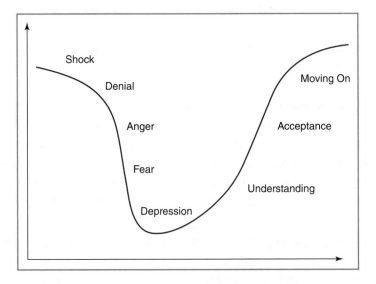

Simplified Kübler-Ross change curve

This simple workshop had a dramatic effect. I feared extreme cynicism from the participants, but the feedback we received was the exact opposite. It was incredibly well received. In fact, some of the attendees became rather emotional during some of the sessions.

And yes, it also helped us to produce the business results we needed. The course preceded a series of restructures and changes. People were able to cope with the resultant uncertainty far better than they would have without the training. Many embraced new roles and many others found the confidence to look, proactively, for new career opportunities.

Through the divestments and restructuring that followed, the size of the workforce reduced by 50% and yet, remarkably, this was done while maintaining high employee satisfaction; moving scores of employees who were 'somewhat satisfied' and upwards from 48% to over 70%. At the same time, we saw customer satisfaction scores increase from 65% to over 90%. Helping people to cope with change was a key preparation for this success.

Of course, a one-day training course cannot solve all ills. It can help, but at best it is just the beginning; merely one way of providing people with the help they need to cope with the change. Your people will also need one-on-one coaching and assistance to take ownership of their personal situation; and, as we discuss in Chapter 18, your managers will need to find the emotional triggers that will help their people to embrace the change.

'Without accepting the fact that everything changes,
we cannot find perfect composure. But unfortunately,
although it is true, it is difficult for us to accept it.
Because we cannot accept the truth of transience,
we suffer.'
Shunryu Suzuki[16]

Chapter 2

Lack of Clarity Regarding What We are Trying to Achieve and Why

'Clarity is the most important thing. If you are not clear, nothing is going to happen.'
Diane von Fürstenberg[17]

Having delved into some of the detail as to why people don't like change, let's continue our exploration of the other reasons why 88% of change initiatives fail.

Change initiatives that fail, fail to provide their people with credible answers to four key questions:

Q1: What are we trying to achieve?

Q2: What does success look like?

Q3: Why do we need to change?

Q4: What is in it for me?

Why change fails:

People don't like change

Lack of clarity

Implications unknown

Process over outcomes

Inertia

Set up to fail

Poor communications

Emotions trump logic

A change-averse culture

Ineffective leadership

Q1: 'What are we trying to achieve?'

This the most important question for every single change initiative to answer. Actually, it is the key question for any leader and any manager to ask themselves a dozen times a day. Too many change projects fail because they don't manage to clear this first and most important of hurdles, and subsequently what they are trying to achieve is:

* unclear

* unrealistic and/or

* immeasurable.

What business outcomes are we trying to deliver? What does success look like? How will we measure it? These questions need to be answered to the satisfaction of all involved – before the change leadership should even contemplate moving on to addressing 'why'.

Clarity of business outcomes

If the desired outcomes are not crystal clear, the probability of the change initiative failing is close to 100%. As the renowned NY Yankees baseball legend-cum-philosopher, Yogi Berra, said, *'If you don't know where you are going, you'll end up someplace else.'*

However, clarity is not as easy to achieve as it may sound. It requires the leadership to be honest, open and objective. It requires perseverance, continual questioning and a willingness to adapt to changing circumstances.

While it may demand significant effort, achieving clarity is the most important, and first, step on the road to success.

Let me give you an example of a terribly worded, but real-life, answer to this most fundamental of questions: 'What are we trying to achieve?'

The sentence below is a ten-year-old Mission Statement from one of the UK's largest banks:

'We will deliver our strategic vision by executing our strategic plan and we will measure progress against this plan using our key performance indicators.'

What is anyone supposed to do with that piece of committee-constructed drivel? The authors probably spent months crafting this piece of self-evident nonsense, somehow thinking it was an accurate description of what they were setting out to achieve. Let us assume that they began the process wanting to state the organisation's key business outcomes clearly. What they ended up with is a superficial and superfluous statement jam-packed with buzzwords that led nowhere.

It is beyond unclear; it is unrealistic and entirely immeasurable. It is meaningless. No wonder the UK taxpayers had to bail them out.

Point-of-Sale Software Development

I have made an executive decision to anonymise the negative case studies (of course, as noted earlier, these are usually the ones from which we can learn the most) and use the actual company names for the positive case studies.

At the point of this particular engagement, this client was one of the UK's largest financial adviser networks with more than 2000 financial advisers and £150m+ turnover.

At the time, the most important change programme for this company was the complete overhaul of its adviser technology system: the software that its financial advisers used to follow a compliant advice process; to document the clients' current financial position goals and attitude to financial risk; and to place orders for insurance and investment products that met their clients' needs. This was supposed to be quite straightforward. However, anything to do with (a) software, (b) financial advisers and (c) financial regulation is never plain sailing, a fact to which anyone in the industry will attest.

This initiative was doomed to failure from the beginning for a few key reasons. The first one was the decision to take an off-the-shelf package and modify it to such an extent that it ended up being unrecognisable, unwieldly and unsupportable. Management suffered from the all-too-common, hubristic notion that 'we are different' from our competitors. They weren't. A school-boy error, but we all seem to make it again and again. They also made the mistake of thinking that a computer system could largely replace people in a company whose business model was built on personal adviser/client relationships based on trust.

But perhaps the key reason for the interminable cost over-runs, multi-year delays and suboptimal system that resulted is that there was nowhere near enough genuine, objective discussion about precisely what the project was trying to achieve. This question was only really answered at a very high level. Yet, as always, Beelzebub was lurking in the details.

The system was being designed to be:

- A pre-sales aid

- A data collection mechanism

- A compliant advice process (or 'a patronising straightjacket' as the advisers referred to it)

- A transaction interface

- A compliance-checking tool

- A portfolio management tool and

- A customer service tool.

In setting out to achieve all of the above, it actually achieved none of them. It was slow, cumbersome, difficult to use, almost impossible to maintain and... well, a waste of money and years of effort. Obviously, it couldn't do all of these things without compromising something. What was needed was prioritisation.

What was the primary purpose of the system? If it was a data collection and pre-sales tool, then they should have focused on that to deliver an exemplary version. If the primary purpose was to force advisers through a very narrow advice process to reduce the number of post-sales complaints, first they should have questioned whether there was a better way to achieve this, and then focused the development on that.

The problem was that everything was a priority. It ended up resembling a miniature Swiss pocket knife – with a blade not quite big enough to be genuinely useful, a fairly useless pair of tiny scissors, a pretty average screwdriver, a passable corkscrew and a tool for cleaning horses' hooves that no one will ever use.

Realistic outcomes

While the outcomes need to be clear and detailed, they also need to be realistic; they need to be credible; they need to be achievable. How many IT projects end up having their scope pared back at an increasing rate of knots as the deadline approaches? Let's be honest – almost all of them. (Worse still, most software projects end up placing all of the 'de-scoped' functionality into a Phase 2 – which is rarely delivered.) Of course, as with anything to do with change, establishing realistic outcomes upfront is more of an art than a science – and it isn't easy. At the start of any change journey, everyone involved is buoyed with optimism and a sense of excitement, so it is no surprise that the expected outcomes may end up looking over-stated in the harsh daylight of hindsight. The intended outcomes will have appeared to be utterly achievable at the start of the journey and hindsight can be a cruel, clear and unfair lens through which to judge whether the intended outcomes were indeed realistic. Nevertheless, setting unrealistic outcomes is a significant reason why projects fail to deliver. 'What are we trying to achieve?' not only needs to be clear; it also needs to be credible.

The previous point-of-sale software example ticks this box, too. The proposed outcomes were completely unrealistic. No system can be asked to do all of the things that this one was originally being asked to do. The expectations were unachievable, and no one was brave enough to question this until a great deal of time and money had been wasted.

Measurable outcomes

If an outcome cannot be measured, how will anyone know if it has been achieved? I have known businesses that have never set measurable outcomes. 'Why would you have me set a target that we may not meet?' asked a senior leader once asked me rhetorically – but genuinely. I would like to think (hope?) that what this particular leader was trying to say was that an obsession with firm targets unleashes its own set of unintended consequences. Targets drive behaviours, sometimes of an unwanted variety; and targets can be wrong in hindsight. While these are all true, they are distractions; they are excuses for not setting measurable objectives, monitoring them over time to see if they are still relevant and planning for the behavioural consequences of driving the organisation to deliver them. The alternative is complacency, which, like a white ant or woodworm, will erode the organisation from the inside.

As understanding as I tried to be regarding the leader's comments, the real reason behind his aversion to measurable outcomes is that without them, no one can ever be blamed if/when they are not achieved. It is the classic consequence of a 'no accountability/no blame' culture. In such an organisation, there is little upside for accepting accountability and therefore little appetite for the sort of stark clarity that comes with measurable outcomes. In such an organisation, association with 'failed' initiatives can be career limiting. However, this sort of complacency cannot last forever. One day, such a company will need to clarify what it is trying to achieve and establish measurable outcomes for the simple reason that the Board, eventually, will be dissatisfied with where the organisation has ended up.

But when a company does set clear objectives, they must be measurable. Outcomes that are difficult to measure are disingenuous and demotivating for staff. A generic Mission Statement cries out for a goal, a target, a number... something measurable to aim for. Otherwise it is just a well-intended statement of intent rather than something that is able to be delivered.

What gets measured gets done.

Q2: 'What does success look like?'

But while metrics are critical, they are rarely sufficient on their own. To embrace the change – to deliver the change – your people need to be able to understand in some detail the sort of future they are being asked to build; and this requires a narrative.

It requires a description of what success looks like – of what the new customer experience will be like; of the new propositions that need to be developed and why; of the increased productivity and efficiency required; of the details and supporting rationale of the new investment strategy; of the benefits of the new talent development programme...

Your people need to have a mental picture of what they are being asked to achieve. It must be more than numbers. While '50% increase in sales, 50% increase in profits, 30% increase in customers and becoming #2 in the market' may all be measurable – they are hardly inspirational. Furthermore, they can be misleading.

When I was with Zurich Insurance back in 2007, as Strategy Director of the new Global Life Emerging Markets business, Zurich's Global CEO proclaimed that he wanted the organisation to become a 'Top 5 global insurer' within five years. This objective was clear and it was measurable. The organisation duly set about defining precisely what was required to achieve this transformation. From memory, Zurich was currently lying seventh in the rankings. The entire Zurich global management team from across the globe was involved in assessing territories, business lines, partners, channels, customer service and propositions. We looked at lessons we could learn from Australia and whether they could be applied elsewhere; lessons from Chile and applying them to Europe; lessons from the US and applying them to Japan...

And while we were in the middle of all this detailed analysis and planning, The Great Recession hit. AIG was bailed out by the US government and several other insurers above Zurich also took a severe hit. Suddenly, without doing anything at all, Zurich was the world's fifth largest insurer.

Zurich had not suffered the same fate as a large number of its competitors simply because it had not invested, to any significant degree at least, in Collateralised Debt Obligations, let alone Synthetic Collateralised Debt Obligations, for the humble reason that the CEO admirably admitted that he couldn't get to the bottom of how they worked and where the real risks were (if only others had been so honest). Meanwhile, the Chief Investment Officer had been gradually moving all of the General Insurance policyholders' funds out of equities and into fixed interest and cash – as he thought the entire market was over-priced and due for a massive correction. How right he was. As the world's major share indices shed 40% of their value, Zurich's GI investment team posted a 1% return in the middle of the worst financial crisis since the Great Depression.

The point of this story is that metrics alone are not enough – Zurich had changed nothing and yet it had achieved its very measurable outcomes. The organisation went on to complete its 'strategy execution' planning and I assume did its utmost to execute the plans over the ensuing years. (Or did it? Fast forward eight years... Zurich now ranks 11th in the world in terms of market capitalisation and 19th in terms of assets[18]... which shows that while clarity of outcomes is important, execution is everything. We will cover that in a later chapter.)

Q3: 'Why do we need to change?'

Clarifying what we are trying to achieve is indeed critical. But a successful change programme will need to go further than that. If we want people to embrace change and adopt new ways of working, we will need to explain why the change is necessary. Then we will have to make it relevant to each and every individual affected.

Too many change initiatives don't explain the reason for the change in enough detail or in the right manner to convince people that it is the right thing to do. Many change leaders simply assume that 'doubling turnover and profit over the next five years' is so obviously a good thing that every employee will instantly get on board. But more often than not, this is not the case. The people don't necessarily share the boss's enthusiasm – or incentive plan either, let's be honest.

The rationale for change not only needs to be clear; it also needs to be credible.

Daryl Connor coined the most used phrase in change management, 'burning platform', to describe his view that people will need a high degree of certainty that the status quo is not an option before embracing the change. This iconic concept is that the only reason one would jump off an oil rig into the pounding ocean is if the platform itself was aflame. People need the motivation to make the change.

Personally, I think this metaphor, while incredibly powerful, is too often used in a 'glass half empty' manner; i.e. we have to make the status quo so uncomfortable that even leaping into an ice-cold, tempestuous sea seems favourable in comparison. I believe that making the status quo uncomfortable is not sufficient. Being 'encouraged' to jump off a burning oil rig will not automatically mean that we will eagerly embrace the freezing cold waters of the North Sea. We may agree with the need to change, but we will be highly reluctant swimmers! As I said in the Introduction, to be encouraged to change we need both the 'carrot' of a better tomorrow and the 'stick' of negative consequences if we were to stay with the status quo – and we don't like to dwell too much on the stick. Just knowing it is there is fine. Just convincing people that the current situation is dire won't deliver long-term, sustainable change.

There is both a 'right reason' and a 'real reason' for almost everything in the world of business. This is particularly true when it comes to change.

To illustrate, let's take a look at two common change scenarios – a 'growth' strategy and a 'batten-down-the-hatches' strategy. In the case of the growth strategy (e.g. a goal to 'double revenue and profit over the next five years'), the 'real reason' may be that the new CEO has been charged with the achievement of this goal to prepare the company for sale: in order to get the best price, the Board will need to show a five-year growth story. This may not be something that the Board wants to publicise at this point in time, which is why the company will need a 'right reason' – a reason that is equally true but far more politically and publicly palatable.

Growth   In the growth scenario, the 'right' reason for the strategy may very well be to take advantage of beneficial market conditions to grow market share, thereby launching new customer propositions and enhancing customer service. This is an exciting change to get behind. It implies more people, new product development, channel development and investing in customer service. It implies training, personal growth and career opportunities. Furthermore, it implies working for the market winner.

But even when the need for change isn't good news, people still need to know *why* they are being asked to change and, even more importantly, they need to *believe* that the change is necessary.

Batten down the hatches   Now let's look at the less positive scenario... the case of a company needing to 'maintain profitability in the face of increasing competition and mounting cost pressures'. Even when it is not a gung-ho, sabre-rattling growth story, the rationale for change will still need to be made clear before people will even consider accepting the change. In fact, when the change story is 'bad news', the rationale needs to be 100% genuine. Employees can tell when bad news is being 'sugar coated' and they don't respond well to it. They respect leaders who treat their employees like adults and tell it like it is.

A 'batten-down-the-hatches' change story implies process improvements, reducing staff numbers, a focus on cost control and a search for efficiency savings. But your people will have a far better chance of accepting, perhaps even embracing, this if they are being treated fairly; if they genuinely believe that this is the reality of the market and this is the best (or perhaps 'least worst') option available.

In both the 'growth' story and the 'batten-down-the-hatches' scenario above, your people will need to believe firmly that the leadership is in control and that they are doing the best thing by the company – and its employees.

Why is the status quo not an option?

In order for someone truly to buy in to the rationale for change, it may be necessary to address the seemingly obvious question of why the current situation is not an option.

Zurich International Life

I was Strategy Director of a classic 'growth' strategy at Zurich International Life in the late Noughties. The new CEO had kicked off the strategy prior to my arrival. When he joined, the company was turning over less than $200m and he set the company an ambitious target of reaching $1 billion turnover within five years. The staff thought he was either mad or ridiculously ambitious – or both. However, within three years, the company had pushed through $500m and if the Great Recession of 2008 hadn't hit, the billion dollar mark was a genuine possibility. People were achieving things they hadn't dreamed were possible.

It was a highly successful change initiative – well led by the CEO, well managed by the executives and managers across the globe. Employee engagement was effective, the business outcome was clear, the implications were thought through by the managers themselves, action plans were in place and monitored, people were motivated and delivering. It would be churlish of me to fault it.

Apart from one little thing. And it is little, but it is also something to learn from. Upon reflection, the answer that we never addressed properly was 'Why was the status quo not an option?' The main reason we didn't spend a great deal of time contemplating this question was that we were caught up in the whole growth story ourselves – and the CEO was very much one who led from the front. But another reason (possibly the 'real' one) is we thought it was a daft question. It wasn't a question that came naturally to our personalities. Growth = good. End of story. Yet, looking back on it, this was a question that was on most people's minds and yet was never voiced openly.

Employees had just been through an intensive 'batten-down-the-hatches' phase and the vast majority of them would have preferred a period of stability if we were to be brutally honest with ourselves. Instead, we embarked upon a dozen new initiatives all at once. Sales took off, customer numbers ballooned, customer service exploded – new propositions, new territories... it was all very exciting.

I now wonder if we could perhaps have spent more time convincing them that staying with the status quo was not a viable option. As it turns out, it would have been disastrous, as during the explosive growth period that followed, our main competitors grew just as fast as we did. They too were scrambling and sprinting just to maintain market share – the market was growing that quickly. If we had taken the more sedate route, we would have lost market share, lost good people and lost customers.

But with the clarity of hindsight, one of the things we could have done, perhaps to make the change even more successful, was to acknowledge the desire for the status quo and to explain fully why this was not an option. Perhaps we could have spent more time convincing

(continued)

our people. Maybe, just maybe, if we had spent time addressing these rarely voiced concerns, we may have been able to out-pace our competitors. This is not to take the gloss off a highly successful growth story; it is just a thought to store away for future use.

Q4: 'What is in it for me?'

This is the key question your people may never voice out loud but it will be played and replayed inside their heads until they get a credible answer that they genuinely believe. *Change must not only be good for the organisation; it must also be good for me personally if I am to embrace it fully.*

Caught up in the thrill of the deal and carried away with the brilliance of our new strategy, we leaders can forget that change is often brutally unsettling for our people – even 'good' change that will deliver growth for the company and opportunities for all.

Change is personal. We must continually remind ourselves of this fact, as it is critical to our future success. As leaders, we are beholden to our people. Our future success depends entirely on their ability to deliver – and they simply won't be able to do this if they are worried about the impact of the change on them personally. We have to tackle this head-on if we wish to succeed.

Most of us have been made redundant at least once in our lives. Even when you are presented with a big fat cheque, it hurts. No matter how well the process was followed; no matter whether you have a juicy contract lined up to jump straight into, the fact that your services are no longer required is a personal blow to the solar plexus. As leaders, we must never forget this – for two reasons. Firstly, because a good leader treats people the way he or she would like to be treated themselves, and secondly, because everyone whom you haven't made redundant will be watching how well you take care of those you have had to let go. You will need the survivors to dust themselves off and deliver – and they won't do this unless you have earned their trust and respect. You will need to address their very human fear that they may be next.

Your people may reluctantly go along with the change if they think it is good for the organisation, but if you want your people genuinely to embrace the change, each one of them will need to understand how it is likely to affect them personally.

Chapter 3

The Implications are not Fully Understood

'Good intentions can often lead to unintended consequences.'

Tim Walberg[19]

'Implications' is the most forgotten word in the business lexicon.

Sir Isaac Newton's third law of motion, which states that *'for every action there is an equal and opposite reaction'*, is just as relevant to the business world.

Every new strategy produces implications for the organisation – implications for customers,

Why change fails:

People don't like change

Lack of clarity

Implications unknown

Process over outcomes

Inertia

Set up to fail

Poor communications

Emotions trump logic

A change-averse culture

Ineffective leadership

implications for shareholders, implications for employees. Yet too few strategic plans and too few change programmes fully explore these implications ahead of time. And, of course, they are critical to success; the 'law of unintended consequences' has scuppered many a good idea and rendered some of the best strategies impotent.

Many a CEO will leave 'implications' for others to think about during the execution phase – especially the big picture leaders who like to paint a vision of the future and then leave it up to the business to get on with it. But such an approach, while admirable in its desire for delegation, is fraught with danger for the simple reason that strategy cannot – or rather should never – be separated from execution.

'Strategy without execution is a daydream. Execution without strategy is a nightmare.'

I found this brilliantly pithy line in 2004 and have carried it with me ever since. I have been unable to verify its provenance and have accepted the unsubstantiated claim that it is the translation of an ancient Chinese/ Japanese proverb. Irrespective of where it originated, it is quite brilliant.

Without proper analysis of the implications of a strategy, the leader will have no idea whether that strategy is able to be implemented. Furthermore, there may be some genuine barriers to execution that should necessitate significant modification of the plan. And a strategy that cannot be implemented is a waste of time.

One approach I used to help one particularly lead-from-the-front, visionary CEO is that, once he and his Commercial Director had determined the new strategic vision, we engaged all of his management team in a detailed assessment of the implications.

The company in question was the UK's largest retail investment platform and the case study is explored in some detail in Chapter 13.

Chapter 4

An Obsession with Process over Outcomes

The operation was a complete success.
Unfortunately, the patient died…

In a previous life, I was consulting to a financial services firm in the UK and one of the first tasks I was asked to do was to assess the efficacy of the Programme Management Office (PMO). The Head of the PMO duly sent me a ream of documentation covering a range of projects and so, with a cold towel applied to my forehead and a bottomless cup of coffee, I began to plough through them.

Why change fails:

People don't like change

Lack of clarity

Implications unknown

Process over outcomes

Inertia

Set up to fail

Poor communications

Emotions trump logic

A change-averse culture

Ineffective leadership

Much to my surprise, the documentation was brilliant. The Project Summary documents were clear and concise. Just scanning them, I knew precisely what each project was setting out to achieve, why, the forecast costs, the expected benefits, the project success measures, who was accountable for what, the key implementation risks... each one was perfect. The Project Initiation Documents (PIDs) took it to another level of detail with Gantt charts, critical path analysis, stakeholder analysis, governance framework, project dependencies, a detailed timeline outlining every meeting and milestone and a sound communications plan. Why on earth did the executive team want me to look into this? It was all flawless.

I then met with the PMO Head, expecting this to be the shortest engagement in the history of consulting. She was a formidable lady; the sort of highly competent, take-no-prisoners deliverer that companies need to throw at seemingly intractable problem areas. A lesser person would have been on the aggressive side of wary in being told to meet with an external consultant who was digging around her department to find out what was going wrong. Not her. She was completely unfazed.

I started with letting her know that it was the best project documentation I had ever seen and then we took a look at each project one by one.

'OK. Let's start with this one. Outcomes, cost benefit, timetable... all clear. Makes complete sense. Where is it up to?'

'That one was cancelled six months ago,' she replied.

'Right. How about this one?'

'In the middle of implementation. Taking longer than we expected.'

'This one?'

'Didn't make it to implementation.'

Almost every project had encountered a major hiccup and delay. A large percentage had been abandoned.

'Why?' I wondered out loud.

To be honest, I cannot remember precisely what she said in reply but she was quite clear that fault lay with the leadership of the company – changing their minds, unrealistic deadlines, lack of focus, inability to prioritise (the project list was incredibly long for a company of its size).

She left and I was in a quandary. A day or so later, my interim verbal report to the CEO was that I had never seen a better organised programme office and yet very little seemed to get delivered. He grinned and said something along the lines of, 'Now you know the problem; I look forward to hearing a solution.'

I spent weeks talking to managers and project managers across the company, following each project timeline, looking at project communication emails and reviewing the prioritisation process before I eventually came to my conclusion.

The resultant report outlined a host of small improvements concerning what should be labelled as a project and what should be somebody's day job, prioritisation, reliance on too few people… but the punchline was:

'Too much focus on the process and not enough on the outcomes.'

The cart was trying to drive the horse.

The process may have been faultless, but very little was delivered. What was needed was a focus on the required outcomes and the quality and relevance of the outputs.

The formidable PMO Head had constructed such a firm process and ruled it with such a rod of iron that everyone was too busy *doing* to focus on *why* they were doing what they were doing, let alone the outcomes that needed to be delivered. Tasks were being done almost because the process said they needed to be done.

Four key actions were required:

1. Outcomes needed to be defined clearly and accountabilities needed to be clarified. There needed to be clarification of what was trying to be achieved, why and who was accountable. The accountable leader and the PMO needed to be incentivised to deliver the outcomes required.

2. The leadership needed to review the business cases and intended outcomes of each project to question openly whether they still stood up to scrutiny – or were necessary.

3. The leadership needed to prioritise objectively. It needed to stop certain projects altogether – and be clear why. It needed to put some on ice. And it needed to focus on a few projects with the biggest bang-for-the-buck and see them through to conclusion.

4. The leadership needed to appoint a senior 'Business Lead' (I was yet to think of the term 'Change Catalyst') to assist the PMO Head. This

needed to be someone who was obsessed with outcomes and genuine communications; someone who could make sure that the process existed to enable delivery of the outputs rather than the other way around; someone senior enough to help the leadership provide the guidance the PMO needed.

In my experience, most PMOs could benefit from the appointment of a 'Business Lead'; not, as is usually the case, an executive appointed to be the 'Project Director' nominally responsible for the project (but who simply doesn't have the time to dedicate to it). What is required is someone reporting to this Director who can be devoted to the task. Such an outcomes-obsessed, empathetic business person will have different skills to the ultra-organised, process-focused project manager. In my experience, it is impossible to find both sets of skills in the one individual. They are the yin and yang of change – and you need both.

So what happened in the example above? They ended up asking me to join the executive team where I learnt the invaluable lesson that dispensing advice is so much easier than implementing it! My new Board colleagues soon became sick of the terms 'outcomes', 'accountability' and 'implications'. But we managed to make some big strides in the right direction – rationalising the project list, vastly improving communications and focusing on delivering the really important things.

Which we did. It was a brilliant learning experience.

Chapter 5

Inertia

'All of a sudden, nothing happened.'[20]

*I*nitial inertia is a very common type of organisational torpor: the difficulty of moving from talk to action.

The design phases of a change initiative are challenging enough. A great deal of work is done in analysis, hypothesis testing, strategy formulation, communication, interviews, meetings, workshops, seminars and seemingly endless presentations and documents. It requires a great deal of time and energy just to get this far. Inevitably, there comes a time when the leadership needs to dedicate its energy to other things. This usually coincides with the implementation phase.

Why change fails:

People don't like change

Lack of clarity

Implications unknown

Process over outcomes

Inertia

Set up to fail

Poor communications

Emotions trump logic

A change-averse culture

Ineffective leadership

Some organisations are heavily influenced by strong personalities for whom the status quo is, and always will be, their preferred option. I have witnessed occasions when a change initiative swiftly fizzles out after the design phase – in spite of the hard work described above – because key members of the leadership found a reason either to postpone the initiative or to slow it down. And, of course, slowing it down equates to a slow death for any change programme. When it comes to successful change, maintaining the momentum of the design phase is critical.

Mid-term inertia is another common cause of failure. Trying to change course mid-stream often proves to be impossible; once the initiative is underway, no one dares to pause and assess whether the planned outcomes are still possible – or still desired.

Allow me to return to the leader I mentioned earlier who was averse to setting measurable outcomes. He is correct in his belief that one of the unintended consequences of setting measurable outcomes can be an obsession with their achievement at all costs. Not achieving them is likely to be regarded as a failure, which is often both unfair and unwise because circumstances can change. *'No battle plan survives contact with the enemy,'* proclaimed German military strategist Helmuth von Moltke (1800–1891). You can set outcomes upfront which, during the strategy and planning phase, look completely clear, realistic and measurable; yet somewhere during implementation, it becomes increasingly apparent that these outcomes are no longer realistic. They need to be questioned; they need to be changed. And this is an awfully difficult thing to do. The change train has left the station with a clear destination. Pulling it up short of that – or even, heaven forbid, changing track – would look like an admission of early failure and, quite frankly, would be unthinkable to many a leader. And yet, so often it would be the right thing to do.

Delivering change requires clarity but it also requires confidence and flexibility. Confidence to pause and objectively reflect upon the progress of the initiative; to re-assess whether the intended outcomes are (a) still achievable and (b) still desirable – and the flexibility to alter course when reality gets in the way of the plan.

Sometimes, changing course or even killing a change programme can be the best thing for the organisation, saving huge sums of money, countless unproductive man hours and many a career.

'Change happens', as Forrest Gump should have said.

Chapter 6

The Project
is Set Up to Fail

'Good managers can cause great people to fail'[21]

The 'set up to fail' syndrome is a well-documented phenomenon.

It occurs when people are put into situations in which, no matter how talented they are, they have very little chance of succeeding. This is almost never done intentionally, but it is always easy to see in hindsight that key elements of the governance structure or process were inadequate and the people were, in effect, 'set up to fail'.

Why change fails:

People don't like change

Lack of clarity

Implications unknown

Process over outcomes

Inertia

Set up to fail

Poor communications

Emotions trump logic

A change-averse culture

Ineffective leadership

Many change projects are handicapped from the very beginning with unclear and/or inappropriate governance.

I have seen change projects where it is unclear who is accountable for what and who is responsible for what.

I have seen change programmes led by steering committees too large to conduct meaningful discussion and debate; too large to arrive at considered decisions.

I have seen change projects where the ultimate decision-maker is unclear – giving the working group carte blanche to disappear down as many rabbit holes as it wishes.

I have seen change initiatives swamped by bureaucracy.

I have seen working groups so large that they have become talking shops rather than doers of the work.

Time and time again, I have seen change projects follow traditional project management methodologies to the letter, only to deliver suboptimal outcomes, if any at all.

And one of the reasons for their failure can lie in their set-up: not enough time is invested in establishing clear governance roles and decision-making processes upfront.

To have a chance of being the one in eight that succeeds, your change initiative will need:

- Clarity as to who the ultimate decision-maker is

- A small and focused Steering Committee with a clear remit and scope

- A small and focused Working Group with a clear remit and scope

- A process that is aligned to your organisation's culture

- A Project Manager to help everyone follow the process

- A Change Catalyst to ensure delivery of the outcomes you require.

These subjects are covered in detail in Part Two: The Necessary Ingredients for Successful Change.

Chapter 7

Poor Communications and Disingenuous Stakeholder Engagement

'Lack of candour, if unchecked, ultimately leads to dysfunctional environments.'

Ed Catmull, President, Pixar

The importance of effective communications cannot be over-stated, and I discuss what it means and how to do it in detail in Part Two, so here I shall be brief.

In order to be effective, communications must be genuine. Genuine communications are only possible in organisations that value openness and honesty; in organisations where facts, knowledge and insight are openly and eagerly shared; in organisations that are open and honest with their employees and promote genuine two-way dialogue.

Why change fails:

People don't like change

Lack of clarity

Implications unknown

Process over outcomes

Inertia

Set up to fail

Poor communications

Emotions trump logic

A change-averse culture

Ineffective leadership

Change projects that fail, fail to communicate effectively.

Change projects that fail, also fail to engage genuinely with their stakeholders.

Change projects that fail, fail to communicate effectively

Effective communication:

- Is a dialogue, enabling genuine understanding of the leadership and by the leadership

- Uses multiple 'channels' rather than relying solely on the 'broadcast' communications media of email and auditorium presentations. Effective communication uses workshops, focus groups, 'brown bag' lunch sessions, FAQs, intranet Q&A sessions, magazines, videos, podcasts... whatever works to ensure understanding at all levels

• Involves listening

• Questions and probes the strategy in order to provide people with the clarity they need

• Answers 'why?'

• Asks 'so what?' – to ensure clarity of the implications and the next steps

• Is tailored to meet the specific audience

• Is genuine

• Involves genuine engagement with the key stakeholders.

The organisation that fails to encourage genuine dialogue with its people – or with communications departments that are unable to enable all of the above – will never be able to deliver genuine, sustainable change.

Change projects that fail, also fail to engage genuinely with their stakeholders

At one point in my career, I was a Senior Manager within the change management division of Andersen Consulting, at the time the world's largest consulting company. AC's programme and project management methodology were intimidating. Actually, I think the official term used was 'comprehensive'. I have never seen so many chevrons. And to accompany each step of the process was a model or tool or template that spelled out in detail the process to follow. It reminded me of the 'colour by numbers' colouring-in books we all had as children – with buckets of added convolutions and complexity.

When you finally waded through the process and reached the 'Stake-holder Management' chevron, you would find several tables to guide you through the process of putting a stakeholder management plan together. I am being more than a little unfair and overly facetious. The content was excellent. It was the way it was used that often went down with clients like a lead balloon. Andersen Consulting had a reputation for hiring the brightest, most capable graduates they could get their hands on and put-ting them all through intensive training at their university campus out-side of Chicago. These intimidatingly clever and hard-working 'Androids' (as many clients came to call them) were then let loose on their clients with their shiny new frameworks to conduct, among many things, 'stake-holder management' exercises. These high-IQ but often not-as-high-EQ[22] graduates couldn't help but run this as a 'tick-the-box' exercise. It wasn't their fault. It is what they were asked to do and very few of them had ex-perience on the other side of the desk. Every form was filled in to perfec-tion but often, limited insight was gained from the interviews.

To me, it starts with the terminology. You can't 'manage' stakeholders; you have to 'engage' with them. This simple word selection is important. One implies a change that is being done *to* you, the other a change that is being done *with* you.

Chapter 8

We Forget that Emotions Trump Logic Every Time

*'Emotions are the great captains of our lives and
we obey them without realizing it.'*
Vincent Van Gogh[23]

W e think we are rational beings. We aren't. Our decisions are driven by our emotions.

Logic may indeed be the foundation of every change initiative (at least, let's hope so!) but just laying out the logical and rational reasons for the change will never, ever be enough to convince people that the change is worthwhile. In order to help someone make a decision to change, we must appeal to their emotions.

Why change fails:

People don't like change

Lack of clarity

Implications unknown

Process over outcomes

Inertia

Set up to fail

Poor communications

Emotions trump logic

A change-averse culture

Ineffective leadership

When preparing for a meeting or a negotiation, how much time do we spend gathering the facts, developing the supporting analysis and preparing the logical arguments versus understanding the motivations of those with whom we are meeting?

And yet, we all instinctively know that emotions, instinct and 'gut feel' are significant components of almost every decision we make. In fact, the ability to make decisions without possession of all the facts to hand is one of the skills admired in great leaders.

Even billion-dollar investment decisions are made, to a significant degree, on emotion. Portfolio managers are swamped with financial data and analysis about every aspect of the stock or country or sector in which they specialise. The one thing they don't have is a crystal ball. So, even with volumes of market data at their disposal, their decision must, in the end, be based on a 'feeling' – as the merit of their decision is only possible in hindsight. There is a genuine risk to every investment decision – for the simple reason that no one actually knows what will happen. Their decisions may be supported by logical analysis of the facts, but, in the end, it is their 'call'. Active investment managers talk about their 'high levels of conviction' about the investment strategy they have chosen. All this means is that they have a high level of belief. This belief may be based on facts, but, in the end, it is not 100% rational.

Incidentally, as a collective, active investment managers are pretty lousy at making good decisions. An in-depth 2016 study by Dow Jones Indices found that over the ten years up to and including 2015, 86% of European active equity funds underperformed their passive benchmark. Now, let's remind ourselves that active fund managers are paid handsomely to beat these benchmarks (otherwise, investors could just track the FTSE 100 or S&P 500 themselves at very little cost). Active fund managers charge high fees to compensate for the brilliance of their insight and decision-making. So the fact that only 14% of European active fund managers did what they were paid to do may seem rather shocking. However, compared to the US, the Europeans look pretty good. Ninety-nine per cent of US active managers underperformed their passive benchmark over the ten years prior to 2016. The figure was 97% for emerging market fund managers and 98% for global equity fund managers.

Over the five years prior to 2016, active managers have performed marginally better – 'only' 80% of European fund managers failed to beat a low-cost, passive index fund. Although 100% of Dutch fund managers failed to justify their existence over the last five years.

Economists, too, are notoriously poor at predicting future events. Their default position suffers from 'status quo bias'; they tend to assume that tomorrow will be more or less the same as today – unless, due to some unforeseen Black Swan[24] event, it isn't. Economists sit atop a long list of professions that failed to forecast the Global Financial Crisis. The fact they missed it so comprehensively has led to quite a deal of soul-searching among the profession. *'It's not just that they missed it, they positively denied that it would happen,'* exclaimed Wharton Professor of Finance, Franklin Allen.[25]

Thirteen countries went into recession during 2008. How many of these did economists predict by September of the year before? None.[26]

Forty-nine countries went into recession during 2009. How many of these did economists predict by September of the year before? None.

Many reasons have been hypothesised for this collective failure – group-think, the human tendency to extrapolate the future from the present, poor data models... but one of the reasons could very well be that economists are, by nature, incredibly logical people. 'You know, things just don't smell right' is not a phrase that will win you a Nobel Prize for Economics.

One industry that has been built around the fact that our emotions rule our decisions is the world of advertising

Strangely enough, Coca-Cola's advertising agency, McCann Erickson, decided against a logical, fact-driven approach to marketing Coca Cola. Instead, they opted for happy, sing-song, beach-loving, healthy, sociable youths supping on a Coke and loving life. A key reason why Coca Cola tastes so great and gives you such a boost (even after extract of coca leaves was removed from the original recipe) is that one can contains more sugar than a healthy person should consume in an entire day, and that the 'sugar rush' provided by these sorts of fizzy drinks is not only addictive but is one of the main causes of the obesity epidemic that has swept the Western world for the last three decades. It has also fuelled the worldwide explosion in diabetes. Of course, leading with these realities would not have sold many of their client's products, so instead McCanns appealed to our emotions.

As an aside, ironically, Coke was first marketed as a health tonic. Confederate Colonel John Pemberton, who was addicted to morphine after being wounded in the American Civil War, began a quest to find a substitute for the dangerous opiate – and so invented Coca Cola. Coke was initially sold as a patent medicine, and the first sale is recorded as having occurred at Jacob's Pharmacy in Atlanta, Georgia, on 8 May, 1886. Pemberton claimed Coca Cola cured many diseases, including morphine addiction, dyspepsia, neurasthenia, headache and impotence. He failed to add that it was also extremely good for polishing jewellery, cleaning barbecues and rotting teeth.

The Economist plays with our emotions!

Is nothing sacred in advertising? Another example of how emotions rule our decisions is how *The Economist* managed to increase the uptake of its online subscriptions and maximise revenue at the same time. The marketing department tried two separate approaches.

Approach 1

In this approach, they offered readers three choices:

1. Website only subscription for $59

2. Print-only subscription for $125

3. Print and Web subscription package for $125.

When confronted with this choice, no one went for option 2 but 84% of people chose the more expensive 'Print and Web' package (option 3).

Approach 2

They then removed the print-only option, presenting readers with a choice of just two packages:

1. Website only subscription for $59

2. Print and Web subscription package for $125.

This time, only 32% of people chose the 'Print and Web' package.

The choices were logically the same, but by playing with our emotions through the simple act of including a 'decoy' option (Approach 1), *The Economist* was almost able to triple the number of people who subscribed via the most expensive option.

Scientific evidence that emotions rule our decisions

But it isn't only during retail purchasing decisions that our hearts rule our brains – emotions play a significant part in every decision we make. In fact, scientists have proven that without emotions, we would not be able to make a decision!

World-renowned Portuguese neuroscientist, Professor Antonio Damasio,[27] discovered this to be true after a study of people with damage in the part of the brain where emotions are generated. He found that these people behaved quite normally apart from one key impairment – they were not able to feel emotions. A surprising consequence of this soon came to light – they also couldn't make decisions. They could describe what they should be doing in logical terms, yet they found it very difficult to make even simple decisions, such as what to eat. With no rational way to decide, these test subjects were unable to arrive at a decision!

Professor Damasio has written several books on this subject. His research has shown that emotions play a central role in social cognition and decision-making. His 'somatic marker hypothesis' is a scientific theory about precisely how emotions and their biological underpinnings are involved in decision-making (both positively and negatively, and often subconsciously).

All this has significant consequences for instigating sustainable change. It underscores the importance of putting ourselves in the shoes of each person who will be affected by the change. We need to understand what motivates them and we need to appreciate that all the logic in the world is likely to be insufficient to help them embrace a new way of doing things. We need to address their emotions.

Emotional commitment is four times stronger than rational commitment

As mentioned briefly in the Introduction, a 2004 study of some 50 000 employees by the Corporate Executive Council showed that, when it comes to engaging employees, emotional commitment is *four times* more powerful than rational commitment.

It is a stunning finding and a stellar report. You can find several links to the final presentation online. Here's one: http://www.usc.edu/programs/cwfl/assets/pdf/Employee%20engagement.pdf.

The study uncovered three cascading facts that have the potential to transform any organisation:

1. Companies with high employee commitment deliver two to three times the total shareholder return than companies with low employee commitment.

2. There are two types of commitment: emotional and rational. Emotional commitment was found to be four times more powerful than rational commitment. Most companies strive for rational commitment, where every employee understands the company's strategy and how their role fits within it. But this will only unlock one-fifth of their potential; if your people bound out of bed in the morning desperate to 'make a difference', they will be four times more capable of delivering outstanding results.

3. And lastly, it was discovered that the single most significant factor in creating high emotional commitment among employees was the employee's manager.

What does motivate people?

Let's build on the subject for a minute and explore what truly motivates people. While the emphasis will differ from person to person, the top six employee motivators according to Frederick Herzberg's Motivator-Hygiene Theory[28] are:

1. A sense of achievement

2. Recognition

3. Challenging and stimulating work

4. Responsibility

5. Advancement

6. Personal development.

According to Herzberg, people are not content with the satisfaction of lower-order needs at work; for example, those needs associated with minimal salary levels or safe and pleasant working conditions. Rather, people look for the gratification of higher-level psychological needs having to do with achievement, recognition, responsibility, advancement and the nature of the work itself.

This goes for everyone at work – at all levels. If we want them to be motivated, we have to address these six key areas. And, of course, this is doubly important for your people managers – we need them to be motivated so that they can, in turn, motivate their staff. Because, as we established earlier, the single most important driver of motivation, and therefore commitment, is the way people are treated by their manager. While the executive team and the Board may be responsible for setting the overall vision of the company, the managers are the only ones who can make sure people believe it, and achieve it.

They are the 'change agents' we need to harness.

Chapter 9

A Change-averse Culture

'He who rejects change is the architect of decay.'
Harold Wilson[29]

A change-averse culture is one of the most difficult change barriers to overcome. If your organisation's culture is averse to change, if your organisation's leaders are averse to change, even the best Change Catalyst doesn't stand a chance.

This aversion to change is most commonly found in large and highly successful companies that have been the dominant

Why change fails:

People don't like change

Lack of clarity

Implications unknown

Process over outcomes

Inertia

Set up to fail

Poor communications

Emotions trump logic

A change-averse culture

Ineffective leadership

player in their market for long periods of time – and, of course, in government departments where the desire to *look* busy often triumphs over the need actually to *be* busy delivering productive work.

In the case of the market leader, while at first this may appear to be counter-intuitive, it is an entirely real and understandable phenomenon. It is extraordinarily difficult to change a successful organisation, as the approach and skills that have made it successful are often the very things that can so easily blind its employees to the challenges posed by new technologies and nimbler competitors.

It takes a brave CEO indeed to turn a market leader on its head in order to react to future market forces that have yet to affect the company to any significant degree. Bill Gates did this at Microsoft in the 1990s but this is one of very few examples. Hayden Christensen clearly articulated the challenge in his brilliant book *The Innovator's Dilemma*, and I have dedicated Chapter 30 to the challenge of overcoming complacency.

Linking everyone's pay to the achievement of the organisation's objectives will certainly influence the way your people deliver your strategy. Another major influence will be the way the leadership behaves. Leaders must lead by example. They must embrace the change. They must encourage their people to challenge the status quo. They must enable their people to be 'change-ready'.

In fact, establishing a 'change-ready' culture is one of the ten ingredients of successful change. We discuss it in detail in Chapter 20.

Chapter 10

The Leadership Doesn't Stay the Course

'And it ought to be remembered that there is nothing more difficult to take in hand, more perilous to conduct, or more uncertain in its success, than to take the lead in the introduction of a new order of things.'

Niccolo Machiavelli[30]

Source: https://www.torbenrick.eu/blog/change-management/change-management-comic-strips/

By now, you have probably deduced that the reason why 88% of change initiatives fail can really be summed up in two words: 'The Leadership'.

The leadership fails to provide clarity about what needs to be achieved and why. The leadership doesn't fully understand the implications of the change. The leadership fails to create a culture where inertia can be overcome. The leadership

Why change fails:

People don't like change

Lack of clarity

Implications unknown

Process over outcomes

Inertia

Set up to fail

Poor communications

Emotions trump logic

A change-averse culture

Ineffective leadership

allows process to rule outcomes. The leadership inadvertently sets the project up to fail.

And here we are at Reason #10 and guess what? It's the leadership's fault again. This time it is because they don't stay the course. The company's leaders cannot take their eyes off the end goal for one minute. If they do, the change initiative will wither and die – like a flower deprived of sun.

Change is tough. I think we have established that. The forces against success are numerous and unrelenting. At the first sign of a diminishing of commitment by senior leadership; at the first sign that the executive team may not be 100% aligned; the forces against change, like a Hogwarts Dementor, will infiltrate this chink in the armour and the momentum for change will start to wane.

There are three key moments when the leadership needs to resist the temptation to have second thoughts:

1. As soon as each layer of management engages in exploring the implications of the new plan. For the wavering leader, this can be difficult as they watch the challenges to their perfect plan being aired so freely.

2. Once the implementation phase begins. Feeling that their job is done, they can hand over the execution of the plan to their underlings and simply look forward to the monthly progress reports.

3. At the first sign that the implementation is starting to hit some real problems that look like affecting cost, timeline and/or outputs.

At each of these phases, the leadership needs to stay strong and stay committed. The leadership needs to be visible throughout the rest of the implementation phase as well.

This is not to say that the leadership shouldn't review what it is trying to achieve and how – this is healthy (and rare, as discussed). It just cannot give up. It cannot turn its attention elsewhere for too long. It needs to stay committed to the change. Otherwise two things will happen: the change initiative will become one of the seven out of eight that don't deliver, and a precedent will be set for the next one, making future change even more difficult.

Notes

1. Charles Franklin Kettering (29 August, 1876–24 or 25 November, 1958) was an American inventor, engineer, businessman and the holder of 186 patents.
2. British Home Stores, having traded since 1927, collapsed mid-2016. Sir Philip Green (CEO) and his wife, Tina (Monaco-based owner of the parent company, Arcadia), were able to sell the business in 2015 for a pound, leaving a potential £571m hole in the staff pension plan. The pension plan was in surplus when the Greens purchased BHS in 2000. In 2005, Arcadia took out a loan of £1.3bn and Tina Green was paid a tax-free dividend of £1.2bn, which was four times the profit of the business. The Greens earned several hundred million more in dividends, rent and interest during their 15-year ownership of BHS. One thing that certainly needs changing – the UK's corporate governance laws!
3. Harvard Business Review Press, 1st edition, 1 May, 1997.
4. American actor and musician (1925–2001). Lemmon was an eight-time Academy Award nominee, with two wins.
5. American author (1890–1937) who achieved posthumous fame through his influential works of horror fiction.
6. Rosabeth Moss Kanter, 'Ten Reasons People Resist Change', *Harvard Business Review*, September 2012.
7. In the same speech, she went on to say that the other half of Trump's supporters 'feel that the government has let them down' and were 'desperate for change.' 'Those are people we have to understand and empathize with as well,' she said. She was right, but no one remembers this part of her statement because she ended up apologising for her 'deplorables' comment rather than focusing on addressing the genuine concerns of the 'other half' of Trump's supporters.
8. George Bernard Shaw (1856–1950) was an Irish playwright, critic and polemicist. He wrote more than 60 plays, including major works such as *Man and Superman* (1902), *Pygmalion* (1912) and *Saint Joan* (1923).

9. Thich Nhat Hahn, Thai Buddhist Monk, Teacher and International Peace Activist (2012) *You are Here: Discover the Magic of the Present Moment*, Shambala Press.

10. American author of 1970s best-sellers, including *Jonathan Livingston Seagull* (1970) and *Illusions: The Adventures of a Reluctant Messiah* (1977).

11. Theologian Reinhold Niebuhr (1892–1971) first wrote the prayer for a sermon at Heath Evangelical Union Church in Massachusetts.

12. Karpman, S. (1968) 'Fairy Tales and Script Drama Analysis', *Transactional Analysis Bulletin*, 7(26), 39–43.

13. Eric Berne, a Canadian-born psychiatrist, created the theory of transactional analysis, in the middle of the 20th century, as a way of explaining human behaviour. Berne's theory of transactional analysis was based on the ideas of Freud but was distinctly different. Freudian psychotherapists focused on talk therapy as a way of gaining insight into their patients' personalities. Berne believed that insight could be better discovered by analysing patients' social transactions.

14. American actress 1942–2013.

15. Dr Laurence J. Peter (1970) *The Peter Principle*, Raymond Hull. The central premise of the book is that all managers are eventually promoted to their level of incompetence to stay there for the remainder of their careers, thus reaching their 'Peter Plateau'. A cynical view without doubt, but not entirely inaccurate.

16. Buddhist monk (1908–1974).

17. Diane von Fürstenberg, formerly Princess Diane of Fürstenberg, is a Belgian-born American fashion designer (1946–).

18. http://www.relbanks.com/top-insurance-companies/world

19. US Politician 1951–

20. A misquote from Monty Python's *Adventures of Ralph Mellish*, 'Matching Tie and Handkerchief' LP.

21. 'The Set-Up-To-Fail Syndrome' Manzoni and Barsoux, *Harvard Business Review* 2002

22. Emotional Quotient (EQ) – a snappy acronym awarded to Emotional Intelligence (EI) to evoke a comparison with IQ (Intelligence Quotient). See Chapter 11.

23. Dutch post-impressionist painter 1853-1890.

24. Excellent book by Nassim Nicholas Taleb about planning for (and betting on) extreme events – with extremely low likelihood and extremely high impact. So named as black swans were assumed not to exist until Dutch explorer Willem de Vlamingh discovered them in 1697 in a remote part of the world that would become known centuries later as Western Australia. The black swan adorns Western Australia's state flag.

25. 'Why Economists Failed to Predict the Financial Crisis', 13 May, 2009, Wharton, University of Pennsylvania.
26. Source: Ahir and Loungani (2014) 'Fail Again? Fail Better? Forecasts by Economists During the Great Recession.
27. Professor of Neuroscience at the University of Southern California and an Adjunct Professor at the Salk Institute.
28. Herzberg, Frederick, Mausner, Bernard, Snyderman, Barbara B. (1959) *The Motivation to Work*, 2nd edition, New York: John Wiley.
29. James Harold Wilson, Baron Wilson of Rievaulx KG OBE PC FRS FSS (11 March 1916–24 May 1995) was a British Labour Party politician who served as the Prime Minister of the United Kingdom from 1964 to 1970 and 1974 to 1976.
30. Machiavelli (1513) *The Prince* Italian Renaissance historian, politician, diplomat, philosopher, humanist and writer (1469–1527).

Part Two

The Necessary Ingredients for Successful Change

'Change is inevitable. Successful change isn't.'

Campbell Macpherson

The necessary ingredients for successful change

We have discussed in some depth why the vast majority of change initiatives fail. Let us now look at the subject from the glass-half-full perspective and discuss what we need to do to ensure our change initiative is the one in eight that succeeds.

To deliver change successfully, your people must understand what needs to be achieved and why – and the organisation, at all levels, must be prepared, equipped, aligned and motivated to follow it through to completion. This requires strong and confident leadership engaging with their people in an open, honest, transparent and genuine manner. It requires the leadership to listen. It requires detailed planning and a governance structure and process that are in tune with the culture of the organisation. It also requires the establishment of a culture that is ready to embrace new ways of working.

I also recommend the identification of a 'Change Catalyst' to help the leadership stay focused, to enable communication and to ensure the organisation delivers the business outcomes it needs to achieve.

Top Ten Ingredients for Successful Change:

1. A Change Catalyst to drive delivery

2. A strong, committed, aligned and unwavering leadership team

3. Complete clarity about what we are trying to achieve and why

4. Laser-like focus on the outcomes

5. Detailed understanding of the implications of the change

6. Identification of the emotional triggers

7. Genuine engagement of people at all levels of the organisation

8. Clear governance and thorough planning

9. A change process that includes a 'pause for reflection'

10. The establishment of a change-ready culture.

Chapter 11

A Change Catalyst to Drive Delivery

'Never believe that a few caring people can't change the world. For, indeed, that's all who ever have.'

Margaret Mead[1]

One of the most important ingredients for successfully instigating sustainable change is the identification and appointment of a Change Catalyst: someone whose role it is to guide the organisation – its people and its processes – to the ultimate delivery of the outcomes the business needs.

Successful change requires:

A 'Change Catalyst'
Clarity of what and why
Implications understood
Outcomes focus
Pause for reflection
Governance and planning
Genuine engagement
Emotional triggers
Strong leadership
A change-ready culture

The Change Catalyst is the ingredient that is most often overlooked, and I believe this common omission is one of the key reasons why 88% of change initiatives fail.

A Change Catalyst is a business person, not a project manager. A Change Catalyst is aligned to your shareholders, not just the stakeholders. A Change Catalyst understands the business: the drivers of profitability, the drivers of shareholder value, the drivers of customer satisfaction, the drivers of employee satisfaction. A Change Catalyst understands the market: the short-, medium- and long-term trends facing the industry and how successful competitors could take advantage of them. A Change Catalyst is regarded as a peer by the 'business end' of the organisation.

A Change Catalyst also possesses an 'EQ'^{2} to match their IQ. They are able to empathise with, and be respected by, people at all levels of the organisation. They are able to gain the trust of the company's leaders, managers and employees alike. A Change Catalyst makes every group feel safe and confident to discuss their concerns and suggestions openly without fear of adverse consequences.

It is vital that the relationship between the Change Catalyst and the leadership is open and transparent. The Change Catalyst must be able to be completely frank with the leadership – also without fear of adverse consequences. Because, if the Change Catalyst is doing his/her job properly, there will be times when they have to tell the organisation's leaders things they may not wish to hear.

On the flip side, the leadership must be able to confide in the Change Catalyst with total confidence that this privileged information will be protected. Ideally, the Change Catalyst needs to be regarded as the leadership's confidante and adviser.

The difference between a Change Catalyst and a Programme Manager

A Change Catalyst's strength lies in his/her focus on outcomes. A Programme or Project Manager's strength lies in his/her ability to drive the process. The Change Catalyst is the yin to the Project Manager's yang.

To illustrate the difference between project/programme management skills and the skills of a Change Catalyst, let me take you back to 1998 and my time with Andersen Consulting. Many of the 'Change Catalyst' skills and responsibilities I have discussed above were contained in the role profiles of either the Programme Manager and/or the Lead Partner. Yet, rarely did I see these traits displayed, for the simple reason that almost everyone was a process person. AC was very hierarchical. Put simply, the Partners sold the work and managed the client engagement, and the managers managed the project teams to deliver the work. So, to make it through the ranks at AC, managers needed to prove themselves as Project Managers and Programme Managers. However, the skills you need to be good at project management are very different to the skills you need to be good at selling and client engagement. The former is focused on deadlines, deliverables, processes and budgets. The latter is focused on business outcomes and understanding client aspirations, needs and motivations.

My time with this global consultancy confirmed my view that these are indeed very different skill sets and that while a Project Manager can improve their relationship management skills and a Relationship Manager can improve their project management skills, each of us is naturally inclined to one or the other. To be successful, a change programme needs both. It needs a Programme Manager to provide the enabling process and structure and a Change Catalyst to engage effectively with stakeholders and focus on the quality of the outputs – to ensure the delivery of the business outcomes the organisation needs.

(In much the same way that it is almost impossible to find a genuine 'Sales and Marketing Director' – as candidates are either dyed-in-the-wool salespeople who regard marketing as 'sales support' or they are dyed-in-the-wool marketeers who regard sales as simply the last step in the marketing process. If you need equal focus on both sales and marketing, you will need separate directors, and you will need to force them to work together. But I digress.)

Andersen Consulting

The Lead Partner I was working for knew the dilemma that his consulting firm was facing: the fact they were brilliant at project management but less so at client engagement and relationship management. The managers within the client organisation respected the Andersen Consultants but also found them to be somewhat aloof and sometimes more than a little intimidating. This is understandable. AC combed the world for the smartest graduates they could find and put them through rigorous training before slotting them into client teams. They were smart, confident, educated, well-trained – but the vast majority had never worked anywhere else. As I remarked earlier, the nickname given to Andersen Consultants by clients the world over was 'Androids'. The firm was very long on IQ but a tad short on EQ.

The Lead Partner for this particular client also happened to be AC's Global Managing Partner for Financial Services. He had decided to relocate to Sydney from the US for the duration of the engagement – which gives you an idea of how lucrative the engagement was for Andersen Consulting. The firm had more than 300 consultants working full time on this one client – completely transforming its technology in preparation for, and to manage the aftermath of, the de-mutualisation and listing of Australia's largest insurance company.

I was what they called 'a senior hire', joining AC in 1997 at the veteran age of 34 having run my own multimedia company for the previous five years. Most of my previous clients had been financial services companies. The firm needed someone with experience in the emerging world of 'eBusiness'.

Six months into my time at AC, the Lead Partner parachuted me in to take a look at the enormous IT procurement project that had gone awry. He knew I knew nothing about procurement, let alone IT procurement; he just needed someone to provide him with an objective view of the situation. His instinct also told him it was probably a relationship management issue. He needed someone that the client's managers would trust so that he could determine precisely what was going wrong. As he expected, the problems had little to do with the processes or the technical aspects of the task. They were all to do with unrealistic expectations, poor communications, poor engagement and a breakdown of trust between the client and the consultants.

He also asked me to produce a sales piece to demonstrate to the client's Board the benefits of a single holistic IT system across all of their legacy systems; one that would provide platform-agnostic and seamless customer service. (This concept was ahead of its time, as

(continued)

smartphones and iPads weren't even a glimmer in Steve Jobs's eye in 1998.) So, I compiled a film crew from people I knew around Sydney, wrote a little script, cast a few actors and produced a four-minute promotional video to highlight the benefits of such a solution. The video was presented at the client's next executive team meeting.

'I want that!' declared the larger-than-life (also American) CEO when the video had finished. 'How much to give me that?' he asked, turning to the AC Partner.

'Oh, about $100 million,' he replied.

'I don't want that,' retorted the CEO, still pointing at the screen. It must be the largest win and the quickest loss I have ever been involved with.

Lastly, when confronted with a poor set of customer satisfaction scores from the client, the Partner asked me to design a training course for Andersen Consultants that would help them improve their client relationship skills – to become less like high-IQ androids and more like high-EQ humans. It took a couple of months, with assistance from many of the L&D professionals throughout this truly global firm, and the course was ready to pilot. It was to be a combination of classroom sessions with independent lecturers, coaching and mentoring. Unfortunately, the Managing Partner moved to London and the momentum for the course was lost. He summonsed me to join him in early 1999, but we never did dust off that development programme. It is a pity. It was such a great idea.

The skills of a Programme/Project Manager and a Change Catalyst are complementary but different. The former will ensure organisation and process. The latter will be focused on delivering the business outcomes you require. If your change initiative is to be the one in eight that succeeds, you will need both.

Should my Change Catalyst be internal or external?

While it depends upon the size of the initiative in question, the expertise you have in-house and your corporate culture, ideally, your Change Catalyst should be internal. *Your* people should drive *your* change.

One of the things I observed during the AC engagement above is that, with 300 consultants in their midst, the client's managers felt powerless; they did not feel in charge of their own destiny. The change was being done *to* them. Many of them couldn't wait for the consultants to leave so that they could start taking back decision-making and ownership of their departments.

However, finding the right person from within your organisation can be a challenge. Most organisations don't employ Change Catalysts to sit around in case they are needed one day, which is one reason why a large number of organisations tend to look externally for this sort of role. Also, sometimes leaders want to shake things up a little and the benefits of external expertise can be seen to outweigh the benefits of nurturing in-house talent. In addition, external consultants, especially from the large multinational firms, come with their own form of intrinsic insurance policy. It used to be said that 'no one got fired for buying IBM'. The large consultancies of McKinseys, PwC, EY, Bain, BCG, *et al.* come with a strong sense of security for the manager who hired them. Most Boards prefer to be presented with a study conducted by McKinseys than a small independent firm, no matter how competent or experienced the latter may be. The bigger the client company, the truer this is.

When I was Strategy Director for a subsidiary of Zurich, the CEO and I realised this. So, once we had mapped out our preferred strategy in conjunction with the rest of the management team, we then brought in KPMG to build upon and endorse the strategic plan. They conducted their own enquiries and brought their own insight to the table. Their final report concurred with the strategy, enhanced it, suggested amendments to the plan and supplied a detailed budget and timeline – and the Board duly signed off on it.

The best of both worlds

I prefer, wherever possible, the synergistic combination of an internal manager paired with an external consultant. This way, the internal manager can benefit from the experience of the external consultant and gradually take over Change Catalyst duties as the initiative progresses, until there comes a point where the external consultant is no longer required. I have always been a big fan of this model – it uses external expertise in the way it should be used – for limited periods of time to get the initiative up and running, imparting knowledge and experience in the process.

A Change Catalyst in Action

I am now about to break one of the rules that I promised I would follow. This is a positive case study but I am not providing the name of the company involved. The company name isn't relevant to the story.

A team was tasked with conducting a review of this organisation's industry. The team was duly established and, purely because of the personalities involved, natural roles emerged:

- **The Team Lead** who happened to be a natural 'Change Catalyst' with a leaning towards stakeholder engagement, communications, the quality of the deliverables and an obsession with outcomes.

- **The Specialist** who knew the technical details of the subject matter inside out and had held senior-level roles with similar organisations.

- *The Analysts* who also understood the technical details and were able to 'crunch the numbers' and conduct much of the desk-based research and analysis the project required.

- *A Project Manager* who understood the importance of governance and was highly organised. This role was critical in the early stages of the project.

This combination was important. The exercise would have failed to deliver anything near the quality that it delivered if just one of these roles had been absent.

Let me be completely honest. The fact that the Team Lead also had the skills of a 'Change Catalyst' was a complete accident. Normally in this company, the Team Lead of such an initiative would have been the 'Specialist' (i.e. the subject matter expert), in the often-mistaken belief that he/she would automatically be good at stakeholder engagement and communication. The lucky accident that the Team Lead in this case was a different person entirely and had the skills of a 'Change Catalyst' meant that the stakeholder engagement was thorough and genuine, the communications were clear and the reports and presentations were tailored for maximal comprehension and impact.

The initiative could not have been more successful.

The approach enabled the senior members of the organisation to compare the most important aspects of the organisation's approach and governance with industry best practice in a way that was completely objective, open, honest, consequence free and fact based. The detailed stakeholder engagement enabled the entire leadership and a large swathe of the senior management to become familiar with the issues and concepts involved ahead of the formal meetings, thus ensuring robust discussions and debates when the report was formally presented. It also ensured that all concerns regarding the report's direction and ultimate recommendations were fleshed out well in advance.

(continued)

In fact, several insights revealed during the stakeholder engagement meetings were incorporated into the final report – a clear sign that the stakeholders were actually being listened to. The clarity of the report and presentation enabled swift decision-making and cleared the way for future projects. And the technical detail and analysis were insightful, relevant and material. The end report and its accompanying presentation were the ideal combination of technical expertise and communications know-how: credible, informative, enlightening and easy to read.

The key recommendations of the final report were consequently adopted and will enable clarity of objectives, clarity of accountabilities and the delivery of even greater shareholder value.

The life of a Change Catalyst

A Change Catalyst is a challenging role.

Change Catalysts care about the organisation; sometimes even more than management. Wanting the best outcomes for the organisation, Change Catalysts are, in a real sense, working for the shareholders. As the business press uncovers almost on a daily basis, the interests of shareholders and the interests of management aren't always aligned. They should be, obviously, but it isn't as easy to achieve as one would think. Shareholders want what is in the best long-term interests of the company – a strategy that is differentiated, achievable and executed; growing revenues; growing profits. Management want those things too, but they are also subject to an additional set of pressures. They have company politics to deal with, issues of pride, personal reputations, personal ambition, and they work to different, often shorter-term timeframes.

It's almost the logical vs the human. Long-term shareholders can afford to be logical. They want return on equity, return on capital, capital gains and dividends. Their personal ambition and careers are rarely closely tied to the company itself. They can afford to be rational. Management, on the other hand, have their careers entirely entwined with the company, and they have to deal with all that messy human stuff.

According to *Fortune* magazine's data, the 500 largest companies in the US have a median CEO tenure of 4.9 years. In the UK, the median is 5.9 years, according to the *FT*. At the other end of the spectrum, long-term investors such as pension funds and sovereign wealth funds are judged on 10, 20 or even 30-year performance and tend to hold on to shares through multiple cycles.

To imply that management doesn't want what is best for the company would be both incorrect and slanderous. They do; but their priorities can be different. No matter how much we want to do the best by the company, we all have personal ambitions, expenses and families. Most of the time, personal goals align with corporate goals, but not always.

Management's priorities are to maintain their income, maintain their reputation, enhance their profile and further their career – while doing the right thing by the company. Shareholders' priorities are the other way around.

The job of a Change Catalyst is, in essence, to try to bridge the gap between shareholders and management; to help the management deliver the outcomes that are in the best interests of the shareholders. When it works, it is a most rewarding role. But, of course, like the light bulb in Chapter 18, both the shareholders and the management must genuinely want to change.

'"You never do things the easy way, do you?" she said.
"There's an easy way?" I asked.'
Patrick Rothfuss[3]

What is EQ?

I bypassed this earlier and it is worthy of greater discussion. EQ stands for Emotional Quotient, which is a snappy acronym awarded to Emotional Intelligence (EI) to evoke a comparison with IQ (Intelligence Quotient).

Harvard's Howard Gardner[4] offers one of the best and most concise definitions:

'Your EQ is the level of your ability to understand other people, what motivates them and how to work cooperatively with them.'

Although the term first appeared in a 1964 paper by Michael Beldoch, it gained popularity in the 1995 best-selling business book, *Emotional Intelligence*, written by the author, psychologist and science journalist, Daniel Goleman. As he says on his website (www.danielgoleman.com), the inspiration for his book came from 'an article in a small academic journal by two psychologists, John Mayer, now at the University of New Hampshire, and Yale's Peter Salovey. Mayer and Salovey offered the first formulation of a concept they called "emotional intelligence."' The *Harvard Business Review* has hailed Emotional Intelligence as 'a ground-breaking, paradigm-shattering idea', one of the most influential business ideas of the decade.

EQ is far more important than IQ when it comes to business

Goleman's research indicated that Emotional Intelligence accounted for 67% of the abilities deemed necessary for superior performance in leaders, and mattered twice as much as technical expertise or IQ.[5] Other psychologist findings report that among the ingredients for success, IQ counts for roughly 10% (at best 25%); the rest depends on everything else – including EQ.[6] A study of Harvard graduates in business, law, medicine and teaching showed a negative or zero correlation between a key IQ indicator (entrance exam scores) and subsequent career success.

Five categories of Emotional Intelligence[7]

1. **Self-awareness.** The ability to recognise your own emotions and feelings is a key component of EQ. If you evaluate your emotions, you can manage them. The major elements of self-awareness are:

   a. *Emotional awareness.* Your ability to recognise your own emotions and their effects.

   b. *Self-confidence.* Sureness about your self-worth and capabilities.

2. **Self-regulation.** The next step is regulating these emotions. We have little control over when we experience emotions, but we can learn to control how we react and how long an emotion lasts. Self-regulation involves:

   a. *Self-control.* Managing disruptive impulses.

   b. *Trustworthiness.* Maintaining standards of honesty and integrity.

   c. *Conscientiousness.* Taking responsibility for your own performance.

   d. *Adaptability.* Handling change with flexibility.

   e. *Innovation.* Being open to new ideas.

3. **Motivation.** Motivating yourself requires clear goals and a positive attitude. Although we all seem to have a predisposition to either a positive or a negative attitude, we can, with effort and practice, learn to think more positively. Motivation is made up of:

   a. *Drive.* Your constant striving to improve or to meet a standard of excellence.

   b. *Commitment.* Aligning with the goals of the group or organisation.

c. *Initiative.* Readying yourself to act on opportunities.

d. *Optimism.* Pursuing goals persistently despite obstacles and setbacks.

4. **Empathy.** The ability to recognise how people feel – the ability genuinely to put yourself in their shoes – is important to success in your life and career. An empathetic person excels at:

   a. *Service orientation.* Anticipating, recognising and meeting clients' needs.

   b. *Developing others.* Sensing what others need to progress and bolstering their abilities.

   c. *Leveraging diversity.* Cultivating opportunities through diverse people.

   d. *Political awareness.* Reading a group's emotional currents and power relationships.

   e. *Understanding others.* Discerning the feelings behind the needs and wants of others.

5. **Social skills.** 'People skills' are the final component of EQ. Skills such as:

   a. *Influence.* Wielding effective persuasion tactics.

   b. *Communication.* Sending clear messages.

   c. *Leadership.* Inspiring and guiding groups and people.

   d. *Change catalyst.* Initiating or managing change.

   e. *Conflict management.* Understanding, negotiating and resolving disagreements.

   f. *Building bonds.* Nurturing instrumental relationships.

   g. *Collaboration and cooperation.* Working with others toward shared goals.

h. *Team capabilities.* Creating group synergy in pursuing collective goals.

Emotional Intelligence is a must-have ingredient in any successful Change Catalyst.

And a Change Catalyst is a must-have ingredient for successfully instigating change.

Chapter 12

Clarity About What we are Trying to Achieve and Why

'Surely clarity is the most beautiful thing in the world.'
Goerge Oppen[8]

W e covered this in detail in Chapter 2, so here I shall be brief.

Successful change requires:

A 'Change Catalyst'

Clarity of what and why

Implications understood

Outcomes focus

Pause for reflection

Governance and planning

Genuine engagement

Emotional triggers

Strong leadership

A change-ready culture

Being clear about what you are trying to achieve and why is critical to success.

The desired business outcomes must be clear, realistic and measurable.

You need to paint a picture of the future for your staff and provide them with a narrative concerning what the future will look like – and ensure this vision of the future is both credible and motivational. The vision of the future must be relevant to everyone; tailored for all levels of the organisation. In my experience, engaging every team in the act of translating the higher-level vision into something that is relevant to them pays enormous dividends.

And lastly, the reasons for the change must be genuine. You may not be able to provide the 'real' reason for the change, but the 'right' reason needs to be sincere, believable and something that people want to get behind.

Chapter 13

Detailed Understanding of the Implications of the Change

'There are downsides to everything; there are unintended consequences to everything.'

Steve Jobs[9]

If you want your desired outcomes to be delivered, you will have to understand who and what will be affected by the proposed changes.

Whether this is a new strategy for the company, a new IT system or an enhancement of a recruitment process, every change comes with its own set of consequences; implications for the team, the department, the organisation and the individuals involved. Obviously, this last one is where effective stakeholder engagement comes in.

Successful change requires:

A 'Change Catalyst'

Clarity of what and why

Implications understood

Outcomes focus

Pause for reflection

Governance and planning

Genuine engagement

Emotional triggers

Strong leadership

A change-ready culture

As many as possible of these implications should be explored in advance, as some of them will be so significant that the strategy itself may need to be altered.

Take the IT system example given earlier – the implications of trying to get an off-the-shelf package to do things that it wasn't originally designed to do were an explosion in costs, a multiplication of development time and incredibly slow system speeds. If, and I admit it is a big if, these could have been discussed openly beforehand, some or even all of them could have been avoided. Or, most likely, the anticipated outcomes could have been re-examined and recalibrated before too much damage had been done.

The implications of streamlining a recruitment process may be that a key step, which may be time-consuming but is critical for quality control purposes, is bypassed. Or the proposed change may mean that critical information will no longer be passed between HR and the department. Understanding the implications of a planned change is critical.

While exploring likely implications in the planning stage is critical, the trick is to keep looking for them throughout the entire change process. And, of course, keep a look out for unintended consequences because no matter how thorough, no change planning activity can possibly capture them all upfront.

Cofunds

Cofunds was, and I believe as of writing this chapter still is, the UK's largest retail investment platform. At the time of the engagement, it had burst through the £50bn under management mark.

The CEO had determined where he wanted the company to go; he had determined his strategic vision. My job was, and I quote, to 'do your workshops and get everybody bought in'. This phrase was accompanied by sweeping hand gestures as though it was a simple exercise that wouldn't require much effort. I gathered that the assumption was that as soon as they heard the brilliance of the strategy, employees would simply applaud and fall into line. My first response was to laugh (the CEO in question was, at the time, and still remains, a good friend) and then to offer the thought that success would not be achieved by attempting to get anyone to 'buy in' to someone else's idea. What we needed to do was genuinely to engage the management team in building upon the CEO's strategy to such an extent that it became *their* strategy – to turn what was a high-level vision with a clear rationale into a strategy and plan that they owned – because they had been genuinely engaged in its development.

'Yes. That is what I meant,' said the CEO, now smiling but still waving his hands in a manner that an independent bystander may have thought was a tad dismissive.

(continued)

The first step was to assist the CEO in communicating this vision and high-level rationale to the executive team and ask for their thoughts and input. The second was to sit with each of the executives one-on-one to understand their genuine feelings and opinions about the new vision – and to start to gauge their personal fears, barriers and ambitions. Several meetings are usually needed: not everyone opens up to a stranger in a 45-minute interview. (Although I am continually amazed at how many people do open up in the first meeting and the degree to which they give their honest opinions. Effective listening is a key skill to develop. It is one that I will forever be improving.)

Engagement must be genuine. Too many times, I have witnessed a 'tick-box' style of disingenuous engagement. This is where the chief protagonist produces a PowerPoint deck and then proceeds to present every page to each and every 'stakeholder' with minimal dialogue. Once that is done, the process box labelled 'engagement' is ticked and they move onto the next audience member. The 'victims' of this style of faux engagement do not feel as though they have been engaged with all, which is simply storing up a problem for later. It is also disrespectful of the stakeholder. Disingenuous engagement tells the stakeholders that their opinions are not important.

Genuine engagement requires genuine dialogue. Genuine dialogue is respectful. It is driven by a genuine desire to understand each stakeholder's opinion. It will also uncover good ideas regarding enhancements or additions to the proposed plan. More importantly, it will bring to the surface reservations and concerns, which will have to be addressed if the new initiative is to be successful. In some of the best engagement meetings I have been involved in, we didn't even open the presentation material; we just talked.

After the one-on-ones, the next step was a session with the executive team to play back a summary of their collective thoughts and enable each team member to voice doubts, concerns and suggestions to their peers. We also started the planning for a wider senior management team offsite – which quickly followed.

Critical to planning the management team offsite was genuine engagement with the wider management team (executive team direct reports and influential others). I met with most of them, again so that I could hear concerns, grievances and suggestions prior to the meeting – and to ensure that people were prepared and ready to 'hit the ground running' offsite. During the Away Day, we revisited the strategic vision – which by now had been enhanced and was well on its way to being 'owned' by the whole executive team – and started to delve into the detail. We went back to basics – discussing the organisation's strengths and weaknesses, the opportunities and threats facing the company – and started to unearth the 'elephants' and the obstacles to success. We did this not just to set the context, but to ensure everyone genuinely engaged in the subject. The ownership of the new vision was starting to widen.

But the most important part of the day was the discussion of implications of the strategy to the business. The 'real' purpose of the preceding sessions was to get the whole management team genuinely engaged in the new plan. The final session was where the rubber started to hit the road. Now that they understood the end goal and the rationale for change, and had added some flesh to the skeleton of the strategy, the final session was where the new insight (and engagement) truly began – when we began to explore the implications of it all. It would mean an overhaul of customer service; greater automation and ultimately fewer employees per customer. It would mean prioritisation – we couldn't do everything; some projects had to stop; some propositions had to be de-prioritised to make way for others. It would require a refocusing of the sales force. It would require seriously questioning the validity of the high-volume/low-margin part of the business. The HR Director queried whether we had the right

(continued)

137

skills and the right people in some of the key positions. Participants rattled off new skills that would be needed and current roles that may not be.

Now we were cooking with gas. Almost everybody was not only engaged but had gone further and made the mental leap into implementation mode – all because we had started to focus on the implications of the change.

The insight that this exercise uncovered resulted in the inevitable refinement of the strategic plan. The strategic intent – the broad vision – remained intact. But the finer details of the strategy were modified and enhanced once the implications and challenges of execution were fully understood.

We went on to engage all of the key people throughout the company in separate workshops of their own – each workshop led by a member of the executive team: the more people who have input into the change, the deeper the sense of ownership and the stronger the engagement. And nothing gets people more engaged than being asked to unearth implications and challenges in the boss's new plan!

Chapter 14

A Laser-like Focus on the Outcomes

'Effort is admirable but what truly matters is the outcome it produces.'

The words that your people will become tired of hearing are 'clarity', 'outcomes', 'implications', 'genuine engagement' and 'accountability'. If organisations were to hang these words from the ceiling rather than their corporate values, a great deal more would be achieved.

We have discussed clarity several times. Now let's look at 'outcomes'.

Successful change requires:

A 'Change Catalyst'

Clarity of what and why

Implications understood

Outcomes focus

Pause for reflection

Governance and planning

Genuine engagement

Emotional triggers

Strong leadership

A change-ready culture

Successful change initiatives have a laser-like focus, to the point of obsession, on 'outcomes' – clarifying them, continually referring to them in progress reports and communications, pausing to check whether they are still valid or desirable... and finally delivering them.

The change programme that obsesses over process, thereby taking its eye off what it is setting out to achieve, is guaranteed to fail. Adapt the process to deliver the outcomes – never the other way around.

One organisation I did some work for a while back set out to design (and perhaps one day implement) a strategy development process. The team responsible for facilitating this task had kindly asked for my input and, as I had helped many a company clarify, develop and implement its strategy, I was eager to assist. So, in advance of the meeting, I drew up a simple diagram that mapped out the inputs that I thought might be required and the outputs I assumed the leadership was trying to produce. I also drafted a high-level process to transform the inputs into the outputs.

My main query concerned the outcomes. What was the CEO and leadership team seeking to achieve – precisely what did they want this process to deliver?

After all, the purpose of a process is to deliver something. Defining the end deliverable helps you to define the required process elements. A process without clearly defined outcomes would be a complete waste of time and effort. It would be a road to nowhere.

So, my colleague and I met with the key team members and thanked them for the opportunity to provide our input. We said that, in our humble opinion, the obvious place to start was with the end in mind; so we wondered what were the precise outcomes and outputs that the leadership was looking for this process to achieve.

'Aah,' said the Team Lead, most wisely. 'We have not been tasked with defining the outputs. We have been tasked with facilitating the development of a process – and have been asked specifically not to offer any recommendations as to what the steps in the process should be.'

We had entered a content-free zone. They were designing a process to develop a process. I felt as though I had accidentally stumbled onto the set of *Yes Minister*.[10]

'The key question here is not a "what" question. It's a "who" question,' he went on to declare with added gravity.

My colleague said afterwards that it was the only time he had seen me lost for words.

My advice: if you wish to instigate genuine change rather than just facilitate the appearance of change – take a different approach. Start with the 'what' and the 'why'. Once these are clear to all concerned, then move on to the 'how' and, finally, the 'who'.

Chapter 15

A Change Process that Includes a 'Pause for Reflection'

'Whenever you find yourself on the side of the majority, it is time to pause and reflect.'

Mark Twain[11]

Throne process, the methodology, you use to instigate your change must be in tune with the culture of your business.

The purpose of the process is to enable the change, not to smother it. Use, adapt or design a process that fits the size of your organisation, the style of your organisation and the type of initiative upon which you are embarking.

Successful change requires:

A 'Change Catalyst'

Clarity of what and why

Implications understood

Outcomes focus

Pause for reflection

Governance and planning

Genuine engagement

Emotional triggers

Strong leadership

A change-ready culture

Any sound project management methodology can be used to keep the project on track and organised. (But organised to achieve what?)

A structured project management process will help you manage risk, manage quality and control changes during the project. Every project needs one.

But while a good process is essential, never forget that it is merely the enabler.

And no matter what process you select, I strongly recommend embedding into it a step entitled 'pause for objective reflection'. This tip is vital to success and yet it is rarely done.

Once a project has set its planned objectives and they have been signed off by the appropriate governance body, it is 'full steam ahead'. Once the project is in mid-stride, it is difficult to stop it – as asking the working group to pause is tantamount to implying that they may be doing a poor job. Unless, of course, an official 'pause for reflection' was pre-ordained ahead of time as part of the process.

'Pausing for objective reflection' should be a feature of every change initiative – and mandatory for IT projects. Time and time again, organisations commit the same error and decide to tailor a system extensively to meet 'the organisation's unique requirements' rather than opting for an off-the-shelf package used by others in their industry. Inevitably, the initial budget is eclipsed, implementation becomes overdue, the new system becomes unsupportable and outdated and the scope of the functionality gets scaled back dramatically.

The correct thing to do at this stage would be to 'pause for objective reflection' – and then, with a clear head and with no blame attached to anyone, abandon the development all together and opt for one of the industry standard packages. This is usually very unlikely to happen, as it would be an admission that the wrong decision was made in the first place. Rather than admit that the train is on the wrong track, it is often far too easy to keep piling coal into the furnaces until eventually the locomotive runs out of track and crashes headlong into the buffers.

But to be fair, pausing for objective reflection is a difficult thing to do. Calling a halt to a doomed IT project is an easy decision to make in hindsight but it is extremely difficult to do when you are in the middle of the implementation mayhem. The only way to have a chance of carrying it off is if, upfront, you make 'pausing for objective reflection' a discrete step in the implementation process – perhaps even going to the trouble of getting independent observers in to assess progress mid-stream with a remit to question whether the intended outcomes and rationale are still valid. If you establish upfront that this type of inertia is a genuine change phenomenon that needs to be anticipated and managed, the change leader can emerge unscathed and even rewarded. It is all about setting expectations upfront.

Formalising such a pause will give everyone involved the opportunity to check whether the intended outcomes are still desirable, whether they are still viable or whether they need adapting in any way. It will provide the leadership with an opportunity to reflect on the project governance structure – what is working and what isn't – and whether there are any extra or different skills required within the working group. It will provide an opportunity to reflect upon the quality and timeliness of communications and stakeholder engagement. It will also provide an opportunity to reflect upon the schedule and milestones.

Such a 'mid-term review' would give the leaders the opportunity to acknowledge that circumstances change and to step away from, and rise above, the day-to-day management of the project. Such a simple step, if conducted objectively and openly, could save the organisation a great deal of time and money. It is another tool in your armoury for giving your project the best chance of delivering the outcomes that the business needs.

Chapter 16

Clear Governance and Thorough Planning

'Governance must not only be clear, it must also be appropriate.'

Aclear governance structure, transparent decision-making processes and thorough planning are the necessary infrastructure for the instigation of sustainable change.

Clear governance

Good governance is simply clarity on the roles required, who is *accountable* for what (the decision-makers), who is *responsible* for what (those actually doing the work) and how decisions are made.

> **Successful change requires:**
>
> A 'Change Catalyst'
>
> Clarity of what and why
>
> Implications understood
>
> Outcomes focus
>
> Pause for reflection
>
> *Governance and planning*
>
> Genuine engagement
>
> Emotional triggers
>
> Strong leadership
>
> A change-ready culture

Investing time upfront to ensure clarity on these four points will pay rich dividends. I have seen too many projects that have rushed through this step and have come to regret it. Lack of clarity on who is accountable has resulted in decisions being delayed or made by people without the authority to do so. I have seen projects take on a life of their own due to the fact that it is unclear who should be making which decision.

Project/programme roles

Traditional project roles, as recommended by renowned project management methodologies such as PRINCE2, are sound – and yet, they are inadequate for, as we know, 88% of change projects fail. In my experience, a crucial role is missing – that of the Change Catalyst.

Traditional project management roles:[12]

- **Project Manager:** Responsible for organising and controlling the project. 'The Project Manager will select people to do the work on the project and will be responsible for making sure the work is done properly and on time.'

- **Customer:** The person who is paying for the project.

- **User:** The person who is going to use the results or outcome of the project, or who will be impacted by the outcome of a project.

- **Specialist:** The person who provides the expertise to do the actual work on the project (i.e. will be designing and building the outcome).

- **Project board:** Made up of the customer (or executive), someone representing the user side and someone representing the supplier or specialist input. The project board is responsible for providing the Project Manager with the necessary decisions for the project to proceed and to overcome any problems.

- **Project assurance:** Can be performed by third parties or the project board. Its purpose is to provide an independent view of how the project is progressing across the three dimensions of 'business assurance' (checking that the project remains viable in terms of costs and benefits), 'user assurance' (checking that the users' requirements are being met) and 'specialist/technical assurance' (checking that the project is delivering a suitable solution).

The above list of roles is sensible. Logically, it should all work. The Project Manager manages the project team to do the work and reports to the project board that makes the decisions, guided by input from the customers and users.

So why then do seven out of every eight change projects fail?

Because, in real life, grey areas occur in any governance structure. Misunderstandings occur at every junction – between the project board and the Project Manager, between the customer and the project board, between the Project Manager and the user... Project boards often need assistance when making decisions and no one is formally tasked with challenging their decisions. There is also an imbalance of time and focus. The project board members may be outcomes-focused but only a small proportion of their time may be allocated to the project. While the Project Manager may be full time, his/her skills lie in managing the process.

A 'Change Catalyst' is outcomes-focused and thrives in the grey areas

The keys to success are contained within the last point on the above list; the role described as 'project assurance' – checking that the project remains viable in terms of costs and benefits, checking that the users' requirements are being met and checking that the project is delivering a suitable solution. When done properly, this works. But to do it properly requires more than just 'checking'. It requires someone to be obsessed with outcomes; someone to drive the results of these checks through to their intended conclusion.

The Change Catalyst is the glue that holds it all together – the person who ensures that the outcomes are delivered.

My recommendations for change governance roles:

1. **The Client:** This may be the Board, the CEO, a specific Director… but every change initiative requires an ultimate 'Client'; someone who has either commissioned the change or approved the change and is ultimately accountable for setting expectations, overseeing delivery and approving the quality of the end result.

2. **Steering Committee:** The Steering Committee works on behalf of the Client. Good Steering Committees have clear remits; they are clear on what they are trying to achieve, why, what lies within their scope and what lies outside of their scope. The Steering Committee

is also clear on who it reports to. It is best if its membership is small, and therefore focused, and it is often helpful if its chair is able to cast a deciding vote – on behalf of the Client.

3. **Working Group:** Consisting of a Change Catalyst (focused on outcomes), a Project/Programme Manager (focused on process) and content specialists. The Working Group should also be small. While a wider group of stakeholders will need to be involved, don't have them all on the Working Group or you will take an inordinate amount of time to deliver very little.

4. **Change Catalyst:** Ideally, the Change Catalyst leads the Working Group. However, if, for some reason, this is not possible, another solution is to have the Change Catalyst act as an adviser to both the Working Group and the Steering Committee – bridging the gap between the two. Whatever the structure, the Change Catalyst's remit is to ensure quality of outputs from the Working Group and Steering Committee, the quality of communications and, ultimately, the delivery of the business outcomes that the organisation needs.

Thorough planning

'If you fail to plan, you are planning to fail.'
Benjamin Franklin[13]

The importance of planning cannot be over-estimated, especially when it comes to instigating change.

The first step of any change plan is to ensure clarity of what the initiative is setting out to achieve and why; ensuring the outcomes are clear, realistic and measurable; and that your people understand and embrace what the future will look like.

The next step is to establish the most appropriate governance structure, ensuring clarity of roles and remits, processes, milestones and the schedule.

A stakeholder engagement plan, a communications plan, a plan for establishing the implications of the change and reviewing the outcomes and timetable accordingly, identifying interdependencies among the workstreams, a detailed project schedule including milestones, deliverables and review points – these are all significant pieces of work in their own right. They need to be done and they need to be coordinated, as they are individual components of a holistic change plan.

Thorough planning will enable the project to set off in the right direction with the right people doing the right things.

But, of course, to re-quote Helmuth von Moltke, 'No battle plan survives contact with the enemy', so your change plan must be living and adaptable – its sole purpose is to help you deliver the outcomes your organisation requires.

Chapter 17

Genuine Engagement with People at all Levels of the Organisation

'Effective two-way communication demands that we capture both content and intent and learn to speak the languages of logic and emotion... Of the two, the language of emotion is far more motivational and powerful...'

Stephen R. Covey,
'Principle Centred Leadership'

By 'genuine engagement', I mean the full gamut of (a) communications and (b) stakeholder engagement. I will discuss each of these separately. I use the word 'genuine' deliberately.

Your communications may be 'professional' but if your employees don't believe they are genuine, they will have very little impact. In fact, they will be damaging to your cause. Disingenuous communications can be worse than none at all.

Successful change requires:

A 'Change Catalyst'

Clarity of what and why

Implications understood

Outcomes focus

Pause for reflection

Governance and planning

Genuine engagement

Emotional triggers

Strong leadership

A change-ready culture

The same is true when it comes to stakeholder engagement. Superficial engagement with stakeholders is disrespectful, counter-productive and a waste of everyone's time. Genuine engagement involves listening and acting upon the insight you receive.

Effective communications

Communications departments that are staffed by spin doctors producing professional but superficial outputs are completely ineffective. Some external communications departments I have stumbled across appear to go out of their way to ensure that very few facts and very little insight are communicated externally. They specialise in highly polished rhetoric but actually say very little. Similarly, some internal communications departments I have witnessed have actually become a barrier to genuine communication internally. Superficial 'broadcast communications' achieve little. Conversely, if you treat people like adults and ensure your communications are two-way, relevant and conducted on an adult-to-adult basis, there is a very good chance that they will respond accordingly.

Please excuse me if some of the following tips are a little obvious. But even as someone who professes to communicate for a living, I have found that returning to this list can be a very useful exercise. I can easily get stuck in my ways and need a gentle reminder of what I should be doing. Think of it as a health check for your communications.

'Tell them what you are going to tell them, tell them, and then tell them what you've told them.'

This was the advice I was given in the very first 'business writing' course I ever attended at the tender age of 17½. Ironically, it was in the Royal Australian Air Force and the instructor, who had modelled himself to sound and look as much like Winston Churchill as possible, was actually teaching us 'Air Force Writing', most of which was about as interesting as reading the instruction manual of your average kitchen appliance. But the three-part structure he recommended and his advice still resonates with me 35 years on.

Make sure your key message is clear and leave the readers in no doubt as to what it is.

What is the purpose of the communication?

Is it simply to inform? Why? To what end? What do you want your audience to think/feel/do as a result of absorbing your communications? This purpose will be the criterion against which the communications should be judged.

'Put yourself in the shoes of your audience and adapt the tone, length and vocabulary accordingly.'

Again, 'Communications 101', but we don't always do it. One of my favourite engagements was to help a Director transform his department's communications with the organisation's Investment Committee. Yes, we defined the purpose of the communications, we made sure the key message of every one of the missives was clear and we tightened up the narrative to make sure all of the analysis and insight was material and supported the key message, but we also had to make sure the tone was appropriate. To do this, we had to get inside the heads of our specific audience – understand their backgrounds, experience, likes and dislikes; and understand how they used our communications. Once armed with this insight, we were able to improve the commentary further: ensuring that the Executive Summary was crystal clear and stood as a communications piece in its own right, minimising asset-specific jargon and adopting a tone that was more relevant to the target audience. The purpose of the communications was to encourage deeper understanding and debate. We couldn't possibly achieve this without tailoring our material to the unique needs of the audience.

In terms of *content*, my advice is to make sure every piece of change communication is relevant and material.

In terms of *tone*, I recommend being genuine, constructive, open and transparent.

Communicate frequently and regularly

This way, communication doesn't become a big deal. If you only communicate when you have something earth-shattering to announce, every communication will be received with fraught anticipation. Infrequent communication is disdainful. It treats people like mushrooms. It signals to your people that they can't be trusted with too many facts. It is the sign of a culture that is afraid of information escaping and of people scared of saying anything that could be misconstrued – however well-intentioned the communications may be. These sorts of cultures cannot communicate in an open, honest and genuine way with their employees. They also find it very hard to change.

Sesame

One of the first things we introduced when we formed Sesame out of five separate IFA Networks was regular, genuine communications. Not glossy, professionally printed and bound, spin-laden brochures chock full of propaganda and staged photographs. We bypassed the glossy paper and went straight for authenticity – in the form of a fortnightly e-Newsletter (a.k.a. a PDF document distributed to all 1000 staff by email). We called it *Open*. My Communications Manager, Paul Wood, came up with the name and my instant reaction was to laugh – which to me is always the sign of a good idea. It was not only a corny/witty pun given the name of the company but it also reflected the tone we were striving to achieve. My brand strategy friends would condemn such a name as a 'Visible Strategy Line' but hey – it worked.

The first page of *Open* was always a timely comment from the CEO which was followed by a host of topics and discussions of interest to the staff. We shone a spotlight on specific teams to enhance understanding of what different teams did across the company, we discussed new HR policies, highlighted customer service stories, celebrated sales wins, gave updates on key projects, summarised new regulations… whatever our people needed to know, and whatever our people wanted to share with one another. We also highlighted social events and congratulated people for passing industry exams and qualifications.

We also did something really cheesy – invented a recognition mechanism that, using no creativity whatsoever, we called 'The 120% Club'. This was purely a column on the final page where people were individually thanked for performing above and beyond the call of duty; for 'going that extra mile'; for giving '120%'. I told you it was cheesy. Staff members could nominate anyone for inclusion in the '120% Club' – and (with a bit of editing) Paul would print them. What did

(continued)

people receive as reward for inclusion in this so-called 'club'? Nothing except for recognition by their peers – which just happens to be the strongest form of motivation that there is. The trick to making such a cheesy thing as the '120% Club' actually work is that it must be genuine – and this starts at the top. It just so happened that I was HR Director and genuinely thought this was a superb idea. But more importantly, so did our HR managers (as the idea for the 120% Club was theirs) – so everyone in HR was as one in support. Once everyone else could see that this wasn't a gimmick, that it was a genuine mechanism for identifying and thanking people for extraordinary effort and for using their initiative, they started to join in. Once they saw the galvanising effect it had on their people, the entire management team got on board. Our Communications Manager was soon inundated with nominations every fortnight.

Open was a great success. It struggled to get traction in its first few months, as it was suspected to be either propaganda or trivia, depending upon whether you were a staff member or a senior manager, and I had to convince my fellow Board members to give it a chance on more than one occasion. But by the end of the 6th or 7th issue, it had gained a momentum all of its own. It had been allowed to improve by trial and error until it had become the company's central communications piece, read by everyone. 'Let's put that in *Open*' became an oft-heard comment at executive team meetings. *Open* underpinned years of often tumultuous change.

Remember that communication is a net-sum gain

Just as with external PR, not every piece of change communication will be good news and not every communication will be well received. Some will be completely misconstrued, no matter how well-intentioned – especially if they are emails. For some reason that I am yet to fathom, people will read negative things into emails even if they aren't really there.

Genuine communication between humans is messy. Actual, real-life conversations involve toing and froing, misunderstandings, clarifications, emotion, persuasion, humour... they don't follow a straightforward Bayesian logic.

Listen

There is much more to communication than writing well. When it comes to change, communication must be a dialogue. Listening is the essence of effective communication, and this is true at all levels of the organisation. The best way to convince someone that the change will be good, to encourage someone to embrace the new way of working, is not to tell them; it is to listen. As my very first Sales Manager once told me when I was an eager 22-year-old fresh graduate recruit:

'Sometimes, Cam, you just have to shut up and let them buy.'

Genuine stakeholder engagement

'Stakeholder engagement' is a strange term. It feels impersonal; it feels like a process. It may be streets ahead of 'stakeholder *management* ' but it is a term that still needs softening and expanding, for the genuine engagement of stakeholders is not a 'colour by numbers' systematic process. It is more of an art than a science. It requires genuine relationship building and genuine dialogue. It requires listening.

What 'stakeholder engagement' also requires is detailed planning.

First let's define 'stakeholder'. Simply put, this is anyone affected by the change. This, of course, will depend upon the change initiative in question. For the implementation of a new strategy, this will include the Board, the executive leadership team, management, departmental teams, customers, regulators, the media, shareholders, corporate investors… anyone affected by the change.

Each *group* of stakeholders needs to be assessed to understand the common perspectives and concerns shared by the group's members. We need to establish how we will address these common concerns, what the change will do for them as a group, the key messages we want to deliver to each one and what we would like them as a group to do and say differently.

Each group needs to be prioritised in terms of the importance to our ultimate success. We then need to plan the most appropriate forms of engagement for each group.

Once we have done that, we can get to finding and evaluating the key individuals within each of these main groups – to ascertain whether the key individuals are for or against the change, to what degree, how influential they are and how to engage them effectively.

Even though we each have our own individual motivations and triggers, it is very useful to segment the individuals into different camps. For example:

Advocates: Those naturally for the change and able to influence others

Acceptors: The ones who are likely to go along with the change

Neutrals: Those who are not fussed one way or the other

Sceptics: Those who are slightly on the wrong side of neutral

Resistors: Those against the change

Saboteurs: Those key negative influencers who could do real damage.

This is such a valuable planning exercise. It is also the one time in this whole process where you do *not* want to be open and transparent. These assessments are purely for the project team. The exercise creates hypotheses of what different people's concerns are likely to be before engaging with them to ascertain whether these hypotheses are, in fact, true and, if not, to amend them – and then what to do about it. Your stakeholder analysis should be re-examined and improved continually throughout the project.

	Advocates *For the change and influential*	Acceptors *Likely to go along with the change*	Neutrals	Sceptics *Able to be persuaded*	Resistors *Against the change*	Saboteurs *Against the change and influential*
Names						
Default actions						

Stakeholder Segmentation

A full-page version of the chart is contained in Chapter 35: The Change Toolbox along with other useful aids for stakeholder impact assessment, analysis and engagement. A full-size colour version of this image may be downloaded from www.changeandstrategy.com.

Methods of engagement

Engagement is not just one-to-one meetings, although these are critical with the key players and need to be conducted several times throughout the programme. Engagement can also include workshops, lunches, anonymous intranet surveys, customer focus groups, telephone interviews... whatever is most appropriate to understand their perspective fully and to engage with them properly. Sometimes companies forget to conduct two-way engagement with their people during normal times, let alone during times of change.

Take employee engagement surveys, for example. Some organisations seem to create an entire industry around their annual employee survey, thereby generating a great deal of heat but very little light on the subject of engagement. If all you do is send each staff member a personalised link to an online survey, distribute home-grown PowerPoint slides of the results to the departments and conduct a broadcast-style 'Town Hall' session to present pages of graphs – your people will undoubtedly respond with an equal amount of disdain and indifference. I even know of one organisation that didn't communicate the results of more than a quarter of its employee survey's questions because HR didn't like the answers.

Call me old-fashioned, but if you are setting out to measure employee engagement, I tend to think you should do your best to engage with your employees in the process.

This should include focus groups to gain a better understanding of the answers provided and to explore some of the key implications. Employee surveys should be driven by a genuine desire to engage your people in improving the way the organisation works. The alternative is a tick-the-box, superficial exercise with pseudo statistics masquerading as engagement. Staff see through this.

As with communications, if engagement is not genuine, it can be worse than doing nothing.

Chapter 18

Identification of the Emotional Triggers

How many social workers does it take
to change a light bulb?
Only one. But the light bulb must want to change.

This is supposed to be a joke about social workers. But it is actually a truism about change. People only genuinely change if they want to. So, in order to help them to want to change, we need to help them find their trigger, and a purely rational trigger will be inadequate, as we have discussed in earlier chapters. Furthermore, everyone's trigger will be different.

Successful change requires:

A 'Change Catalyst'

Clarity of what and why

Implications understood

Outcomes focus

Pause for reflection

Governance and planning

Genuine engagement

Emotional triggers

Strong leadership

A change-ready culture

'Change or you will be fired' is a strong motivator – but not enough for anyone genuinely to embrace new ways of working. 'Change and you will learn new skills and help the company move into new areas, but, even more importantly, it will make you even more employable' is the sort of emotional motivation that may enthuse people to put their heart and soul into a new way of doing things.

If we are successfully to instigate change that is sustainable, we need to find the appropriate emotional triggers at all levels of the organisation. While there will be certain emotional triggers that will be common to the members of specific groups (the executive team, managers, team leaders, sales, investment departments, compliance, legal, operations...), everyone will also possess personal triggers that are unique to them. Each individual will have their own unique emotional motivations. Some will be motivated by status, others by the opportunity to develop, some by career advancement – we genuinely are all individuals.

To illustrate just how important it is to find your people's emotional triggers if you wish to instigate change, allow me tell you a story that has nothing to do with work.

I know of a young man who is beyond clinically obese. He is in his early 30s and is unlikely to work another day in his (probably shortened) life. He hasn't suffered any physical injuries. His legally recognised incapacity is entirely down to his weight. Why is he so obese? Well, logically that is easy. He eats far too much, especially far too much sugar and processed foods. He drinks too many sugary drinks and he drinks too much alcohol. In fact, he displays all the signs of being an alcoholic. And he gets no exercise. The repercussions of his obesity? His body is shutting down, his internal organs are struggling to cope, his legs and knees can't stand the strain and he is now diabetic. He is jobless, hopeless and he gives all the appearance of someone who has a very low regard for himself.

Surely, you can't get more of a 'burning platform' for change than that? Yet, he does not possess the ability or the motivation to change. He can't even make the first step, let alone see the whole transformation through to its slimmer, healthier and happier conclusion.

Rational logic is a totally inadequate driver of change. Logically, this young man would rather be healthy, employed and live a longer life. But even when the situation is dire, logic is insufficient. Logic won't fix this young man. Deeply rooted psychological barriers are preventing him from saving his own life. He lacks the emotional motivation to change.

I know of a second man who was once in much the same predicament – he too was morbidly obese. I know this to be true; he has shown me the photographs. At the time the photographs were taken, his wife had just had their first child and they had decided to buy a house. The bank demanded that the man obtained life insurance before they would release the mortgage. He dutifully went along for a medical check-up to enable the insurance company to price the life insurance premiums. He knew the price of the insurance was going to be astronomical. But it wasn't the cost that proved to be his trigger. It was the doctor – and his baby daughter. The doctor said to him, 'I know the premiums are ridiculously high, but if I were you, I would take the life insurance contract (it was ten-year term insurance). You will be lucky to see your daughter's tenth birthday anyway and your wife could do with the money.'

Our man was outraged and stormed out of the doctor's surgery. But on the drive home, he gradually came to the realisation that the doctor was right. The realistic possibility of not living to see his daughter's tenth birthday was the trigger he needed. Today he is quite literally half the size he used to be: 34-inch waist, fit and healthy. He carries around a photo on his phone of his wife holding up a pair of his old trousers – she could climb into one of the legs with plenty of room to spare. His wife has asked him to keep the photo on his iPhone to remind him that she stuck with him 'through the fat times'.

The second man found his trigger; he found his emotional motivation. The first man hasn't. Without help, he may never find it.

I have used this highly dramatic example to underline the importance of helping your people find their emotional change triggers, for the simple reason that they will only change if they genuinely wish to do so – and their decision will be based largely on emotion.

To help them find their triggers, you will need to engage your best HR people and your most influential people managers, because, as we discussed in Chapter 8, your managers are the number one influencers of their people's emotional commitment. You will need to help your people managers find the emotional change triggers for each one of their people – as sustainable change will be the culmination of commitment from individuals across your organisation.

Chapter 19

A Strong, Committed, Aligned and Unwavering Leadership Team

'All for one and one for all.'
Alexandre Dumas[14]

Successful change requires strong leadership.

But more than that, it requires leaders who genuinely and actively embrace the change – and are seen to do so. It requires a leadership team whose members are all aligned and working together to achieve the desired outcomes; outcomes that every one of them genuinely cares about delivering. It requires leaders who will 'stay the course' in the face of future obstructions and challenges. It requires leaders who 'walk the walk', not just 'talk the talk'. And when it comes time for implementation, the leaders must be the first ones to embrace the new ways of working.

Successful change requires:

A 'Change Catalyst'

Clarity of what and why

Implications understood

Outcomes focus

Pause for reflection

Governance and planning

Genuine engagement

Emotional triggers

Strong leadership

A change-ready culture

Any chink in this armour, any gap in the alignment, any hint of disagreement, any sign of hesitation and the change effort will begin to crumble – quickly.

Of course, to achieve this unity and clarity of purpose will require each member of the leadership team to be motivated personally and emotionally to support the change fully and actively. Like every other member of staff, the leadership will also be wondering, 'What is in it for me?' and they will need their individual concerns and needs addressed before they will genuinely be committed to the new world.

I once witnessed a highly Alpha-male CEO completely ignore this essential ingredient in a quite spectacular fashion. He had decided to reorganise the entire front end of the company along product lines; centralising control and demoting country managers in the process. He also decided not to share any of this with anyone but the HR Director until the two of them had worked out the details. Together they decided the structure and composition of the new top team. The CEO then called a high priority meeting of all of his direct reports at which he announced everyone's new job titles. When he had finished his pronouncements, there was complete and stunned silence around the table. You could have heard a pin drop.

'What's the problem?' the CEO half-asked, half-shouted in mounting exasperation. For some reason he had expected the gathered executives to be instantly excited and completely enthused – after all, the HR Director and he had worked hard on this.

Gradually, one by one, the executives began asking a few questions – tentatively at first. 'Why change from the current account-centric model? Won't this mean clients end up getting visits from three or four different sales reps rather than one? What is going to happen to the existing account managers? What is going to happen to the Country Managers?' All reasonable questions. This was the first any of them had heard about the plan, after all.

The CEO's face became redder and redder with every question and he gripped the table ever more tightly as time went on. Finally, after the trickle of questions had gained momentum and was heading towards flood proportions, the CEO snapped. He stood up and roared, 'You had all better get used to it! Either you are on the bus or you are under it!' and then stormed out of the room.

It took the change consultants, of which I was one, months to try to obtain some semblance of unity among the new leadership team. But to be honest, we were fighting a losing battle. From Day 1, it was obvious that the change was being done *to* everyone not *with* them. The individual needs, concerns and wants of the CEO's direct reports were not taken into consideration. This was the CEO's plan; no one else's. The leadership team was, therefore, never genuinely aligned – and this fact was obvious to everyone else in the organisation.

Chapter 20

A Change-ready Culture

*'Before everything else,
getting ready is the secret to success.'*
Henry Ford

Creation of a culture that embraces, encourages and rewards change is our final key ingredient for success.

As we have seen in Part One, people need help if they are to embrace change willingly. They need help to overcome their fear of the unknown, their fear of failure and/or their fear of being blamed. And to enable this on an organisation-wide scale requires the establishment of an environment where people eagerly look for improvements in the way things are done, are allowed to question the status quo, are encouraged to learn from failure and are open to new processes, procedures and structures.

Successful change requires:

A 'Change Catalyst'

Clarity of what and why

Implications understood

Outcomes focus

Pause for reflection

Governance and planning

Genuine engagement

Emotional triggers

Strong leadership

A change-ready culture

It requires the establishment of a change-ready culture.

The ever-increasing pace of change in the modern business world means that today's leaders must be able to take their organisations in new directions swiftly and decisively when the need arises.

Building a 'change-ready' culture requires the leadership to be empathetic and communicate constantly, clearly and genuinely. You should also:

- **Assess the change-readiness of your people, your managers, your leaders and your organisation as a whole.** The best way to do this is through a combination of employee culture survey and focus groups – both run by genuinely independent external professionals. (For the former, I recommend Insync, www.insyncsurveys.com.au, an Australian-based firm used by hundreds of major corporations across the world for precisely this purpose.)

- **Remove 'blame'** that may exist within your organisation. Seeking to improve things must not reflect poorly on those who have designed or manage the current process.

- **But keep 'accountability'.** In my first year at Sesame, we removed the blame culture so successfully that no one was being blamed for anything – even non-delivery! We had created a no-blame, no-accountability culture, which we then had to set about rectifying.

- **Ensure your people are focused on outcomes.** Make sure that accountabilities are clear and your people take pride in delivering. Celebrate success.

- **Treat 'failure' as a learning experience rather than a hang-able offence.** Successful people fail time and time again. Obviously there are limits to this, but if managers set clear objectives and clear guidelines and provide the support their people need, the impact of mistakes should be containable. But most importantly, mistakes can be the most powerful learning mechanism possible.

  One of the world's most successful hospitality companies, Four Seasons, has abandoned the word 'failure' from its corporate lexicon altogether. Instead, they use the word 'glitch', because a 'failure' or a 'mistake' is something you can't take back. A glitch is an opportunity to recover from and improve things as a result.

  At Facebook, whose corporate motto is 'move fast and break things', no one is criticised for failing. Instead, they may be criticised for not trying hard enough.[15]

  An example of victorious failure was the launch of Virgin Wines in the UK. It was so successful that our warehousing and distribution processes couldn't cope. Customers waited weeks for their delivery, which was utter failure in our books and very expensive as we had promised that delivery would be free if we didn't get it to them within three days. But the way we responded to solve our clients' problems turned this glitch into an opportunity. Those affected during our launch week ended up being the company's most loyal group of customers.

Another, possibly apocryphal, story about treating failure as a learning experience is the tale of the share trader who, after a spectacular run of bad luck/form, was several millions of dollars in the red and consequently tendered his resignation. 'Don't be daft,' allegedly replied his manager as he rejected his offer. 'I have just invested millions in your training. Get back to work.'

- **Genuinely encourage continuous improvement and new ideas.** Doing this effectively will require you to set clear parameters upfront – ensuring that the new ideas that are generated are material enough to make a difference but not so large that implementation will be too challenging. The worst result of any innovation or continuous improvement programme is when the initial sparks of enthusiasm are snuffed out because almost every new idea is rejected.

- **Reward people for seeking improvements, being innovative, taking risks and solving problems.** Make it positive and rewarding, perhaps even 'cool', to want to change things for the better.

- **Encourage your people to question the status quo.** This will be a challenge for some of your 'old school' command-and-control managers. If your people think they are insulting their managers by pointing out areas for potential improvement, they will never do it.

- **Help them to think 'and' not 'or'.** Help your people to frame their new ideas constructively. Help them to build upon what the organisation does well. Help them to be builders rather than destroyers.

- **Make change normal.** Change shouldn't be something that is done to your people; something they have to endure periodically at the whim of the firm's leaders. It should be part of Business as Usual; part of your company's DNA; integral to the way your people think, act and operate. After all, change *is* normal. Not changing is the anomaly. *'Permanent change is a fundamental part of what it means to be human'* (Professor Brian Cox, *Wonders of the Universe*, BBC 2015).

- **Give your people the tools to cope with change.** Help them to avoid the lure of victimhood. Help them to feel personally responsible for their future success. We discussed some ideas for this in Chapter 1.

- **Get your managers change-ready.** As we discussed in Chapter 8, your people managers need to be at the vanguard of every change. They need to be looking forward to change. They need to be continually on the lookout for ways to improve the way the business works and genuinely committed to supporting changes – not just going through the motions.

  You need to know what your people managers feel about the proposed changes and you need to turn them into advocates for change. Your people managers have the power to make or break any new initiative.

- **Ensure the leadership is change-ready.** Every single member of the leadership team must genuinely be ready and willing to embrace change. They set the tone for the rest of the organisation. If the leaders are not advocates of change, the likelihood of success of any significant new initiative will be dismally low. The old adage 'If you can't change the people, you will have to change the people' is never truer than when applied to a firm's leaders.

As we saw in Part One, the barriers to change are formidable – hence the 88% failure rate. Building an environment in which change is normal and where seeking ways to improve the way the organisation works is actively encouraged will improve your odds of victory significantly. Creating a 'change-ready' culture will lay the foundation for success.

In fact, culture is such an important component of instigating successful and sustainable change that Part Three is dedicated entirely to the subject.

Notes

1. US cultural anthropologist, author and speaker (1901–1978).
2. For more information about EQ, please refer to the section at the end of Chapter 11, creatively entitled, 'What is EQ?'
3. Author (2011), *The Wise Man's Fear* (The Kingkiller Chronicle: Day Two) DAW Books.
4. Howard Gardner is the John H. and Elisabeth A. Hobbs Professor of Cognition and Education at the Harvard Graduate School of Education.
5. Goleman, D. (1998) *Working With Emotional Intelligence*, New York: Bantam Books.
6. http://psychcentral.com/lib/what-is-emotional-intelligence-eq/
7. http://psychcentral.com/lib/what-is-emotional-intelligence-eq/
8. American Poet 1908–1984.
9. Co-founder, former Chairman and CEO of Apple Inc.; former CEO and majority shareholder of Pixar Animation Studios (1951–2011).
10. Classic BBC comedy (1980–1984) about the ineffectiveness but utter control of the British Civil Service. www.youtube.com/watch?v=dIto5mwDLxo
11. American author 1835–1910.
12. Wording taken from www.prince2.com.
13. Benjamin Franklin (1706–1790) was one of the Founding Fathers of the United States. A renowned polymath, Franklin was a leading author, printer, political theorist, politician, freemason, postmaster, scientist, inventor, civic activist, statesman and diplomat.
14. *The Three Musketeers* 1844.
15. These two insights regarding Four Seasons and Facebook are courtesy of the WhatIf? innovation agency.

Part Three

Culture Change

'Culture eats strategy for breakfast.'
Peter Drucker[1]

Culture change

Creating the right corporate culture is one of the golden keys to sustainable and enhanced performance. How you decide to treat your people will
impact every single aspect of your organisation – the types of products
you sell, the kind of service you deliver, your sales, your profits – everything. Your culture will determine your success.

'Culture is critically important to business success', according to 84%
of the more than 2200 global participants in Strategy&'s 2013 culture and
change management survey.[2] Yet, less than half of the respondents believe their companies do a good job of managing culture or that culture is
a priority in their companies' transformation initiatives.

A senior colleague once told me that corporate culture is something
that simply happens; that it is the culmination of far too many random
factors to be managed. She was wrong. Culture is not an esoteric phenomenon. It is real, it is tangible and it can be changed.

Corporate culture is the lingering effect of every interaction between the leadership, the management and the employees. It manifests itself in every interaction between the employees and the customer.

It boils down to one simple equation: Culture = Behaviour. Culture is the way your organisation works; *how* your people deliver your strategy. Of course, to change your culture you need to understand fully *why* your people behave the way they do.

Culture change fails when it is de-coupled from strategy. Culture is not the remit of HR; it is the remit of the CEO and the entire leadership team.

This section of the book dedicates itself to the art of culture change. We discuss the importance of 'Cultural Intelligence', what culture is and, more importantly, how to change it.

'The thing I have learned at IBM is that culture is everything.'
Louis V. Gerstner, Jr[3]

Chapter 21

Cultural Intelligence

'Cultural Intelligence' is a relatively recent term coined by P. Christopher Ealey and Soon Ang.[4] They defined Cultural Intelligence as a person's capability to adapt as he/she interacts with others from different cultures. They also posited that these capabilities are a form of intelligence that can be measured and developed. They suggested calling it CQ (Cultural Quotient).

Cultural Intelligence is related to Emotional Intelligence, but, in the words of Christopher Ealey, *'It picks up where Emotional Intelligence leaves off'.*[5]

'A person with high Emotional Intelligence grasps what makes us human and, at the same time, what makes each of us different from one another. A person with high Cultural Intelligence can somehow tease out of a person's or group's behaviour those features that would be true of all people and all groups, those peculiar to this person or this group, and those that are neither universal nor idiosyncratic. The vast realm that lies between those two poles is culture.'

The key hypothesis behind Cultural Intelligence is that understanding the impact of an individual's cultural background on their behaviour is essential for effective business.

Furthermore, we can develop strategies and skills to improve our cultural perception – to enable us to distinguish behaviours that are driven by someone's background from those that are specific to them as individuals. Of course, the implicit assumption is that appreciating the difference between the two will enable us to react appropriately once we recognise the genesis of the behaviours we are witnessing. In turn, this should result in a better working environment and, ultimately, better outcomes for the organisation.

Originally, I perceived that the concept of 'Cultural Intelligence' was only relevant for organisations with a multinational workforce. I was mistaken.

The concept of 'Cultural Intelligence' was originally based on under-standing and appreciating other people's default national cultures. This is of increasing importance as an expanding number of organisations be-come increasingly multicultural, especially those located in the world's large metropolitan centres. I recently worked within a department of a large institutional investor where the 50 people in the department were from 19 different nations – USA, UK, Ireland, Canada, France, Germany, Slovenia, Brazil, Argentina, Russia, China, Hong Kong, South Africa, Pakistan, India, Lebanon, Australia, Egypt and the UAE.

However, while a great deal of focus has been placed on the clash of cultures in organisations where multiple nationalities co-exist, clashes of different cultures occur in every organisation – even in those where every single employee is from the same country and speaks the same mother tongue.

The four components of Cultural Intelligence

The inventors of 'Cultural Intelligence' describe four different CQ capa-bilities: motivation (CQ Drive), cognition (CQ Knowledge), meta-cognition (CQ Strategy) and behaviour (CQ Action).

CQ-Drive is a person's interest and confidence in functioning effectively in culturally diverse settings. It includes: Intrinsic interest – deriving en-joyment from culturally diverse experiences; Extrinsic interest – gaining benefits from culturally diverse experiences; and Self-efficacy – having the confidence to be effective in culturally diverse situations.

CQ-Knowledge is a person's knowledge about how cultures are similar and how cultures are different. It includes: Business – knowledge about eco-nomic and legal systems; Interpersonal – knowledge about values, social interaction norms and religious beliefs; and Socio-linguistics – knowledge about rules of languages and rules for expressing non-verbal behaviours.

CQ-Strategy is how a person makes sense of culturally diverse experiences. It occurs when people make judgements about their own thought processes and those of others. It includes: Awareness – knowing about one's existing cultural knowledge; Planning – strategising before a culturally diverse encounter; and Checking – checking assumptions and adjusting mental maps when actual experiences differ from expectations.

CQ-Action is a person's capability to adapt verbal and nonverbal behaviour to make it appropriate to diverse cultures.

In my opinion, CQ-Drive cannot be taught. You either have it or you don't. But the other three can be improved through training, coaching and experience.

The sources of Cultural Intelligence – head, body and heart

OK. Bear with me for a paragraph or two. It may appear that I have gone all 'New Age' on you, but stick with me. It will be worth it.

The inventors of CQ also proclaim that Cultural Intelligence resides in the 'head, body and heart' (or, if you prefer: 'understanding', 'action' and 'commitment'). They also declare that rarely are people equally strong in all three areas – yet all three are necessary.

Head

This involves understanding the beliefs, customs and taboos of foreign cultures. It is often not straightforward, as few people are able to analyse themselves or their own culture objectively to any great degree, let alone capable of explaining the nuances to strangers. So, other ways need to be found to obtain this understanding. While this can include reading books and blogs and attending training courses, genuine awareness requires interaction with the foreign cultures in question and it takes time.

Body

Your new-found understanding will not be enough. It will have to be backed up by action. Adopting some of the traits and habits of the new culture will help you deepen your understanding and will demonstrate respect for the other culture.

In France, it is normal to greet female colleagues and clients with a kiss on both cheeks; three if Swiss. In many Middle Eastern countries it is an insult and a sign of ignorance if you even offer to shake the hand of a local woman. Not offering a hand to a European lady would be dismissive and rude. Kissing a Middle Eastern woman could get you arrested.

Heart

Adapting to a new culture requires confidence, perseverance, the willingness to get it wrong and the ability to recover. The alternative is to give up after unsuccessful efforts either to understand or engage.

Actually, this head/body/heart concept is useful for any type of change. As change leaders, we need to appeal to our people's 'heads' (the logical rationale for the change), their 'hearts' (the emotional rationale for the change) and their 'bodies' (help them turn both into action).

Observing the default settings of other cultures

'You mustn't judge Australia
by the Australians.'
Dame Edna Everage[6]

Stereotypes can be insulting, patronising, simplistic and inappropriate. But as a shorthand method of observing different cultures, they can also be unnervingly accurate.

The English are polite, well-mannered, love a good process and carry the faint whiff of Empire with them wherever they go. Many a British leader has been known to quote something along the lines of, *'When it comes to democracy and the rule of law, it is the first five hundred years that are the hardest.'*[7] Let's face it; the British Empire was an exercise in cultural enforcement rather than cultural engagement. It was the exportation of British culture, values, military might and law to the four corners of the globe.

Americans are direct, enthusiastic, energetic and action-oriented with a 'can do' mentality that is simultaneously invigorating and exhausting. Americans see black and white where the English see innumerable shades of grey. Americans turn nouns into verbs with alarming regularity and use imprecise language, often stemming from a 'Wild West' pioneering heritage, to convey mental pictures in a manner that is about as non-British as it is possible to be without speaking a different language altogether. *'Two countries separated by a common language'* as George Bernard Shaw is alleged to have penned. Americans too have a sense of superiority – which is not completely unearned (a use of the double-negative of which an Englishman would be proud). After all, 'The American Way' has produced the world's largest economy and the world's sole superpower – from nothing. *The Economist* recently reported that UK companies that are acquired by US firms experience, on average, a 10% increase in productivity.

Australians are a fascinating combination of the two. They possess the 'can do' attitude of the Americans but are even more direct. Meanwhile, they have maintained a very British sense of humour and love of irony. But unlike the Brits, Aussies are underwhelmed by rank and status, and they tend to get straight to the point. They avoid both the American fondness for marketing spin sound-bites and the British art of subtle phrasing and word-smithery. When disagreeing with a statement, Britons may say something along the lines of, 'I don't disagree with the point being made but I think that perhaps the matter could do with a little more research.' Americans will think 'this isn't how it is done back home' but say something along the lines of: 'I can't see that position gaining any traction in the marketplace!.' The Australian reaction will be, 'That's bullshit, mate.'

The Italians use elaborate hand gestures and are passionate in almost everything they do. In the same way that there is no Portuguese word that conveys quite the sense of urgency as the Spanish 'mañana', there appears to be no Italian equivalent for 'punctuality' or 'deadline'. The French think the Italians possess a ridiculous and completely unwarranted sense of superiority.

The French know they are superior – culturally, intellectually, gastronomically and enologically.

The Dutch can be blunt to a degree that is often considered by others to be rude. Because it is.

The Germans are efficient and effective. There is only one correct way to do things and the sooner everybody else realises this, the sooner we can all get on with delivering the outcome that is required.

The Japanese are inscrutable. Honour and respect for both elders and position are of utmost importance. As a gaijin,[8] the verbal language barrier will not be the only challenge to understanding what is happening in a meeting, as your hosts possess an entire lexicon of nonverbal communication and will keep their cards very close to their chests.

The Chinese are ordered, respectful and much less individualistic than Westerners. The concept of 'saving face' is as important in China as it is in Japan. Truth is in the eye of the beholder. This can be a complete anathema to a Western mind-set where, more often than not, truth is almost regarded as an absolute.

Arabs are driven by family, honour and an acceptance of fate. 'Insh'allah' is the most-uttered phrase in the Arab world. Translated as 'god willing' or 'if god wills', the phrase concludes almost any statement about the future. *We will discuss this at the next meeting, insh'allah. I will see you after the holiday, insh'allah. Your telephone and Internet will be connected next Tuesday, insh'allah.* (Yes, insh'allah can also be used as an abdication of responsibility.) The acceptance of god's will may be the reason why a significant number of people don't use seatbelts, don't secure their babies during car journeys and/or don't take out life insurance. Truth is both relative and contextual. 'Face' is all-important. Arabs talk in stories and love grand visions. When will they be delivered? Insh'allah.

I could go on as I have only scratched the surface of a small number of the 193 countries and countless cultures across the world. But I think you get the idea. However, while stereotypes may be able to provide a snapshot of how other cultures think and behave, a detailed understanding of the mind-sets, approaches and nuances of other cultures is the first step towards improving our Cultural Intelligence and thereby our effectiveness in multicultural environments.

Even within nations, we find different cultures. Britain may be a small island or, more correctly, a collection of small islands, but it is also a patchwork of innumerable cultures. Put a cockney, a Scouser, a Somerset farmer and a Glaswegian in the same room and very little will be understood by any of them. Not only is the 'United Kingdom' made up of four separate nations (England, Scotland, Wales and Northern Ireland just in case you were in any doubt), each of these home nations contains many dozens of distinctly different cultures within its national borders. The number of accents across England is almost too numerous to count; the language changes recognisably (or some may argue, unrecognisably) within just a few miles. Our home is in West Oxfordshire. The accents of some of the farmers in Gloucestershire (the county starts at the end of our village) are so pronounced that I have trouble understanding them at times. And accents are only one indicator of cultural difference; each county and each region has a sense of humour, attitudes and behaviours that are distinctive and common to people from that area. To some degree, the same can also be said about people from different regions of Australia, states in the US, different parts of Germany, etc.

But it isn't just our geographical background that makes us think and behave differently. Our educational background will also have an influence – state school, private school or public school; university or trade; which type of university, which type of degree? The culturally intelligent among us will need to understand and decipher a number of factors that influence the way we behave and the way we interact with others.

Observing your own default settings

> 'It is well, when judging a friend,
> to remember that he is judging you with
> the same godlike and superior impartiality.'
> Arnold Bennett[9]

Of course, observing others is only one half of the battle. The far more difficult half is observing yourself.

Cultural Intelligence profiles

Ealey and Mosakowski believe that most managers fit at least one of the following six profiles. Which one do you think best describes you?

1. **The provincial** is effective when working with people of similar background to them but runs into trouble when venturing farther afield. The provincial has one way of doing things and finds it almost impossible to adapt.

A particular senior manager springs to mind when I read this profile. His nationality, his natural inclinations and, to some extent, his age combined to ensure that his management style was of the old-fashioned and immovable command-and-control variety; a style of management that I thought had died out decades ago. As did his direct reports, many of whom had previously run substantial teams in their own right. The end result was an unnecessarily tense team culture that was unable to get the best out of the senior and talented team members.

2. **The analyst** methodically deciphers a foreign culture's rules and expectations.

3. **The natural** relies entirely on his intuition rather than on a systematic learning style.

4. **The ambassador** may not know much about the culture he has just entered, but he convincingly communicates his certainty that he belongs there. A good ambassador doesn't underestimate cultural differences. However, 'ambassadors' that I have met remain slightly aloof; respectful but essentially reserved.

5. **The mimic** uses his head and his body, but his heart is not in it. The definition of mimicry in this context is not, however, the same as pure imitation, which can be interpreted as mocking. It is mirroring the behaviours, intonations and actions of others – in a respectful fashion – to put others at ease and to enhance communication.

6. **The chameleon** possesses high levels of all three CQ components and is very rare. Some are able to achieve results that natives cannot, due to their insider's skills and outsider's perspective. Ealey and Mosakowski found that only about 5% of the managers they surveyed fell into this category.

Here is a brilliant example of uber Cultural Intelligence from Ealey and Mosakowski's 2004 HBR article:

'One (such chameleon) is Nigel, a British entrepreneur who has started businesses in Australia, France and Germany. The son of diplomats, Nigel grew up all over the world. Most of his childhood, however, was spent in Saudi Arabia. After several successes of his own, some venture capitalists asked him to represent them in dealings with the founder of a money-losing Pakistani start-up.

To the founder, his company existed chiefly to employ members of his extended family and, secondarily, the citizens of Lahore. The VCs, naturally, had a different idea. They were tired of losses and wanted Nigel to persuade the founder to close down the business.

Upon relocating to Lahore, Nigel realized that the interests of family and community were not aligned. So he called in several community leaders, who agreed to meet with managers and try to convince them that the larger community of Lahore would be hurt if potential investors came to view it as full of businesspeople unconcerned with a company's solvency. Nigel's Saudi upbringing had made him aware of Islamic principles of personal responsibility to the wider community, while his British origins tempered what in another person's hands might have been the mechanical application of those tenets. Throughout the negotiations, he displayed an authoritative style appropriate to the Pakistani setting. In relatively short order, the managers and the family agreed to terminate operations.'

Jump in: the water's fine

Awareness of other cultures and our own default settings may be interesting, but, like all knowledge, it only becomes useful if we do something with it.

And while training courses can be fashioned around improving different aspects of Cultural Intelligence, the best way to learn is to get among it.

A great deal of CQ-Knowledge can be obtained through reading and training. One organisation I worked with in the Middle East conducted a one-day 'Cultural Awareness Workshop' for its expats as a first step in obtaining such knowledge.

CQ-Strategy techniques can be developed through training and coaching.

But the only way to improve the all-important 'CQ-Action' is to start interacting.

Moving beyond differences

A few years ago I was staying in a hotel in Abu Dhabi. As I was ambling out to the pool area, I was overtaken by a gaggle of Japanese guests shuffling past me in one amorphous throng – each one dressed in the hotel's complimentary white robes and white slippers. Seconds later, heading the other way, came a tightly knit cabal of young Emirati women, chatting and laughing with one another; each one dressed head-to-toe in their jet black abayas. I laughed. What was next? A bus load of Germans laying their identical red towels out across all the best sun loungers? We humans; we love our tribes. We like to belong.

We are forever dividing ourselves into different categories; different clubs. Unfortunately, this quickly becomes different ways to define 'us' versus 'them'. United vs City, Republican vs Democrat, Conservative vs Labour, Country Bumpkin vs City Slicker, Black vs White, East vs West, North vs South, Expert vs Man-on-the-Street, Pro-Life vs Pro-Choice, Arab vs Jew, Muslim vs Christian, Muslim vs Hindu, Hindu vs Christian, Scientologists, Catholic vs Protestant vs Mormon vs Seventh Day

Adventists vs Baptist vs Evangelical vs...Sunni vs Shia vs Wahabi vs Sufis vs Ahmadiyyas vs Baha'is vs...

A basic flaw exists in the human condition (probably an innate evolutionary survival instinct) that compels us to gather together in groups and look for enemies. Our default setting appears to focus on our differences rather than our similarities. As a species, we need to work on this as it repeatedly ends in tears.

We see it in business all the time. The moment we move people from one department to another, even one team to another, is the instant when they switch allegiances. Sadly, one of the best ways to motivate and bring people together is to find a common enemy, as politicians of all persuasions know too well. Adam Morgan called it identifying the 'big fish'; the market leader you needed to 'eat'.[10] Honda was decidedly less subtle with its publicly declared Mission in 1970: 'We will destroy Yamaha.'

Find a common goal

Understanding the differences between cultures is important because it will affect how people think and behave and therefore how a change is delivered, but the ultimate aim in any change situation is to bring people together to deliver the shared outcomes you require.

We change leaders need to understand what drives the behaviours of our people – no matter what their cultural backgrounds and influences may be – so that we can bring them all together to embrace a common purpose and achieve a common goal.

This was just one of the many lessons that I learned during my years of working with different international cultures.

Chapter 22

Instigating Change
in a Foreign Culture

L eading, managing and instigating change is hard enough when you are in your own country and within a familiar corporate culture. It becomes considerably more challenging in a foreign country.

The fundamentals are the same – define the outcomes and the rationale for change, engage stakeholders, assess options, clarify the implications, clarify accountabilities, constant communication...

But how you go about it and the pace at which you approach it will be completely different.

I suppose this shouldn't have come as a surprise to me. After all, change is entirely cultural. Changing outcomes, changing outputs, changing processes all require the adoption of new behaviours. Changing 'what' is delivered is only done through changing 'how' it is delivered (and people will only do that if they understand 'why').

But it did.

I grew up in Australia. I went to school in Australia. I went to university in Australia. My first seven full-time jobs were in Australia. Then, in 1999, at the ripe old age of 35, I moved to the UK. Since then, I have helped organisations to instigate strategic change throughout the UK, Europe, the US, Asia and the Middle East.

One of the key things I have learned from an eclectic mix of successes, near-misses, disappointments and outright failures across all of these continents is that your change process needs to be entirely flexible. It needs to flex with the culture of the organisation, which, in turn, is heavily influenced by the nationality in which it resides. A rigid process and a rigid approach will be doomed to failure.

Another lesson concerns communication. Communication is definitely an art – and art is very different in different cultures. US-style broadcast communications laden with hyperbole, Wild West metaphors and posi-tive thinking go down like a lead balloon in Britain. British reserve and the desire not to offend are often taken at face value in Australia, thereby translating into complete agreement with the change, when the opposite may be the reality. In Asia, saving face is critical: communications that may appear to be disingenuous and meaningless to a Western eye will be considered respectful to an Eastern sensibility. In the West, we tend to create the need for change by first pointing out what is wrong with the current situation (creating a 'burning platform'). In the Middle East, this can be insulting. No matter how strong the desire for change, spelling out all the weaknesses of the status quo can be regarded as denigrating to, and belittling the efforts of, all those who have gone before you. This is not the Middle Eastern way – at least not in public and certainly not in writing.

My experience in working in many parts of the world has reinforced all of the theory I have read regarding 'Cultural Intelligence' – especially the existence of group-wide commonalities in terms of attitudes, customs and ways of thinking among people of a certain nationality and common ethnic background. Plus the fact that these group-wide behaviours are not the only drivers of our conduct – we all have idiosyncrasies, habits and biases of our own that we overlay on top of any background traits that we may share with others.

Australia to England

The differences in moving from Australia to England were greater than I had expected, even though the two countries are arguably more alike than any other two you could name. The first thing that struck me was just how small and remote the land of my birth actually was. If it wasn't for sport, Australia would hardly rate a mention in the UK newspapers. In the US, we don't even make it onto the sports pages.

Australia in the late 90s was significantly more advanced than the UK in so many ways. In 1999 Sydney, I was used to proper web-based grocery shopping and online banking, chip-and-pin point-of-sale debit card payments, smoke-free restaurants and all taxis taking credit cards. In 1999 London, Tescos and RBS both handed me CD-ROMs, which made fetching coasters but were of little other use, I was forever visiting the 'cash machine', we were dismissively shown to the dingy little 'no smoking' section at the rear of restaurants (to ingest inferior quality food) and a cabbie threatened to beat me up when I handed him an American Express card at the end of a journey to Twickenham.

Yet, the ghost of the Australian 'cultural cringe' was never far away. This is a term coined in Australia after WWII by the Melbourne critic and social commentator A. A. Phillips. It gives a label to the ingrained feelings of inferiority that local intellectuals struggled against at the time, and which were most clearly pronounced in Australian theatre, music, art and letters. In essence, Phillips pointed out that the Australian public widely assumed that anything produced by local dramatists, actors, musicians, artists and writers was necessarily deficient when compared against the works of their British and European counterparts. The only way local arts professionals could build themselves up in the public esteem was either to follow overseas fashions, or, more often, to spend a period of time working in Britain.

I still felt it 50 years later. Whether perception or reality, the fact that something had been done in Australia didn't mean it was up to London standards. Jokes about Australia and Australians from even the closest of my London friends seemed to be tinged with a slight edge of superiority. Upon reflection, I think it was 99% in my head, but, as they say, perception is reality. (Actually, it was also around this time that I first heard the colonial and completely unfair term 'The Hong Kong FILTH' – Failed In London Try Hong Kong – so maybe it wasn't entirely imagined on my behalf.) I have long since stopped suffering from the curse of the cultural cringe and I don't see it in the next generation at all – quite the opposite;

my children parade the fact that they were born in Australia as a badge of honour. As indeed it is. But it is just one little example of how national identities can frame and affect an individual's attitudes and behaviour – and how people from other nationalities may not even be aware of its existence.

It made me wonder what little cultural idiosyncrasies other nationalities harboured.

Translating for the Americans

One of the most enjoyable engagements of my career was advising a brilliant, entrepreneurial American insurance technology and service business called iPipeline. After systematically transforming the paper-heavy US life insurance industry, the VC-backed entrepreneurs of iPipeline set their sights on the UK where they wished to perform the same miracles on the British insurance industry and eventually use a British base to launch themselves into Europe. The optimism and enthusiasm of the iPipeline executives were contagious; this is still true today. Their business results were exciting – again, still true today. And their belief that they could transform the UK's insurance industry burned fiercely – so, in spite of my advice that they focus their efforts on the US market and ignore the paper-less, highly competitive and concentrated UK market, we set about identifying a suitable acquisition target and meeting with their myriad shareholders. In the proceedings, it became clear that my 'real' job was as a translator: translating UK English into American English and back again.

We were all speaking the same language and we were all from the same industry, yet the potential for misunderstanding was enormous. These misunderstandings sent many of the conversations down blind alleys. For example, the simple term 'annuity' means completely different things to Americans than it does to Brits. The moment the word was uttered, it gave the charismatic iPipeline CEO an excuse to launch into the story of how his company was the market leader in annuity processing. However, before the story had reached its cruising altitude, I had to bring it back down to earth to explain that UK annuities were reverse pension contracts and not the types of savings plans that used the same name in the States. When I first interrupted him, the CEO gave me a look that was designed simultaneously to pierce and melt the recipient, but as soon as my brief explanation was over, he thanked me as he would have wasted everybody's time disappearing off on a tangent.

But the clash of cultures really started post-acquisition when The American Way came up against British Reticence. I learned that seeking to understand another nation's markets, ways of working, motivations and working practices only works when it works both ways. As indeed it has; the acquisition has been a great success.

Nonverbal communication in Asia

I read somewhere that 'Westerners send 1–2 people to a meeting to *tell* you everything they think you need to know. Asians, on the other hand, send 20 people to a meeting to *learn* everything you know'.

In Japan, meetings are primarily held to acquire information. Ideas are discussed and decisions made through a long and involved consensus-building process – not in a single meeting.

I have been to Tokyo twice on business. Once in the early 90s as an entrepreneur, trying to sell our interactive golf tutorial 'Nick Price's Troubleshooting Golf' to a Japanese video games distributor; and then 15 years later with Zurich when Japan became part of the new division of which I was Strategy Director. Both times, I found the Japanese people I met to be among the most polite, most hospitable and most opaque I have ever encountered. To the uninitiated, their thoughts, motivations and priorities can be completely hidden from view. And I was firmly among the uninitiated.

Every meeting I had in Japan was good-mannered, orderly, respect-ful... and unfruitful – because I was culturally ignorant. Oh, I was aware of the niceties of business etiquette but I had zero ability to read the room, to decipher body language or to see the real meaning behind the words that were spoken. And I have since learned that these forms of commu-nication are the 'real' forms in Japan. *What* is actually said can be banal and may even carry very little meaning. *How* something is said is where the real communication occurs. The Japanese rely heavily on nonverbal cues and the context of what they say, rather than the literal meaning of the words they use to say it. This is, of course, the complete opposite of the direct way that the likes of Americans, Australians, South Africans and the Dutch conduct business.

The Japanese can derive significant meaning from what is left 'unsaid' and context is critical. For example, asking for a fork when dining with Japanese hosts could signal that you have no desire to learn about their culture. Whereas if they see you are struggling with chopsticks, they may indeed offer you a fork, which you would be free to accept without insult-ing their culture in any way.

The Zurich experience was telling. We flew in from the UK to discuss the performance of the Japanese subsidiary, review their strategy and fu-ture plans, and to outline our plans for the new division. We had lengthy and detailed presentations and meetings to help us better understand the nuances of the Japanese market, the strengths and weaknesses of Zurich Life Japan and how they planned to take advantage of the opportunities. We provided suggestions, ideas to leverage experience from other parts of the Group, and genuine debate and discussion ensued. And nothing changed as a result.

We thought our Japanese colleagues were in complete agreement with our divisional strategy and the role we saw them playing in it. Part of the reason for this misconception was that they didn't once say 'no' in any of the meetings. Of course, their mouths may not have uttered the word, but

I have since learned that they would have been projecting disagreement in any number of ways that we were too culturally ignorant to pick up on – through indicating that something might be difficult or sucking air between teeth or suggesting an alternative, changing the conversation or simply staying silent. Sometimes, I now understand, confirming that they understand can actually mean no.

In Japan, silence is highly valued and is linked to credibility. 'The duck that quacks is the first to get shot.' Upon reflection, I think we did a great deal of quacking. We head office gaijins were wined, dined and treated with the utmost respect. We were also politely ignored. But as none of us were able to read the nonverbal cues or properly understand the context, what did we expect?

Hong Kong and Singapore are different – and yet several similarities remain. While seniority is, as in Japan, accorded a heightened level of respect, all of the business meetings were conducted in a very similar fashion to the UK, apart from one small but vital aspect – 'face'. The concept of 'face' is of critical importance. This affected how we could talk about performance numbers, for example. We couldn't dwell on poor numbers or discuss the potential reasons for the slump in sales in a public forum as this would have been disrespectful to the local CEO and Sales Director. Those discussions had to happen in private, preferably before the meeting. In fact, private meetings were where the real business took place. Public meetings were for PR and corporate communication.

Across Asia, as in Japan, meetings are held primarily to acquire information. Ideas are discussed and decisions made through a long and involved consensus-building process, not in a single meeting.

Relationships are also vitally important and require a considerable investment of time – and, quite often, alcohol. A brief flying visit for a few meetings will achieve nothing.

Majilis-style decision-making in the Middle East

Of course, alcohol will not feature in any Middle Eastern relationship-building exercise. But trust and respect are just as essential. I have found Arabs to be extremely welcoming and friendly. They are also very tactile – with members of their own sex anyway. Almost every greeting, however casual, involves a warm and firm handshake, and occasionally even an arm draped across a shoulder to the sound of 'my friend!' They will genuinely be pleased to see you. In the UAE, good friends may touch noses upon meeting and delight in walking together, sometimes holding hands. Their sense of humour also took me by surprise; they love to laugh.

Business in the Middle East is conducted in layers. The vast majority of foreigners only get to see the most external, outer layer. The big decisions are usually made in the other layers. It may appear that important decisions are being made in public meetings, but more often than not they are only being endorsed in such gatherings.

Truth is more relative than it is in the West – and this statement is not meant to be pejorative. It is simply an observation. In business, the same person can adopt completely contrarian viewpoints on the same subject depending upon the size, composition, timing and tone of the meeting in question – and this is completely acceptable.

Seniority, status and respect for elders are ingrained into society and business. The flow of meetings – and the outcomes they produce – can often depend upon what the senior people say and when they say it. The quickest way to stifle debate is for the most senior person to proclaim his opinion at the start of the meeting. Consequently, good Arab Chairmen will provide the opportunity for all participants to speak – before they themselves offer their views. Conversations in meetings can be circular and decisions can be revisited at later meetings. To the Western mind-set, decisions can sometimes be vague or obtuse – firstly, due to the imprecise nature of Arabic and secondly, because clarity of desired outcomes and clarity of accountabilities are not as important as they are in the West.

When I first did some work in the UAE many years ago, I was at a loss to understand the decision-making process. My Western mind-set instantly regarded such a time-consuming way of making decisions as completely unproductive.

It wasn't until I visited the Al Ain Palace Museum, where Sheik Zayed[11] used to hold court in the sweltering summer months, that I began to experience a first glimpse of understanding. I sat in the Sheik's old, open majilis[12] tent at 8:30 one clear spring morning, enveloped by local bird song, and could easily imagine the process that would have unfolded on a daily basis as Zayed was approached by one person after another to discuss the affairs of the day. Discussion groups would fragment and come back together to discuss the same matters from different angles. They would continue throughout the day or days in different parts of the Palace grounds until a consensus and a decision would finally percolate to the surface. This was the way that the tribal elders would have made decisions for centuries. It has some distinct advantages, the chief among them being that everyone genuinely has had input to a decision, so that once a decision is declared, the opposition to it has been significantly diminished and everyone should be ready and willing to get on with implementing it. The West could learn a lot from such a process.

But, of course, 'for every action…' The main challenge with a majilis-style of decision-making is avoiding group-think.

As Thaler and Sunstein illustrated so brilliantly in their best-selling book *Nudge*,[13] we humans have an ingrained tendency to follow other people's views and opinions, even when the logical part of our brain disagrees with it. The *Nudge* authors suggest that this phenomenon goes some way to explain such extremes as the inexplicable rise of Hitler and the Nazi party in pre-WWII Germany, the 1978 Jonestown mass suicide in the

US where 909 followers of the Reverend Jim Jones poisoned their children and then themselves for no logical reason (which is the genesis of the term 'drinking the Kool-Aid' as a short-hand reference to swallowing the company line without question), and why it is so important for US Presidential candidates to win early primaries – because 'momentum' will then almost certainly carry them to wins in future states. Group-think also goes some way to explain the sub-prime mortgage crisis that brought the world to the brink of depression in 2008 (although greed and hubris played even bigger roles). It certainly helps explain many of the disastrous decisions made by the leadership of the Royal Bank of Scotland (briefly the world's biggest bank) at around the same time. It played a significant role in the dotcom bubble and may even explain the current situation when stock markets continue to rise even as corporate earnings fall. Group-think can be dangerous.

'If you can find something everyone agrees on, it's wrong.'
Mo Udall[14]

However, while group-think is indeed something to guard against, consensus is of vital importance when it comes to change – although, as I have outlined, the consensus must be genuine. One of the great things about Emirati culture in particular is that they genuinely involve even the most junior and inexperienced Emirati managers and leaders in the decision-making process. However, when many Westerners go about the process of 'stakeholder engagement', they tend to focus only on the most senior decision-makers and, at best, pay lip service to the more junior or peripheral members of the management team. In the Middle East, this is a mistake as very swiftly this derisory approach will become known throughout the whole leadership team – to the detriment of the expat's standing and the initiative in question.

Arabs care about all members of their group – even the less skilled and the less experienced. This may stem from the fact that not too many years ago, their grandparents were eking out a harsh existence and every single member of the family was needed for the survival of the tribe, especially those families who had to endure long treks across the desert. The family kept together and travelled at the speed of its weakest member.

Family

Family sits at the epicentre of Arab life, something we seem to have lost a little in the West. Consequently, familial duties occupy an inordinate amount of their time. The family comes with a plethora of pre-ordained responsibilities for each and every member, depending upon gender, age and order of birth. Most evenings and weekends are taken up with family obligations, which is one of the reasons why locals and expats rarely mix outside of the office.

Layers of belonging

Your family is at the heart of your identity and this, in turn, defines the sect of Islam to which you belong. Your Emirate is your next layer of definition, then your country and finally your status as an Arab (as opposed to a Persian). Each layer not only defines the 'club' to which you belong but, ipso facto, also defines those to whom you are naturally opposed.

Of course, we humans are all like this to some degree; we are fundamentally tribal by nature. But it seems to be a little more pronounced in the Middle East; the lines of demarcation a little clearer; the walls a little higher; and the foundations a little deeper. People are arguably more inclined to follow the beliefs and biases of their pre-ordained groups.

And, of course, the concepts of 'face' and 'honour' in the Arab world are arguably even more important than they are in Asia. It is very important that someone is not made to look bad or embarrassed in any public meeting – even if they may be ill-prepared, off-beam or wrong.

But then, why should anyone make anyone be made to look bad in public – even if they are ill-prepared, off-beam or wrong? In business, things are rarely black or white; wrong or right. Another thing we Westerners can tend to forget.

Learnings from working in foreign lands

Take your time   Sustainable change needs time. Take your time genuinely to understand the culture in which you find yourself – not just the business etiquette but how decisions are made and why.

Patience   Taking one's time requires patience. People will react to perceived change in ways you won't have imagined. Stay calm; stay patient.

Don't give up   Perseverance is critical. Some cultures are more change averse than others and may test your perseverance – but don't give up. As an Emirati leader said to me, 'Don't stop knocking on the door. After a while, take a pause and think about why the door isn't opening – and then try another way. But keep going until the door opens.'

Respect   Don't just observe the other culture – respect it. Embrace it and learn from the differences.

Genuine engagement   This is the same for any change in any culture, even one with which you are familiar. But it is worth repeating.

Care   If you genuinely care – about the company, about the change and about the people – your colleagues and clients will eventually understand that you are sincerely trying to do the right thing. Try to fake it and you are doomed. In fact, once you stop genuinely caring, it is time to move on.

Enjoy yourself   No matter where they are from, people like to smile and laugh. Life's too short.

Chapter 23

Understanding Your Organisation's Culture

In order to instigate sustainable change successfully, you need to be completely aware of how your people interact with one another; of how your company goes about its business. You need to become aware of your own company's culture – its pros, its cons and how your social norms have developed. Only then can you hope to (a) work with your company's culture to instigate the change you require, or (b) change it.

Observing your organisation's culture will require you to be objective. You will need to look at your organisation anew – from the perspectives of your employees and from the perspectives of your customers. Andy Grove, founder and CEO of Intel, took this quite literally. In order to shake his Board out of its malaise, he and his fellow directors literally walked out the front door, regrouped and then walked back in the front entrance of Intel with 'fresh pairs of eyes'.

You will need to look at how your employees interact with one another, watching out for emotional hotspots – times and types of interactions which cause the greatest angst, excitement, joy or frustration. Take a fresh look at the corporate paraphernalia that adorns your walls, how your employees decorate their desks, the notice boards and common areas – what does it all say about your intended culture? Does this match your desired culture?

How do people interact with one another? What is the tone of their communications? What is the tone of your corporate communications?

Insight via culture surveys

Online culture surveys can be a valuable source of insight – if done well. A successful culture survey:

- Is genuinely anonymous and, more importantly, is regarded by employees to be anonymous

- Is designed by organisational psychologists with a proven track record from a renowned employee survey firm

- Consists of relevant questions that strike the balance between being specific enough to uncover issues specific to your organisation and generic enough to enable you to benchmark yourselves against peers and like-minded companies

- Provides you with detailed and insightful reporting and online portals to help you get the most out of the data provided.

Do not compromise on any of the above points.

I helped a UK client tender for such a survey among the world's leading survey firms and the firm that impressed us the most was, again, Insync (www.insyncsurveys.com.au).

Insight from employee focus groups and interviews

An online survey is only the beginning. However well designed and executed, it will not tell you everything you need to know. Focus groups and interviews with key influencers from across your organisation will give you the opportunity to explore the subject in greater depth – and help you to understand the meaning behind the key survey responses. The focus groups and interviews also need to be treated as highly confidential and conducted using the 'Chatham House Rule'[15] – where participants are free to use the information received, but neither the identity nor the affiliation of the speaker(s), or those of any other participant, may be revealed.

Focus groups and interviews are ideal ways to explore what it is like to work for an organisation and how an organisation works using open-ended, conversational questions such as, 'How would you describe to a friend what it is like to work for the organisation?', 'What is the one thing you would most like to change about this organisation?', 'What kinds of people succeed or fail in this company?'. These face-to-face sessions are also ideal situations to listen and watch out for the things that are left unsaid.

Insight from outside

Similar surveys and focus groups with customers will provide you with another perspective of how the company's culture translates into actual customer interactions. How would your customers or providers or partners describe your organisation's culture?

Chapter 24

Teaching People
to Walk in the Rain

As a young teenager, my son's favourite television show was *Mythbusters*; a cool, science-based programme from the US featuring a trio of hip young science grads and a couple of mad experienced guys conducting scientific experiments that almost inevitably ended with blowing something up in a spectacular fashion.

One episode sticks in my mind; the episode where they set out to prove or bust the myth that you get wetter if you run in the rain.

To do this, the *Mythbusters* team set up a row of ceiling sprinklers in an empty warehouse. One of the team donned a dry pair of blue cotton overalls and proceeded to walk from one end of the warehouse to the other through the simulated rain. Once he cleared the sprinklers, he stripped off the overalls and placed them in a dry and empty bin to be weighed. He then donned another identical pair of blue cotton overalls and repeated the exercise, but this time he ran the length of the warehouse through the man-made rain shower. He placed this second pair of wet overalls into an identical dry, empty bin to be weighed.

The result? The second pair of overalls contained more water than the first! He absorbed more water by running through the rain than by walking through it. This is completely counter-intuitive. We all run when it's raining – to minimise the time in the rain as much as possible. It's just common sense. But it's wrong.

That's what culture change is – teaching people to walk in the rain.

A company's culture is how its people behave, individually and in teams

Or, somewhat ironically, as Bob Diamond, CEO of Barclays, put it only weeks before the Libor-fixing scandal first broke, *'A company's culture is how people behave when they think no one is watching.'*

In the aftermath of the Global Financial Crisis, the UK experienced one new failure of culture in its banking sector after another. Barclays was fined for fixing the Libor exchange rate. HSBC was sanctioned and fined by numerous jurisdictions for permitting money laundering. Standard Chartered was fined for similar misdemeanours.

The culture of UK banks was in the spotlight from the moment that Northern Rock was first bailed out in September of 2007 right through to the slew of mis-selling and rate-fixing scandals that plagued the UK banking industry in the years that followed. I wrote several articles on the subject back in 2012. They are still so relevant that I have included a couple of them at the end of this chapter.

But culture failure wasn't only confined to banks. The Prime Minister, Health Minister, Education Minister, the Minister responsible for Media, Culture and Sport, the Leveson Inquiry, the Governor of the Bank of England and a further slew of journalists were all baying for 'culture change' across a wide range of industries and organisations. We needed to change the bonus culture in our banks, the targets culture in our schools, the scoop-at-all-costs culture in our press, the tick-box culture in the Care Quality Commission and the lack of accountability in our hospitals. George Osborne, the UK Chancellor, introduced the 2014 Government Spending Review with the promise that he would make sure that *'the unfairness of the something-for-nothing culture is changed'*. Culture was all the rage. But apart from George's controversial reduction of welfare benefits, very little happened in terms of culture change. A large quantity of sincerely expressed and fine words were uttered but very little action was taken actually to change the way that Western banks and institutions operated.

This is still true today. As evidence of this, I submit an article that was on the front page of the *FT* as recently as 21 September 2016 – nine years after the bail-out of Northern Rock: *'Wells chief savaged in Congress over fake accounts'*. John Stumpf, Chairman and CEO of Wells Fargo Bank, was summonsed to testify in front of the US Senate banking committee after regulators found that bank staff had created as many as two million fee-generating bank accounts and credit cards without consumers' knowledge. Democratic Senator, Elizabeth Warren, told Mr Stumpf that he should be 'criminally investigated'. She went on to berate him for 'gutless leadership' and declared that his 'definition of accountability is to push the blame to your low-level employees'. She went on to say, 'The only way that Wall Street will change is if executives face jail time when they preside over massive frauds.' Senator Warren put it in even stronger terms than I did in my articles.

Change? What change?

Is this lack of action when it comes to culture change due to the fact that the Chairs and CEOs aren't interested in changing the way their companies work? Or is it because they don't actually know how to instigate long-term, sustainable change?

Making the bold and perhaps naive assumption that it is the latter...

If you have a genuine wish to change your company's culture, I recommend treating it as a programme of work just like any other change initiative. And this culture change programme needs to cover every step of the following checklist.

But before you start changing your culture, you first genuinely have to understand what it is today. Identifying what you are going to change is, in effect, Step 0.

Culture change checklist

1. **Clarity.** The first step is to define and articulate clearly the new behaviours required – and why they are necessary. The high-level generic behaviours that are applicable for everyone in the

214

organisation need to be tailored for each department and made personal for every employee. *'What does good look like for me?'*

2. **Motivation.** While the rational reasons for adopting the new behaviours will be of interest, the emotional reasons for committing to these new behaviours will be the ones that actually drive the changes in behaviour you need. *'What's my personal motivation for adopting new ways of working?'*

3. **Tools and Processes.** What tools and processes do your people need to make it easier for them to start behaving differently? What tools and processes are currently getting in the way of the adoption of the desired behaviours? *'What tools can you give me to help me change?'*

4. **Learning and Development.** You can't expect your people to sit through a PowerPoint presentation on new behaviours and immediately change the way they do things. We humans don't operate that way. Your people will need training, coaching and mentoring to help them use the new tools and start working differently. *'What assistance can you give me to help me change?'*

5. **Reward.** Employees need carrots. How will you reward people when they do display the desired behaviours? As we have seen earlier, the reward may not have to be monetary. Highlighting and rewarding the early adopters is important to encourage more people to follow their example. *'What is in it for me?'*

6. **Consequences.** And they need sticks. What are the consequences of not adopting the new behaviours? If there are no consequences, people simply won't change. (By the way, this goes double for the leadership team.) *'What happens if I don't change?'*

7. **Leadership.** The most influential of all is leadership. A culture stems directly from the behaviour of the organisation's leaders. Leaders must be the first to adopt the new behaviours, leading very much by example. If leaders aren't seen adopting the new behaviours, no matter how much well-intentioned work has gone on each of the above, the culture simply won't change.

However...

...like the light bulb of Chapter 18, the leaders of an organisation must genuinely want their company to change. They also need to be willing to drive through a culture change programme against significant resistance. Then, armed with the above checklist and a Change Catalyst, they have a good chance of succeeding.

The following is taken from an article published in *Money Marketing* on 7 March 2014:

'Response to Martin Wheatley's concerns over culture change in financial services.'

'You must force our banks to change their cultures'

'Corporate cultures won't change in financial services unless CEOs and Boards are forced to do it,' says Campbell Macpherson.

Financial Conduct Authority (FCA) Chief Executive Martin Wheatley's speech at the gloriously-named Worshipful Company of International Bankers last Tuesday was a timely intervention but the FCA must start getting tough if we are going to see a genuine change in the culture in our banks and financial institutions.

Mr Wheatley is right to have serious concerns that economic recovery may drown out the call for culture change at the top end of our industry. This is precisely what will happen unless the FCA is willing to force our banks to change the way they work.

Without clear rules on culture change and genuine penalties for the reticent, too many institutions will simply continue to pay lip-service to the issue – to the continued detriment of their clients and, of course, the taxpayer, who again will be forced to bail them out come their next financial crisis.

The charge sheet against our banks is long and ugly.

It begins with the acts of (1) selling mortgages to people who couldn't afford to repay them, (2) packaging these up into opaque investment instruments in an attempt to mask the level of risk involved, and then (3) convincing rating agencies and investors alike that these piles of toxic nonsense were actually A-rated investments. To my non-legally-trained mind, these are three unconscionable cases of fraud that, in combination, brought the Western economy to its knees.

Yet no executive in any bank has been charged with any sort of criminal negligence. This is not solely due to the difficulty of finding conclusive evidence of personal fraudulent behaviour, but also due to a lack of regulatory or political will to take on The City/Wall Street in such a direct manner.

The charge sheet continues with the systemic manipulation of the Libor exchange rate, the universal mis-selling of mortgage payment and protection insurance and the mis-selling of interest rate swaps to businesses. 'Mis-selling' is such a gentler word than 'fraud'. The end result is the same of course, with customers conned out of their money by seemingly unscrupulous individuals who were aided and abetted by the sales-at-all-costs culture of the organisations that employed them.

And 5½ years since the collapse of Lehman Brothers, very little has really changed, culturally speaking. Bankers are still earning massive bonuses. Almost 500 Barclays employees enjoyed pay packets of more than £1 million in the last year. Even the serially disgraced RBS has come out in defence of big bonuses, citing the universal excuse that it is a global war for talent and if they didn't pay their traders outrageous sums, the 'talent' would simply ply their trade elsewhere.

I know that every good fib contains a grain of truth, but I can't help but wonder how many of these roles genuinely require such an astronomical remuneration package to deliver the investment results the bank needs. But that isn't the issue...

Through Quantitative Easing (QE), the Bank of England has merely exacerbated the problem; rewarding the banks and bankers who caused the financial crisis with the ability to replenish their balance sheets and bonuses respectively through the selling of hundreds of billions of government bonds.

And the government, too, has done little to encourage the banks to change their cultures. In fact, George Osborne has actively gone into battle with the European Commission on behalf of The City in defence of their right to pay large bonuses.

Let me be clear; I am not against paying people a lot of money when they genuinely add a lot of value to an organisation; the bigger the value, the bigger the pay they deserve. But if the government and the regulator genuinely want to change the culture in our banks and thus avoid another dramatic economic collapse, they must understand that the fact that the City's blatant bonus culture still remains intact is a major sign that, culturally speaking, it is 'business as usual' for bankers.

Further proof of the lack of genuine desire for culture change is the Economist Intelligence Unit's findings that 53% of financial services executives believe career progression at their firm will be difficult without 'flexibility over ethical standards'. Un-be-lievable.

Martin Wheatley thinks this suggests some business leaders are still struggling to get their message across. Surely it is far worse than that. Surely it indicates that more than half of our CEOs are simply not seen as being genuine in their desire for culture change. They may broadcast politically correct sound bites regarding the need to change the way their companies work; about the need to be 'aligned to the needs of the customer' ... but their people see these pronouncements merely as something you have to say to keep the regulator at bay; something to distract the media until the next boom takes off and all will be forgotten.

According to Martin Wheatley, 'The key issue here is how do firms create cultures that are genuinely different from those pre-crisis?'

That bit is actually quite straightforward. Successful culture change requires the adoption of a seven-point checklist, the most important of which is Leadership. A culture stems directly from the behaviour of the organisation's leaders. Leaders must be the first to adopt the new behaviours, leading very much by example. Otherwise the culture simply will never change.

And to get our banking leaders to change will obviously take a great deal more than fine words of encouragement. It will require direct instruction from the authorities.

It's time to bring out the big stick.

Campbell Macpherson

The following is taken from an article published in *Money Marketing* on 9 February 2013:

'It's the culture, Stupid. Why graduates are underwhelmed by financial services.'

In this first of a three-part series on 'The Next Generation', covering the next generation of employees, advisers and customers, Campbell Macpherson looks at the next generation of employees and asks what FS firms will need to do to attract them.

The next generation is different. Every generation says this, but this time I think it just might be true.

The previous generation aspired to the corner office with the uber-efficient secretary standing guard outside. They yearned for the big house in the country, the apartment in the city, the annual first class season ticket and the holiday home in the sun. They coveted the Mercedes AMG, the Range Rover, the offshore investment portfolio and the Coutts cheque account. They aspired to pay off their mortgages, to pay off their previous wives and to being able to quit work in their fifties. They were the generation of Gordon Gecko, Donald Trump, Conrad Black, Alan Bond, Fred Goodwin and Rupert Murdoch. They were the work-hard, play-hard, take-no-prisoners but thanks-for-the-final-salary-pension generation. This generation is passing on a world that is drowning in debt with an ever-widening gap between rich and poor, young and old, and they have decimated the very concept of employer–employee loyalty. Many of the companies they are leaving behind are dripping in in-sincerity; from the corporate values that hang from their ceilings to their tick-box corporate social responsibility charters.

The next generation wants none of it.

The next generation has no use for an office, let alone one in the corner. They carry their PA around in their pockets. They avoid com-muting as much as possible and have enough debt from their time at university, thanks very much. They're not into status; they are into making things happen. They're not into the status quo either; they want to change the world. They are the Apple generation; the Google, YouTube, Facebook generation. To them, email is a near-extinct form of communication. They are 'generation social' who understand the power of networks; the power of connections; the power of sharing ideas and building upon them. They have a moral contract with their employer which roughly equates to 'as long as both parties are winning from the relationship, it will continue'. Very few of them will ever be wedded to one company – or even one industry. They believe that business is about more than simply mak-ing money; their employer needs to be doing something for the com-munity; for the world. They have no plans to retire – late or early. The very word 'retirement' makes no sense to them whatsoever. A significant proportion of the next generation will live to 100; they are in this for the long haul. Oh, and they can spot insincerity a mile off.

How on earth are you going to attract these people to your business?

Well, the truth is, when it comes to Financial Services – very few companies will, unless they make some dramatic changes to the way their businesses work.

Only nine financial services firms made it into the top 100 companies for graduates, according to the latest rankings from The Job Crowd (www.thejobcrowd.com), which is ridiculously low given the importance of financial services to our economy. The ranking is based on thousands of reviews written on TheJobCrowd.com by employees in their first three years of work at hundreds of UK graduate employers. The nine FS companies that made it into the top 100 were The Kiln Group at number 10 (who are insurance and pensions specialists according to their website), Nationwide at number 17, Mitsubishi Securities at 38, Morgan Stanley at 48, Citibank at 49, HSBC at 59, Marsh at 65, Fidelity at 75 and Aon at 85.

Where's Prudential? Aviva? L&G? Zurich? Where's Barclays? RBS? Lloyds? Where's Goldman Sachs? Where's Jupiter? Henderson? For goodness sake, the Bank of England was ranked 89 and even the FSA snuck into number 96!

Perhaps we can ascertain some of the reasons for the dismal performance by FS firms if we take a look at some of the comments received by the top ranking companies, and ask ourselves:

'Would your employees say the same things about your organisation?'

1. 'The people here are amazing!' (Microsoft, ranked #1)

2. 'There is a culture of openness where ideas are shared and welcomed on all levels of this incredibly dynamic and rapidly-growing company.' (Newton Management Consultants #2)

3. 'Everyone is so helpful, approachable and very enthusiastic.' (National Grid #3)

4. 'It is an incredibly friendly and positive place to work. Everyone works really hard to achieve the company's goals, but we also have a laugh together.' (FDM Group #4)

5. 'A strong reputation for upholding ethical standards. The feeling that you are contributing to the whole community.' (The Co-operative Group #5)

Other comments for those companies ranked in the top 20 include:

- 'Hunger for change and innovation.'

- 'Incredibly open and fun atmosphere within the company.'

- 'Great support, training and opportunity to progress.'

- 'Exciting and vibrant place to work.'

- 'Genuinely cares about work/life balance.'

- 'Awesome, relaxed, very open and transparent.'

One thing you notice straight away from the above is that it is all about culture; how people feel, act and behave – and in the eyes of the next generation, very few FS companies measure up.

How many insurance firms would their employees describe as 'hungry for change and innovation'?

How many banks would be praised for 'a strong reputation for upholding ethical standards'?

How many fund managers could be said to 'genuinely care about work/life balance'?

How many FS companies could be said to revel in a 'culture of openness where ideas are shared and welcomed on all levels'?

According to The Job Crowd, the answer to the last question is nine.

That is not enough.

Campbell Macpherson

Notes

1. Austrian-born American management consultant, educator and author, whose writings contributed to the philosophical and practical foundations of the modern business corporation (1909–2005).
2. Strategy& used to be Booz Allen strategy consultants until its acquisition by PWC in 2014.
3. Chairman and CEO of IBM 1993–2002.
4. (2003) *Cultural Intelligence: Individual Interactions Across Cultures*, Stanford Business Books.
5. P. Christopher Ealey and Elaine Mosakowski, 'Cultural Intelligence', *Harvard Business Review*, October 2004.
6. International sage and self-proclaimed television 'Gigastar' originally from Moonee Ponds, a suburb of Melbourne; allegedly a creation of Australian comedian, Barry Humphries, which she denies.
7. Most recently, Gordon Brown, ex British PM and Chancellor 2012.
8. Japanese term for foreigner. 'While the term itself has no derogatory meaning, it emphasizes the exclusiveness of Japanese attitude and has therefore picked up pejorative connotations that many Westerners resent.' Mayumi Itoh (1995).
9. English writer (1867–1931).
10. Adam Morgan, (2009) *Eating the Big Fish*, second edition, John Wiley & Sons.
11. Founder of the UAE and ruler of Abu Dhabi from 1966 until his death in 2004. An incredible man whose leadership was the driving force behind the transformation of a collection of desperately poor but proud tribes into one of the world's richest and most advanced countries.
12. An Arabic term meaning 'a place of sitting', used in the name of legislative councils or assemblies and to describe various types of special gatherings among common interest groups be they administrative, social or religious. Also used to refer to a private place where guests are received and entertained.
13. (2008) Yale University Press.

14. Former US Member of Congress 1961–1991 and Democrat Presidential candidate from Arizona.
15. The rule originated in 1927 in Chatham House London to encourage active participation in discussions and debates. https://www.chathamhouse.org/about/chatham-house-rule

Part Four

Getting Down to Business

We have discussed why 88% of change initiatives fail. We have identified the essential ingredients for successful change. We have talked about the importance of culture and how to change it.

Now, it's time to get down to the business of planning and implementing specific change.

Successful change starts with strategy, which is why the first three chapters are all about this important topic – setting a Vision, Mission and/ or Purpose; understanding values and exploring what a good strategy looks like. In this section, you will encounter a Strategy Framework that was developed for one of my clients to help him engage his leadership team in the development of a holistic strategy for the company.

Then we discuss strategy execution, as even the most expensive and innovative strategy will be a complete waste of time if it can't be executed. The Strategy Execution Framework you meet in this chapter may also come in handy.

But to execute your strategy successfully, you will need to attend to what some people incorrectly term the 'softer side' of business. So, in the following chapters we cover designing an organisation to deliver (and how Organisation Design is not just about structure), overcoming complacency, what good leadership looks like, building extraordinary leadership teams and managing and developing your people.

Finally, we wrap the section up with some pertinent case studies and a Change Toolbox which contains the key tools, models and methodologies that I have found useful over the years. I hope you do, too.

Chapter 25

Vision, Mission and Other Buzzwords

Every strategy needs an anchor and a North Star. Something to ground it in reality and a neat set of words or phrases that capture what it is we are trying to achieve, why and how. We consultants love to lead executive teams in endless hours of word-smithing in the quest to develop motivational mantras to enthuse and engage their businesses in exciting new directions. But do they work? Or perhaps a more useful question – which ones would work best for my organisation?

This should be a straightforward topic, yet if you put a dozen different strategy consultants in a room, you would hear 12 different definitions of what a Vision or Mission Statement should comprise and how they should be phrased. In this chapter, I have tried to cut a swathe through the jungle of jargon and simplify the whole subject. I shall let you be the judge as to whether I have succeeded or not. We will take a peek at the 'Big 5' – Vision, Mission, Purpose, Capabilities and Values – and discuss the pros and cons of each to help you cherry pick the ones that are best suited to your company. Then I will share with you my view on the key guiding questions I recommend you answer to give your strategy the direction and guidance it needs.

To Vision or not to Vision?

Visions are for dreamers. There is nothing wrong with dreaming.

A vision is the ideal. The word is defined as *'the act or power of anticipating that which will or may come to be'* (Dictionary.com) or *'the ability to think about or plan the future with imagination or wisdom'* (Oxford Dictionaries).

A Vision Statement is a description of the ideal sort of organisation you want to become; sometimes even the future state of the industry or society in which your organisation operates. If compelling, credible and achievable, a Vision Statement can be a source of inspiration for employees.

In the past, I have been an evangelical exponent of Vision Statements. I have spent untold man hours crafting and re-crafting them and then valiantly attempting to obtain 'buy-in' to these beautifully designed sets of words from as many people as possible. However, I have come to realise with the clarity of hindsight that, for a larger number of these organisations than I would care to admit, it has been a complete waste of time.

The answer to the question of whether one should proceed with a Vision Statement is 'Yes,' if...

- The end result truly inspires people to do great things (or at least greater things)

- It genuinely provides a compelling picture of the sort of company that you want to build

- It is credible, i.e. the end result doesn't sound like something that a Hallmark copywriter could have written over a medium-sized cappuccino.

And the answer is 'No' if...

- None of the above is true

- The end result is little more than fluff – however lovingly crafted

- It doesn't stand up to objective scrutiny

- It is incongruous to the culture of the business.

Here are a few examples of Vision Statements that do what Visions should do – sum up a desired future state:

- 'Our vision is to be Earth's most customer centric company; to build a place where people can come to find and discover anything they might want to buy online.' (Amazon)

- 'Be the world's beer company. Through all of our products, services and relationships, we will add to life's enjoyment.' (Anheuser-Busch)

- 'To be the global energy company most admired for its people, partnership and performance.' (Chevron)

- 'To be the world's premier food company, offering nutritious, superior tasting foods to people everywhere.' (Heinz)

- 'Helping People Around the World Eat and Live Better.' (Kraft)

- 'Saving people money to help them live better.' (Walmart)

- 'To be the best-loved provider of books, music, movies, and other entertainment and informational products and services.' (Borders)

- 'To make the best possible ice-cream in the nicest possible way.' (Ben & Jerry's)

If you have to go on to define every word of your Vision, start again. Your Vision Statement should be easy to understand. Any Vision that requires an accompanying dictionary has missed the mark. Here is a wonderful example of such a beast from Office Depot:[1]

Vision = Delivering Winning Solutions That Inspire Worklife.™

Delivering = Our actions speak louder than words. We are accountable: doing what we say we're going to do efficiently and on time.

Winning = We act with confidence. We're proud to win. We push ourselves to greater heights. And we don't settle for less than being the best.

Solutions = We listen to our customers and understand their needs. We offer products, services and innovative thinking that enable our customers to achieve success.

Inspire = Our inspiration is contagious and enables us to unleash creativity to help people achieve their goals. Our motivation and enthusiasm inspire others to succeed.

Worklife™ = We combine our energy for work with our passion for life. We are creating a fuller, more enriched lifestyle. We share the desire to maximise human potential to achieve personal dreams.

(I must admit, I stopped reading after the second line.)

Fundamentally, you are either a Vision company or you are not. If the majority of your leadership team and employees will genuinely respond to a compelling vision of what the company will look like in the future, then do it. But keep it short, clear and ensure it is compelling and genuine.

Mission

I believe a Mission is crucial no matter whether you opt for a Vision Statement or not. A good Mission Statement is action-oriented; the word 'mission' deriving from the Latin 'mittere' – 'to send'.

A good way to think of a Mission is to pretend you are in the military. To a military commander, a 'mission' may be to capture a town. It has a defined goal. The Vision may be the creation of a free and democratic country. Visions are lofty. Missions are tangible.

In my opinion, there are two generic types of Mission Statement:

1. A pithy, action-oriented version of a Vision Statement

2. A detailed statement that encompasses *what* you are seeking to achieve, *for whom* and then goes on to outline *how* you intend to achieve it.

Either way, a Mission Statement is just the tip of the strategy iceberg (as we will discuss in Chapters 27 and 28). It sets the direction and the guidelines.

Here are a few examples of Mission Statements. They start off with type 1 above and morph into type 2 the farther you go down the list:

- 'To organise the world's information and make it universally accessible and useful.' (Google)

- 'To constantly improve what is essential to human progress by mastering science and technology.' (Dow Chemical)

- 'To emotionally touch and excite our customers.' (Sony)

- 'To help people find better ways to do great work – by constantly leading in document technologies, products and services that improve our customers' work processes and business results.' (Xerox)

- 'To invest in the best interests of Canada Pension Plan contributors and beneficiaries and to maximise investment returns without undue risk of loss.' (CPPIB)

- 'To grow our business by providing quality products and services at great value when and where our customers want them, and by building positive, lasting relationships with our customers.' (Sears)

- 'The mission of Merck is to provide society with superior products and services by developing innovations and solutions that improve the quality of life and satisfy customer needs, and to provide employees with meaningful work and advancement opportunities, and investors with a superior rate of return.'

- 'The mission of Southwest Airlines is dedication to the highest quality of Customer Service delivered with a sense of warmth, friendliness, individual pride, and Company Spirit.'

Knowing that employee satisfaction is the key to delivering customer service, Southwest Airlines then goes on to make a commitment to its employees:

'To Our Employees: We are committed to provide our Employees a stable work environment with equal opportunity for learning and personal growth. Creativity and innovation are encouraged for improving the effectiveness of Southwest Airlines. Above all, Employees will be provided the same concern, respect, and caring attitude within the organisation that they are expected to share externally with every Southwest Customer.'

Other organisations concur with Southwest Airlines and believe that a pithy statement is not enough. *Ben & Jerry's* splits its Mission Statement into three:

Product Mission To make, distribute and sell the finest quality all natural ice cream and euphoric concoctions with a continued commitment to incorporating wholesome, natural ingredients and promoting business practices that respect the Earth and the Environment.

Economic Mission To operate the company on a sustainable financial basis of profitable growth, increasing value for our stakeholders and expanding opportunities for development and career growth for our employees.

Social Mission To operate the company in a way that actively recognises the central role that business plays in society by initiating innovative ways to improve the quality of life locally, nationally and internationally.

Central to the Mission of Ben & Jerry's is the belief that all three parts must thrive equally in a manner that commands deep respect for individuals in and outside the company and supports the communities of which they are a part.

Other Mission variants

The Vision/Mission combo

Sometimes companies choose to conflate Vision and Mission in one flowing paragraph. They articulate the future state and follow this up with a statement of how this will be delivered. 'Our vision is... To accomplish this...' e.g.:

> 'The IKEA vision is to create a better everyday life for the many people. We make this possible by offering a wide range of well-designed, functional home furnishing products at prices so low that as many people as possible will be able to afford them.'

It's a bit formulaic, but this approach can work too. As long as it is aspirational, credible, achievable, clear and helps guide your people to deliver the strategy – it works.

What we do

Sometimes companies simply opt for a statement that clearly states what they do and how they do it:

- 'We are a global family with a proud heritage passionately committed to providing personal mobility for people around the world. We anticipate consumer need and deliver outstanding products and services that improve people's lives.' (Ford)

- 'At Gap Inc. we never stop moving. It takes thousands of passionate, dedicated and talented employees around the world to deliver the merchandise and shopping experience our customers expect and deserve.'

Several of my clients have started their strategy development phase by answering this question. It provides the anchor for all that is to follow.

It is also surprising just how much debate and discussion such a simple question can generate among the leadership team.

Credos

The Ritz-Carlton has a different approach. They have set a credo and a motto to establish customer expectations and guide their people to deliver their strategy.

Credo The Ritz-Carlton Hotel is a place where the genuine care and comfort of our guests is our highest mission.

We pledge to provide the finest personal service and facilities for our guests who will always enjoy a warm, relaxed, yet refined ambience.

The Ritz-Carlton experience enlivens the senses, instils well-being, and fulfils even the unexpressed wishes and needs of our guests.

Motto At The Ritz-Carlton Hotel Company, L.L.C., 'We are ladies and gentlemen serving ladies and gentlemen.' This motto exemplifies the anticipatory service provided by all staff members.

Johnson & Johnson's 'anti-Mission Statement' Mission Statement

J&J have also opted for prose rather than pithy statements:

'At Johnson & Johnson there is no mission statement that hangs on the wall. Instead, for more than 60 years, a simple, one-page document – Our Credo – has guided our actions in fulfilling our responsibilities to our customers, our employees, the community and our stockholders. Our worldwide Family of Companies shares this value system in 36 languages spreading across Africa, Asia/Pacific, Eastern Europe, Europe, Latin America, Middle East and North America. The English version of the Credo is below, or you may choose to view it in another language by selecting a country from the box on the right. You can also learn more about the history of Our Credo and its development.'

Our Credo 'We believe our first responsibility is to the doctors, nurses and patients, to mothers and fathers and all others who use our products and services. In meeting their needs, everything we do must be of high quality. We must constantly strive to reduce our costs in order to maintain reasonable prices. Customers' orders must be serviced promptly and accurately. Our suppliers and distributors must have an opportunity to make a fair profit.

We are responsible to our employees, the men and women who work with us throughout the world. Everyone must be considered as an individual. We must respect their dignity and recognise their merit. They must have a sense of security in their jobs. Compensation must be fair and adequate, and working conditions clean, orderly and safe. We must be mindful of ways to help our employees fulfil their family responsibilities. Employees must feel free to make suggestions and complaints. There must be equal opportunity for employment, development and advancement for those qualified. We must provide competent management, and their actions must be just and ethical.

We are responsible to the communities in which we live and work and to the world community as well. We must be good citizens – support good works and charities and bear our fair share of taxes. We must encourage civic improvements and better health and education. We must maintain in good order the property we are privileged to use, protecting the environment and natural resources.

Our final responsibility is to our stockholders. Business must make a sound profit. We must experiment with new ideas. Research must be carried on, innovative programs developed and mistakes paid for. New equipment must be purchased, new facilities provided and new products launched. Reserves must be created to provide for adverse times. When we operate according to these principles, the stockholders should realise a fair return.'

Phew. I need a cup of tea and a lie down after that one.

Purpose

I love a good Purpose Statement; a clear and concise statement of what we do and, more importantly, *why* the organisation exists. I love it for the simple reason that a good one brings clarity to an organisation. The surprising thing is that the purpose can often be rather difficult to describe as it must be done in as few words as possible – and brevity takes time; as Blaise Pascal[2] once penned, '*I'm sorry I wrote you such a long letter; I didn't have time to write a short one.*'

Your Purpose must be simple and it must tread the fine line between being generic enough to be relevant to every part of the business and yet specific to your business or at least your part of the industry. And it must encourage/enable your people to take a new look at what they do – while giving them a constant reference to ensure what they are doing and how they are doing it is in line with the core reason for the company's existence. It is quite a challenge for a concise statement to pass all of these tests, but it is well worth the effort.

The answer to 'Why do we exist?' cannot be a Blinding Glimpse of the Obvious (BGO) such as to maximise profit or shareholder return. Like 'comply with the regulator', these are givens. A successful Purpose Statement must be customer-facing (e.g. 'Our purpose is to enable our clients to build highly successful businesses'), and it must help to guide your managers and employees in their decision-making and actions.

Here are a few examples of good Purpose Statements:

- 'To create a better everyday life for the many people.' (IKEA)

- 'To make investing easier for our customers and the investors they serve.' (Cofunds)

- 'Our purpose is to solve unsolved problems innovatively.' (3M)

- 'Our purpose is to make people happy.' (Disney)

The difference between a Vision, a Purpose and a Mission

To illustrate the difference, let me show you a trio that I compiled many years ago for a financial services firm – a company that provided services to thousands of financial advisers.

Vision   To transform the way financial advice is provided and regarded in the UK.

Purpose   To help financial advisers run highly successful businesses.

Mission   To build a profitable and sustainable market leader renowned for the quality of its services and people.

The Vision was a lofty aspiration for the company and the industry. The Purpose was a clear and customer-centric statement of why we existed. The Mission was practical, clear and achievable. Together, they make a very compelling 'strategic picture'. But, of course, they are only the beginning.

Capabilities (a.k.a. 'What do we have to excel at?')

While 'capabilities' is the correct label for this, I think the phrase above is more meaningful. Describing 'what we have to excel at' brings the purpose to life and gives it context. You have articulated a concise, simple, relevant and compelling Purpose Statement that has encouraged your people to take a new look at what they are doing and why, but they need some boundaries; they need some guidelines to ensure that the work they set off on doing is focused and prioritised.

The full question is: *'In order to fulfil our Purpose and deliver our Mission, what must we excel at?'* Is it sales? Customer service? Market research? Efficiency? Major account management? What will give us the biggest bang for our buck? What do we want to be famous for? What type of customer experience? What sort of pricing strategy? What skills do we need?

Identifying the high priority areas you need in order to be successful will provide your people with focus and the drive to deliver the things that will matter the most.

Behaviours

'Values Schmalues' to quote the title of the next chapter. Whether you need to display values publicly or not is open to conjecture – and discussed at some length in a few pages hence. But what you definitely need to define is how you want your organisation to go about delivering the strategy; how you want your people to behave.

It is difficult to measure values; but you can measure behaviours. If you must have publicly displayed values, use them to underpin the behaviours you need. Spell out the behaviours you require from the company's leaders and then spell out the behaviours you require from everyone else. Note these behaviours must be designed to enable the company to deliver better results. This is not just being nice to one another for the sake of it; it is adopting the key behaviours you need in order to deliver what you are trying to achieve – better customer experience, increased cross-sales, improved staff retention… whatever your key corporate objectives may be.

Finally, of utmost importance (so important that if you don't do this, just ignore the whole concept of values and behaviours entirely), make sure everyone lives up to these behaviours. And the only way to do that is to link them to rewards. Change your incentive scheme to ensure that how things are done is just as important as what is done. Only when poor behaviour hits someone's back pocket or affects their career opportunities will you have developed the culture you need for your business to deliver what it needs to achieve.

Summary

This chapter contained a great deal of information, jargon and opinion splattered throughout. Let me attempt to bring it all together.

In establishing the anchor for your strategy, in identifying your 'North Star' that will guide the organisation to its ultimate destination, it doesn't matter whether you decide to use a Vision Statement, a Mission Statement, a Vision/Mission combo, a statement of 'What we do', a Credo, a Customer Charter or any other mechanism you come up with – as long as it suits your culture and resonates with your people.

The purpose of these words is purely to set the direction and guidelines for your strategy. As long as they are aspirational, credible, achievable, clear and help guide your people to deliver the strategy, they will have done their job.

No matter which types of statement and phrases you opt for, they must provide compelling answers to the following key questions:

1. What are we trying to achieve and why?

2. For whom?

3. What does the future look like?

4. How will we achieve it?

5. Why does the company exist?

6. What do we need to excel at?

7. How do we need to behave to deliver optimal results?

And remember, such statements are just the tip of the iceberg. They will need to be transformed into an actionable strategy and a clear strategy execution plan. Or all of the effort will merely have been a time-consuming exercise in futile word-smithery.

Chapter 26

Values Schmalues

Conventional wisdom is that every company needs a set of corporate values that will not only look rather fetching adorning the Annual Report, but will also lay the foundation for every client interaction and employee behaviour.

Conventional wisdom is not always right.

Companies spend untold sums engaging their workforce in coming up with a list of prospective qualities that are eventually narrowed down to a list of half a dozen pithy words, heavily laden with meaning. A separate paragraph is then written for each 'Value' to explain the meaning of the word in the context of the organisation. Each of these paragraphs is edited several times before they are all sent to the graphic designers, and finally every screen, mouse mat, coffee mug and spare wall is adorned with these shiny new Corporate Values. They are 'embedded' into the HR appraisal system and every employee is told they must have a personal objective that reflects each one of these wonderful new corporate principles.

And then, to plagiarise my favourite Monty Python quote yet again, all of a sudden… nothing happens. Why?

Because we humans don't work like that. We are free-thinking and independently-minded individuals with values of our own. We may not have workshopped them with our friends and handed them out as Christmas cards, but each of us has our own views of what is wrong and what is right.

By the way, using corporate values as titles for appraisal objectives does not, in any way, shape or form, make one iota of difference to how things are done. It is a lazy, superficial, process-oriented exercise that gives the impression of action but actually achieves very little. I have worked for, with and sometimes against several companies who have commanded their employees to align their personal objectives with the corporate values – and all the employees have done is write their objectives and then allocate them to the imposed buckets. Any attempt to embed your values into your appraisal system (if you must have an appraisal system, which is another topic entirely) must be genuine. Glad to have got that off my chest.

Corporate values also have a significant and almost impossible challenge in the UK and Australia, in that our inherent cynicism towards such things cannot help but give the vast majority of us cause to chuckle at 'Integrity' and the bewilderingly superficial 'Customer Centricity' as they beam pompously down at us as we alight from the lifts of a morning.

There are two types of corporate values – 'right' ones and 'real' ones. The values that you see hanging from ceilings and adorning office walls are almost always the 'right' values; those values the leadership has decided it wants the organisation to aspire to. Rarely are they the 'real' values that actually exist within the organisation and underpin how your people actually behave. And, ironically, the 'real' values can often be far more powerful than the 'right' ones.

Richard Branson inherently understood this. When I was asked to be part of the team that devised and launched Virgin Wines in 2000, I discovered that the Virgin Group didn't possess a brand manual, let alone display its values on the walls of every Virgin company's office. There is no Virgin slogan, by-line or catchphrase. It's just Virgin. I eventually came to the realisation that if you had to spell out what Virgin stood for; if you were to try and distil the 'brand essence' into a few overt corporate values, the very act of doing this would actually diminish the brand. Like looking at stars in the night sky; if you look at a star directly, its brightness diminishes. It is only when the star lies in your peripheral vision that its full brightness becomes apparent. (Or maybe a better metaphor is Heisenberg's uncertainty principle, which states that the very act of measuring an object or a system affects the very thing you are measuring. Anyway, you get the idea.) For someone like me who is so devoted to clarity, this was a terrible thing to learn. But it is true. The moment you state your values is the moment that they start to lose their value.

Your brand values are whatever your customers believe them to be.

Your corporate values are whatever your employees believe them to be.

The 'right' values

The values you proudly display in your Annual Report are usually aspirational rather than actual – but they are almost never described as such. All 'right' values are commendable and laudable. They sound good. They look good. But they must be genuine or they will back-fire. The likes of 'customer first', 'integrity', 'respect', 'trust' and 'teamwork' are brilliant values to aspire to, but I recommend you ask yourself two questions: (1) are they actual or aspirational, and (2) are they appropriate?

For example, a growing number of companies around the world seem to be adding the word 'innovation' to their list of corporate values. It is an admirable word and difficult to object to (as all 'right' values are). But is it always appropriate? Game-changing, revolutionary innovation is for the likes of Google, Amazon, Tesla, Anaplan and iPipeline. It is for fintech start-ups and nimble hedge funds (back when hedge funds actually added value, but again, another subject entirely). A much larger number of companies could benefit from a more evolutionary style of innovation – adding new products to their mix, completely re-engineering their customer experience, transforming their products into services or vice versa. However, a significant proportion of organisations find even this more evolutionary flavour of innovation incredibly difficult; their innately conservative cultures fight against innovative ideas like antibodies attacking an unwelcome virus. At these times, innovation's more conservative cousin, 'continual improvement', will be far more apt. It depends upon shareholder expectations and the inherent culture of the company.

If you do opt for publicly stating your company's values, they should at least be the ones that you have determined to be critical to delivering your strategy. This, in turn, means that you need to be clear on what your strategy is – and what needs to be done to deliver it.

'Real' values

A far more interesting exercise is to identify your company's inherent values: the 'real' values that are ingrained in your organisation's culture. These values are often unique – and powerful.

A company I knew of many years ago had the usual 'right' values exhibited in its Annual Report, embedded within its appraisal system and ingrained within its recruitment process – but its 'real' values were much more powerful. I would describe these values as 'honour' and another admirable quality that I will clumsily label 'fairness'. These values are very rarely found in large companies and yet they occupied centre stage in this one. The concept of 'honour' is almost unheard of; it hails from a different era. It conjures up images of King Arthur and Camelot. Dr Samuel Johnson, in his *Dictionary of the English Language* (1755), defined honour as 'nobility of soul, magnanimity, and a scorn of meanness' and yet this is indeed the term I would use to describe one of the core 'real' values of this organisation. It was honourable in the way it dealt with its partners, providers and employees. It paid its debts on time and in full. It did its best to honour the spirit of contracts as well as the letter of the law and it completely understood the benefit of 'win:win' relationships; that a relationship where one party loses is no recipe for long-term success for either party. When it came to its treatment of employees, it was extremely fair. I have not seen a company that treated its employees better and, most unusually, treated them well at all stages of employment – at entry, during employment and at exit. Consequently, it had a reputation as an excellent employer, inevitably enhancing the quality of potential recruits.

But here comes the rub. The ironic truth about values is such that, to hark back to Heisenberg and Branson, if this company had adorned its walls with the words 'Honour' and 'Fairness', the power of these real values would have been diminished instantly. Stating them so blatantly would have invited people to question their veracity – much as it would if Richard Branson had decided to put the words 'consumer champion' beneath the Virgin logo. Branson has built an incredible empire by looking for industries that are ripe for disruption; where there is room for a new entrant to deliver the sort of products and services that people want; to give consumers a better deal. But overtly labelling him and his businesses as 'consumer champions' would have invited people to look for instances when they did not live up to this expectation. It would have de-valued the brand.

The moment you state your values is the moment they start to lose their value.

Three types of values

I have had an epiphany while writing this chapter. (My definition of an epiphany is an idea so good that when it is voiced it seems so blindingly obvious you wonder why on earth you hadn't realised it before.)

Companies possess three categories of values – and each one should be identified.

An organisation should determine, and declare:

1. What its customers think its **brand values** are;

2. What its employees believe its **corporate values** to be; and

3. The **aspirational values** that the leadership has determined to be critical to deliver the strategy.

If you genuinely want to align the culture of your organisation to your strategy, defining these three sets of values would be a great place to start!

Chapter 27

What Does a Good Strategy Look Like?

B efore we answer that question, let's take a look at the opposite end of the spectrum.

Poor strategy comes in many forms. The main reason for this is that delivering an insightful, transformational strategy is difficult; it requires objectivity, diligence, confidence, clear decision-making, the ability to change tack when necessary, an honest appraisal of the organisation's challenges and a great deal of effort.

Poor strategy, in comparison, is easy, and therefore ubiquitous. It comes in many guises, the most common varieties of which could be labelled:

- Utopia

- Stretch targets

- Verbal nonsense

- To-do lists

- Wish lists

- Spreadsheets and hockey sticks.

Some of the above are welcome as individual components of a good strategy, but they are not stand-alone strategies in their own right. Let's take a little peek at each one.

Utopia

'Describing a destination is no substitute for developing a comprehensive roadmap for how an organisation will achieve its stated goals.'

I adapted this quote ever so slightly from Richard Rumelt's excellent book *Good Strategy Bad Strategy*. The actual quote is an analysis of the Bush Administration National Security Strategy during a Seminar on US National Security Strategy in Washington DC 2007. Rumelt's actual quotation is perhaps even more telling on a number of levels:

'The articulation of a national vision that describes America's purpose in the post-September 11th world is useful – indeed, it is vital – but describing a destination is no substitute for developing a comprehensive roadmap for how the country will achieve its stated goals.'

Painting a picture of the future is a good idea, but on its own it is not a strategy. It is not even a strategic direction; it is simply a desired destination. Describing the sort of company you want to become can be a useful tool but it must be supported by an actual plan of how to get there.

Stretch targets

'Our strategy is to achieve $500m revenue at a gross margin of 20%.' This isn't a strategy; it is a stretch target (unless it is widely regarded as completely unachievable, when it becomes a meaningless set of numbers, a.k.a. 'the CEO's folly'). Again, stretch targets can be very useful but to be achieved, they need to be supported by a plan to engage your people to deliver.

Verbal nonsense

Richard Rumelt uses a brilliant description of this version of poor strategy: 'a superficial restatement of the obvious combined with a generous sprinkling of buzzwords'.

You can see this in any organisation aiming to 'be the provider of choice', 'become an employer of choice', 'become the leading (insert noun here)', or 'be the best (insert a different noun here)'.

A strategy is not a collection of greeting card slogans and consulting jargon. Statements of strategic intent have their place, but alone they will not transform your organisation.

To-do lists

Another management tool masquerading as strategy is an all-encompassing list of corporate, departmental and personal objectives. Don't get me wrong, I believe these are vital elements of an implementation plan, but they do not, of themselves, make up a strategy. They are simply a list of things that need to be done.

> *'While the Bush Administration's 2002 National Security Strategy did articulate a set of US national goals and objectives, it was not the product of a serious attempt at strategic planning. When you look closely at either the 2002 or 2006 national security strategy documents, all you find are lists of goals and sub-goals, not strategies.'*[3]

Wish lists

When a CEO/Board/executive team finds it too difficult to make some difficult choices, the resultant 'strategy' can be a hotchpotch of actions that the committee has decreed to be desirable. The company's strategy is to reduce costs, get closer to the customer, become the dominant player in its core market, enter new markets, implement three new IT systems and become an employer of choice. It is a lovely list, and every single component has its merits, but the company does not have the resources to attempt half of these. It is a platypus of a plan, designed by committee; it is a wish list.

Spreadsheets and hockey sticks

Another pseudo-strategy, and one much loved by the financial services industry, is the financial plan. Financial plans invariably start with a numerical version of the desired end game ('20% revenue growth at 20% margin') and work backwards. Cost centre budgets are worked out to the nth degree with FTEs calculated to the second decimal point and revenue neatly divided into 12 monthly parcels. The next 3–5 years are then graphed, showing a hockey-stick style recovery (if we are currently in the middle of a recession) or a neat straight line of revenue and profit increasing ad infinitum to and through the top-right corner of the page (if we are between recessions). What could possibly go wrong?

This is a particularly dangerous form of faux strategy. Due to the amount of effort expended on its production and the professional appearance of the finished product, too many companies become lulled into the belief that compiling such a work of financial finger-crossing is, in fact, a work of strategic insight. It isn't. The strategy should drive the financial plan, not the other way around.

'What are the components of a good strategy?'

This was an actual question that one of my CEO clients put to me a few years back. And it was a great question, for the word 'strategy' means very different things to different people. A Finance Director will regard his business plan and detailed five-year spreadsheets to be the heart of the organisation's strategy; and will often bemoan the lack of detail coming from the Marketing Department. The Marketing Department will regard Finance's business plan and spreadsheets to be precisely that; belonging to Finance: a numerical wish list at best with only a passing resemblance to what is going on in the marketplace. The reality is that a company needs both a business plan and a market-facing vision; for both are key elements of any good strategy.

In my experience, a *good strategy*:

- is anchored in reality (internal as well as external)

- is customer-centric

- is aspirational yet achievable

- is based on an honest appraisal of future risks

- overcomes obstacles

- includes implementation.

The CEO asked me to paint a picture of the elements of a good strategy and how they interacted with one another. He wanted his executive team to work together to build a holistic plan for the future that contained all of the essential components of a good strategy.

And thus the *Strategy Framework* was born.

Its purpose is to enable every executive to work together to deliver their piece of the puzzle, while ensuring all of the pieces add up to a credible whole. It provides a strategic checklist in pictorial form that is both comprehensive and easy to digest. A larger version can be found in Chapter 35's Change Toolbox and a colour version can be downloaded from www.changeandstrategy.com.

A winning strategy …

- is anchored in reality
- is customer-centric
- is aspirational yet achievable
- is based on an honest appraisal of capability and risks
- is compelling and clear
- includes all of the components below – including execution.

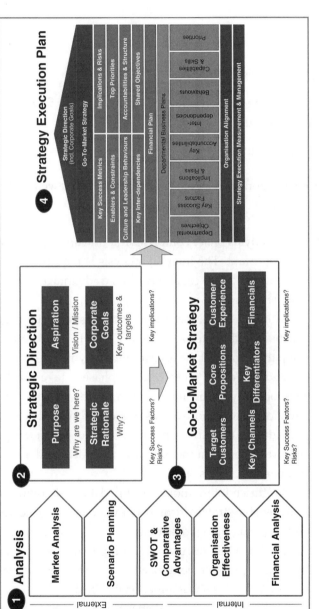

Source: www.changeandstrategy.com

Strategy Framework

257

The *Strategy Framework* visually describes four key components of a holistic strategy:

1. The Analysis

2. The Strategic Direction

3. The Go-to-Market Strategy (or 'Investment Strategy' for an investment firm)

4. The Execution Plan.

Each component is essential and carries equal weight. Let's take a look at each one.

1. **The Analysis** phase comprises internal and external analysis – both are important. The internal analysis is required to ensure your organisation has the capability to take advantage of the market-facing opportunities you uncover.

   In my opinion, the *market analysis* should be pragmatic. By all means hire a strategy consulting firm to assist, but manage them. Help them to resist the urge to smother you in reams of data, spreadsheets and PowerPoints. Use this phase to take a realistic and objective look at your business and to identify market opportunities. In my view, the purpose of this phase is to aid decision-making, not to provide the definitive answer. Use it to size and prioritise market opportunities – but the only way to understand a market truly is to jump in and start selling.

   At Zurich International, we hired a well-known and outrageously expensive strategy firm to analyse the US market for us. Not only did it cost us a great deal of money and time, in hindsight, it was of little value. Only once we had jumped into the market and started designing products and meeting distributors did we discover that the initial analysis was superficial at best.

   I like to start with a realistic hypothesis, or hypotheses, and look for data that support and or challenge it. Along with hypothesis-led analysis of the market, I am a big fan of the good old-fashioned *SWOT* (although I prefer SWTO, leaving the Opportunities section to last). Many an executive may roll their eyes at the thought of conducting one of these old staples, yet you may be surprised at how much constructive debate the activity encourages. Identifying your *comparative advantages* will also be a highly useful piece of analysis. What are your natural (some organisations call these 'structural') advantages compared to competitors or peers (geography, size, financial strength, ownership structure, culture...) and what comparative advantages would you like to develop (skills, capabilities...)?

Another personal favourite is the oft-maligned *Scenario Planning*. I highly recommend it, as some incredible nuggets of wisdom can emerge from an open-minded exercise of 'what if?' The collapse in oil price from a high of c$110 a barrel in 2014 to a low point of c$25 in January of 2016 is a perfect example of where scenario planning would have been invaluable. Rather than assuming that oil would stay at $100+ a barrel forever (as a large number of oil producers and oil-rich countries seem to have believed), planning for a scenario where oil may be considerably less valuable would have been a rather useful exercise. Some oil-producing countries established sovereign wealth funds long ago to help fill the financial gap for the day when oil revenues were considerably lower. Others are only just starting to think about it after the event.

The other two components of a robust Analysis are:

Organisation effectiveness   How effective is your organisation? What is it capable of delivering? Future success will depend upon you possessing the capabilities you need to be successful. But first you need to analyse your capabilities objectively today.

Financial analysis   What are your costs? Per product? Per channel? Per customer segment? This analysis is often difficult to calculate but is critical to success. The answers will dictate your response to the market opportunities identified above.

2. The Strategic Direction does exactly what it says on the tin. It provides the organisation not only with a 'strategic picture' (Purpose/Vision/Mission) but also the rationale for the strategy and the measurable goals you are setting out to achieve. It should serve to inform, enthuse, engage and guide. It will be what will cause your people to bounce into work every morning.

3. The Go-to-Market Strategy covers the key market-facing elements in detail – your core customers and their needs, wants and expectations; your service and product propositions; the customer experience you wish to deliver; your key differentiators, the channels you will focus on and the financial implications that will underpin the strategy. This phase must be developed in tandem with the prior phase. Your Go-to-Market Strategy and your Strategic Direction are intertwined. They will need to be developed in an iterative process.

By the way, for an institutional investor, replace 'Go-to-Market Strategy' with 'Investment Strategy' and a different set of components including shareholder expectations (risk, return, AUM...), guiding principles to guide the investment strategy, the key ratios (internal vs external, active vs passive, liquid vs illiquid...), your approach to asset and/or risk allocation, your active strategy and performance benchmarks and investment guidelines.

4. The Execution Plan. Without this final phase, nothing will be delivered. Even the most innovative strategy is a waste of time unless the organisation is ready, willing and able to deliver. Execution is paramount.

Here are some interesting statistics:

'90% of strategies fail due to poor execution.' (*Fortune* magazine)

'70% of CEO failures are due to the poor execution of good strategy.' (HBR)

'Only 5% of employees understand their company's strategy.' (HBR)

Without this phase, you will have insightful analysis, an inspirational vision of the future, a detailed financial plan… and yet everyone will be sitting back and waiting to see if the results come in.

Once the Strategic Direction and the Go-to-Market Strategy are clear, your people will need a *Strategy Execution Plan* detailing how the strategy is to be achieved – success metrics, implications, enablers, interdependencies, accountabilities – a blueprint for delivery. The next chapter is dedicated to this.

Armed with this level of guidance, each department will be able to produce its own business plan.

I also strongly recommend assigning a central coordination group to oversee the overall delivery – monitoring progress, ensuring employee engagement and alignment to the new strategy, making sure the departments work together to deliver and identifying and resolving execution challenges.

The Execution Plan is the toughest stage of all – but it is arguably the most important. Any CEO with a surplus can pay a strategy firm to produce a beautifully crafted strategy document amply supported by forests' worth of spreadsheets, pie charts and mathematical wizardry, but this 'investment' will be little more than a sunk cost without the plan and the ability to deliver.

Chapter 28

It's the Delivery, Stupid![4]
(Execution is Everything)

Execution is paramount.

Ninety per cent of strategies fail due to poor execution. Every CEO has a strategy. It may be clear and it may be eminently achievable. Yet, nine times out of ten, it is not delivered.

The CEO's biggest challenge is not formulating the strategy; it is getting their organisation to execute it.

As the CEO of Heineken Americas put it to me a few years ago, *'Having a clearly defined strategy execution plan is critical to our success. The process of having every executive present their business execution plans to each other, including the interdependencies between their departments, is invaluable.'*

So why do most strategies fail? Thousands of business pages have been dedicated to answering this rather straightforward question, but in my experience it boils down to four main reasons:

1. Lack of genuine commitment from the top

2. Insufficient engagement with managers and key influencers

3. Poor communication

4. The absence of a robust strategy execution plan.

Commit

It may not seem so at the time, but developing a strategy is the easy bit. Delivering it is tough. It demands unwavering commitment from the Chairman, the Board, the CEO and every single member of the executive team. If these people aren't fully aligned and totally committed to the delivery of the strategy, or if they fold at the first sign of resistance, the strategy will never be delivered.

Engage your people in strategy development

Successful strategies (i.e. strategies that are actually delivered) cannot be developed in a vacuum. The recipe for almost certain failure is for the CEO and one of his/her trusted colleagues to disappear into a room and reappear some days or weeks later with the new strategy à la Moses returning from Mount Sinai with his tablets. No matter how innovative, these strategic pronouncements will rarely be greeted with the rapturous applause and glowing acclaim that the CEO expected. Instead, they will be dismissed with a mixture of thinly veiled disdain, cynicism, lip service or outright ridicule by the senior managers who were not involved in their development. The 'not invented here' syndrome is a powerful force and difficult to overcome. It is a fact of life with us humans that the earlier we get involved in a project, the more committed we will be in seeing it through to a successful conclusion.

If a CEO wishes to produce a strategy that has a significant chance of being delivered, he/she needs to engage all of their lieutenants and key influencers in the development of the strategy. It is as simple, and as complex, as that.

Communicate properly

Effective communication is two-way. When it comes to strategy, too many CEOs rely on what I call 'broadcast communications'; the one-way transmission of messages to the rest of the organisation. Over the years, quite a number of CEOs have asked for my help to 'get buy-in' to their strategy and to get their people to 'understand' the new direction. This is one-way communication and it is woefully insufficient.

Effective communication must be relevant and understood. How often do we pause to check whether the people we are communicating with fully understand the implications of what we are saying and what they now need to do differently? Putting ourselves in each audience's shoes and making sure the subject matter is relevant to them and phrased in such a way to ensure maximal understanding are critical if we want our people to embrace a new direction and change their behaviour and actions accordingly. Your people will want to know how this new strategy affects them and they will be asking themselves, 'What is in it for me?' They will need answers.

Develop a robust Strategy Execution Plan

This is not a job for your programme office. It is a job for you. If you genuinely wish for your organisation to deliver your strategy, don't leave it to chance. Too many times CEOs define their strategy and effectively step back and 'let their people get on with it'. This isn't empowerment, it's abdication of responsibility. Genuine empowerment involves giving people clear outcomes, clear guidelines, clear actions and clear expectations. Some CEOs are wary of micro-managing their people. This is admirable, but making sure they have a clear Strategy Execution Plan isn't micro-managing, it is giving them the tools they need to succeed.

So what does a robust *Strategy Execution Plan* look like? The following figure shows a framework that provides an outline of the key components I recommend addressing.

A larger version of this figure can be found in Chapter 35's Change Toolbox and a colour version can be downloaded from www.changeandstrategy.com.

Your Strategy Execution Plan should spell out all the elements your people need to deliver your corporate goals.

A robust strategy execution plan is critical to enable every department to work together to deliver the outcomes that the business requires.

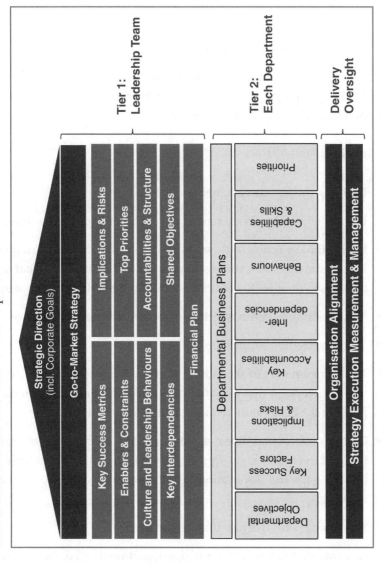

Source: www.changeandstrategy.com

Strategy Execution

The top of the pyramid/house (or 'rocket' if you prefer) is a restatement of your Strategic Direction and Go-to-Market Strategy – keeping the end goals top of mind at all times.

Tier 1 is for the leadership team to deliver

Not only does it deliver the blueprint for success for the organisation, the very act of developing it can be an invaluable process to forge an aligned, collaborative and focused leadership team.

It involves:

- Defining the key success metrics

- Identifying the implications and risks inherent within the strategy

- Listing the key enablers (those skills/capabilities that will be required for the strategy to be successful plus the key deliverables that must be realised in order to deliver the short- and medium-term goals)

- The constraints within which your people will need to operate

- The organisation's top priorities

- The key elements of the culture that success will require – i.e. the ways of working that must be adopted to deliver the outcomes, especially the behaviours required by the leadership team

- Clarity of accountabilities: starting with the executive team, ensuring that everyone knows precisely what they are accountable for and the gaps and duplications in accountability are uncovered and resolved

- Any changes to structure that will be needed

- Key interdependencies among the departments – i.e. the key areas where departments need to work together to deliver the required outcomes

- Key objectives that need to be shared by two or more parts of the organisation

- The financial plan that will guide the implementation.

Tier 1 provides the organisation with the tools it needs to deliver; it gives every department clear direction, priorities, high-level outcomes and the guidelines they need to compile their department business plans.

Tier 2 is owned by the department leadership teams

Each department's business plan should clarify what they need to deliver, who needs to deliver it, how and when. Each business plan should contain:

- The department's objectives

- Key success factors

- Risks to delivery – and plans to mitigate those risks

- Key implications for the department

- Key accountabilities within the department

- Key interdependencies

- Behaviours required to deliver – tailoring the organisation-wide behaviours to the department

- Capabilities and skills required to hone or develop

- The department's priorities.

Last of all comes the *'Delivery Oversight'* piece of the puzzle; a small team to ensure that all of the department business plans are aligned, that together they will deliver the results required, that there are no significant gaps and that duplications are minimised. This team is also responsible for measuring progress towards the end goals and helping the leadership team to act when things go astray and challenges arise.

The leader of this team should be a Change Catalyst.

Chapter 29

Where Are Your Walls?
(Organisation Design)

T he last thing you need is a new structure – and I mean that quite literally.

Organisation Design is far more than deciding who reports to whom, yet when businesses launch into reorganisation mode, the majority of executives head straight for the white board and start drawing up new org charts. At first glance this approach may appear to be decisive and action-oriented, but it is almost guaranteed to fail.

If a company is looking for sustainable change, for an organisation structure that will not only deliver short-term results but also stand the test of time, the approach to organisation design must be thorough and inclusive. It must also start with the strategy; clearly articulating what the organisation is being designed to achieve.

Organisation Design is strategic planning to ensure the organisation is able to deliver its short-, medium- and long-term objectives.

Organisation Design is much more than working out reporting lines. In fact, 'structure' is Step 6 in the process I recommend you follow – shown in the following diagram. (A larger version of this figure is shown in Chapter 35 and a colour version may be downloaded from www .changeandstrategy.com.)

The Organisation Design methodology outlined in the figure has been used, re-used and repeatedly refined by many dozens of consultants over the last 20 years. It has been used to guide organisation design efforts within such companies as Virgin Media, Misys, Sesame, Warburtons, Mothercare, International Personal Finance, Aviva, IFDS, BBC, Guardian, Avis and John Lewis to name but a few. It is a tool to guide companies through the process of designing and implementing the most appropriate organisation as swiftly and as effectively as possible, and it can be used at any and all levels of an organisation.

Organisation Design is much more than structure. It involves clarifying the organisation's strategy and the implications of the strategic direction, then designing every aspect of the organisation to make sure it is capable of delivering the required results.

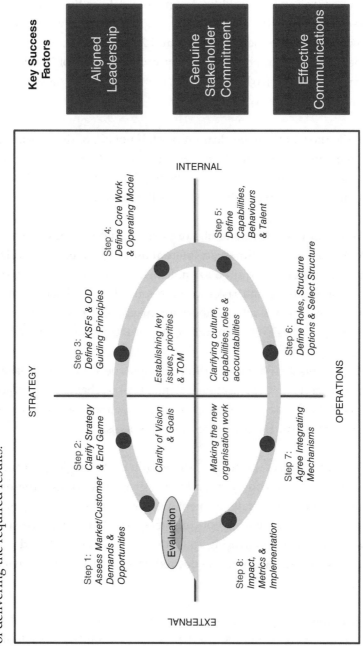

Source: www.changeandstrategy.com

Organisation Design

273

Any organisation should be designed to deliver the strategy, so that is precisely where the methodology begins. It starts with adopting a Strategic/External mind-set. **Steps 1 and 2** involve establishing what the business is trying to achieve – its Purpose, Vision and/or Mission for the future, what it wants to be famous for, the type of organisation it wants to become – and the key corporate goals.

While the CEO may be clear on most, if not all, of this, his or her top team may not be, let alone the rest of the organisation. Clarifying the end game among the top team is vital to laying the foundations for future success – and the boundaries for the rest of the process.

Once that has been done, the org design methodology moves on to **Steps 3 and 4** where a Strategic/Internal mind-set is required – identifying the key elements required to implement the strategy. The key success factors, implications and risks to success need to be determined. What 'magic' do we wish to retain after reorganisation? What are the organisation's key priorities? What should we stop/start/continue doing?

The organisation design guiding principles need to be established and the 'non-negotiable' organisational elements (size, shape, cost, outputs...). These will be the design boundaries and guidelines for the team to refer back to continually during the rest of the process.

The fourth step of the process, still within the Strategic/Internal quadrant, is to define the core work and the key processes of the organisation. Given the company's strategic intent, what work is core to delivery of the key outcomes and what is less core/peripheral? Which processes have the most impact on delivering the required outcomes? How do the existing processes compare to the desired end game and/or industry best practice?

Then, the methodology moves more towards the Operational end of the Y-axis where, in **Step 5**, we define the capabilities, behaviours and talents required to deliver future success – again benchmarked against the desired end game and/or industry best practice.

Then, not until **Step 6**, do we get to structure. Actually, the first part of Step 6 is to identify the key roles that will be required to deliver the outcomes and which of these roles are pivotal.

Then we get to explore the **options** for roles and structure, and I must stress the word 'options'. No structure is perfect. Every single structure has its pros and cons, and I strongly urge you to spell these out for each feasible option. Companies don't do this often enough. Even when companies follow each and every step of this OD process to the letter, they often don't proceed to spell out the pros and cons of the prescribed structure, let alone the fact that other alternatives have been identified and discarded.

If people are to be fully supportive of the new structure, they need to know that this is the best option – and why. They also need to know that you know that the selected structure has its downsides – and implications. If a structure is simply presented as the answer, without this honest analysis, people will simply focus on its downsides. They will compare the pros of the structure they would prefer vs the cons of the structure that has been forced upon them.

Every structure decision comes with its inherent compromises. The trick is to be aware of the compromises you have made – and, even more importantly, for the entire team to be aware of the compromises that have been made. For, without their complete and utter buy-in to the process, and without every new team member going into the new structure with their eyes wide open, the odds of the new structure failing will increase. Once a structure has been decided, every key stakeholder needs to be on board and working to do whatever needs to be done to make it work.

So, you have a new structure. What next? My advice is to **pause for reflection** and double check a few things.

Check whether this has been an inclusive process, where key people have been engaged in the process and feel that they have been part of the development of this new structure.

Check that the key members of the new structure understand the rationale behind the change and are all behind it – or at least able to accept it and move on with a positive frame of mind.

Review or perform a detailed stakeholder analysis. Who is most affected by this change, have their concerns been understood and addressed, how have they been engaged/communicated with?

Check that this wasn't the only structure option put on the table. If it was, check that the pros and cons of the structure were clearly articulated and that these are clear to the key people affected.

Are the key accountabilities clear? Are there any grey areas of accountability, any areas of duplication?

Have the pivotal roles been identified and does the new structure do them justice, incorporating them in a way that will enable the pivotal role holders to deliver the outstanding results expected of them?

Have all of the key capabilities that the organisation needs in order to be successful been incorporated successfully into the new structure?

Ask yourself one key over-riding question: *Will this new structure best deliver the organisation's strategy?*

Then move on to **Step 7**: making the new structure work by designing the 'integrating mechanisms' needed to mitigate the cons, implications and compromises inherent within the new structure. What decision-making processes, management forums, communication forums and processes will be needed to make the new structure work?

Step 8 is to define the success metrics – how you plan to measure the success of the newly shaped organisation.

A colleague and I ran a workshop for Aviva's HR Department to introduce them to the methodology to guide their OD engagements with their internal clients. The number one question that the HR professionals asked us was:

'But all of our business leader clients leap straight to structure. They almost always turn up to the first re-organisation meeting with a new org chart. What do I do then?'

That is the beauty of this methodology. It is ideal for challenging a desired structure. It can be used as a checklist to help the department head make sure he or she develops all of the other components necessary for a structure to work. Our advice was to start with the 'pause for reflection' part of Step 6. Assume the desired structure is appropriate and use the methodology to fill in the gaps. Check that the strategy is clear, measurable and understood; that the implications of the strategy have been identified; that the core work, key processes, behaviours and roles have been recognised; that the pros and cons of the desired structure have been articulated clearly; that the other structure options have been considered and that the reasons for discounting them are clear.

Then you can get on with the invaluable task of making the new structure work.

Secrets to successful Organisation Design:

- Clarity of what success looks like

- Unwavering focus on why we are doing this and delivering the business outcomes required

- Unwavering commitment from the top

- Involvement and engagement of every key individual as early as possible in the process

- Objective and honest assessment of market opportunities and internal strengths and weaknesses

- Not afraid to back-track to early stages of the process when necessary

- Being prepared to compromise; fully aware of why compromise is necessary and the implications

- Acknowledgement that no structure is perfect

- The behaviour of the Senior Management Team:

  o Cabinet responsibility

  o Leaders putting the best interests of the company ahead of their own personal interests

  o Strong collective desire to make any structure work

  o Trust among the leadership team

  o Confidentiality during the design stage; open, honest and transparent communications afterwards

- Clear decisions once the design and implementation process has been agreed

- Clear understanding of the implications of decisions

- Clear, reliable data on which to base decisions – people costs, $ per product/channel...

- Clear communications plan and execution

- Proven Organisation Design methodology.

Chapter 30

Overcoming Complacency (The Innovator's Dilemma)

*'Success breeds complacency. Complacency breeds failure.
Only the paranoid survive.'*

Andy Grove[5]

Complacency has destroyed many a successful organisation. It is one of the most powerful barriers to change there is.

In my career, I have worked with several successful organisations whose leadership teams had become complacent. I have also worked with a large number of companies whose leaders managed to avoid the trap that befalls many a market leader; the trap that has become known as 'The Innovator's Dilemma'.[6]

In his 1997 best-selling book, regarded as one of the best business books ever written, Hayden Christensen details the challenges faced by market leaders and successful organisations. And the problem is that the approach and skills that have made them so successful are the very things that will cause them to come undone in the future.

The decision-making and resource allocation processes that are key to the success of established companies are the very processes that reject disruptive technologies and market changes: listening to customers, tracking competitors' actions and investing in higher-quality products that will yield greater profits. Christensen concluded that these are the reasons why great firms stumbled or failed when confronted with disruptive technological change.

Disruptive technologies start out being small, low-margin and unprofitable. The new entrants, often founded by frustrated ex-employees of the incumbents, have little or nothing to lose. Initially, these small upstarts don't pose a threat and the new entrants find new markets for these technologies largely by trial and error, at low margins.

These new entrants certainly don't start by asking customers what they want. As Henry Ford famously said of his Model T automobile, 'If I had asked the customer what they wanted, they would have said "faster horses".' Usually, the new entrants come up with an idea and then start to find, or create, a market for it. This is the reverse process that market leaders use. But 'product first, market second' was precisely how the Walkman was born, along with Corn Flakes, Kleenex, Post-it Notes, chewing gum, the Polaroid camera... we didn't know we needed them until they were invented.

And with the Internet and smartphones, these innovations are now occurring on a daily basis. Who knew we needed Facebook?

Imagine you were a Venture Capital executive and someone pitched an idea to you for a business – and the pitch went something like this: 'I have invented this smartphone app where people can share text and pictures with one another or a group of their friends – for free!' 'But you can already do that with iMessage from any iPhone,' you would have sensibly replied as you showed the eager young upstart the door. WhatsApp was sold (to Facebook) in 2014 for $19 billion.

Or even more improbable – a different entrepreneur bursts into your office to declare he has invented an app that allows you to send pictures and photos to your friends... but, wait for it – the images are only viewable for ten seconds! This time you would call security. In 2014, Snapchat's CEO rejected an offer (again from Facebook) to buy the company for $3 billion.

It isn't that market leaders fail to spot and develop new technologies. The problem is that they fail to value new innovations properly because they try to shoe-horn them into their existing product lines, margins and the ways of working that have made them so successful. It is very hard for a company to invest in new products that offer lower profit, will initially underperform existing technologies and can only be sold in insignificant markets.

Once the disruptive technologies emerge, they are treated with hostility – as they will inevitably necessitate the cannibalisation of some, or all, of the market leader's market share, products or profits.

How to overcome complacency

First, don't ever take your company's success for granted. Stay paranoid. Keep looking for improvements; for better ways to do things. Keep questioning performance. Keep questioning the viability of your products and services. Stay hungry. Make continuous improvement an integral part of the way your organisation works.

Successful companies are restless. They are never content, even when they have grown to dominate their marketplace, they don't rest on their laurels. They look for the next opportunity; for the next market they can change for the better.

Second, keep a constant lookout for disruptive technologies and new entrants.

Third, prepare a war chest to (a) invest in new entrants at an early stage, (b) buy new entrants as they start to succeed, (c) start a new entrant incubator of your own or (d) all of the above.

IFDS: The value of continuous improvement, thorough planning and never being complacent

International Financial Data Services is a 50/50 joint venture between State Street and DST. Famous for keeping a low profile due to the back-room nature of its work, it was described to me by one of its senior executives as 'the best financial services company you've never heard of'. IFDS was conceived in 1995 and has since grown to be the market leader in funds administration with its 3500+ people processing two out of every three of the investment funds traded in the UK. Most financial advisers and UK investors will have come into contact with IFDS, many without even knowing it, as the company provides white-labelled administration and customer services to such a significant proportion of the industry.

What impressed me most about the business is that having reached the summit of its chosen market, rather than pausing for breath and admiring the view, the IFDS leadership came to the conclusion that the Business Process Outsourcing (BPO) skills and technologies they had developed so successfully for fund managers would be equally valuable to insurers and investment platforms.

So, in 2013, they launched two new businesses: IFDS Retirement & Insurance Solutions to provide outsourced technology and admin services to the pension industry and IFDS Platform Solutions to provide outsourced technology and admin services to the investment industry. And only a year after launch, these bold moves had already started to pay off, with the prize scalps of Old Mutual and St James Place. Both of these industry leaders signed 20-year contracts for IFDS to provide their platform technology and administration services.

But these bold new moves did not come 'out of the blue'. They were the ultimate result of IFDS's culture – which is based, genuinely, on the tenet of 'continuous improvement'.

'Continuous improvement is part of our DNA. It is our most important value. Every one of our employees is actively encouraged to look for new ways of doing things, reducing inefficiencies and improving the experience for the end customer. Creating a culture in which innovation can thrive is the responsibility of every executive and manager at IFDS.'

Simon Hudson-Lund, Executive Chairman of IFDS

The driver of IFDS's expansion strategy was that the leadership saw that it could not afford to be complacent.

(continued)

'The key driver behind our diversification strategy was the fact that we could see our core business would reach a saturation point as we captured an increasing percentage of the funds administration market. To continue growing, we would need to branch out into new markets with new propositions. In fact, we could foresee a scenario where our core funds admin business could even start to enter a phase of natural decline due to the rise of platforms. Both of our parent organisations actively pursued growth strategies, so we received all the support we needed to explore expansion opportunities.'

Simon Hudson-Lund, Executive Chairman of IFDS

In 2014, I asked Simon for his top tips for other CEOs and Boards looking to innovate. These were his top three:

1. Innovate within your sphere of excellence. Carefully think through what your organisation is actually good at and stay close to this.
2. Build your strategy around these key skills.
3. Communicate effectively across the entire company, focusing on *why* you are doing what you are doing. Make sure everyone genuinely understands and believes in the new direction. We started communicating internally about our diversification strategy some 4–5 years ago and month after month we talked about why it was the right thing to do and why it was going to be successful.

I think there are a number of lessons we could learn from IFDS's stunningly successful diversification into two new markets.

The first one that jumps out at me is the importance of planning. IFDS didn't wait until it had a 'burning platform' before it had an eyes-wide-open look into the future. It assessed its challenges objectively and started to put plans together well in advance. Simon Hudson-Lund did not see the expansion strategy as bold. Because of the detailed planning, it was regarded to be common sense and a natural extension of the 'continuous improvement' culture.

The second lesson is the crucial importance of people. IFDS built its future business around its core skills and culture rather than taking a desperate leap into the unknown.

The third concerns the importance of internal communication. Too often, companies under-value this critical component of business success, and they do so at their peril. For if your people don't genuinely understand what needs to change and why, how on Earth will they be able to deliver it?

The fourth is the value of resisting the urge to become complacent.

Chapter 31

What Does a Good Leader Look Like?

'Leadership: it's the art of getting someone else to do something you want done because he wants to do it.'
Dwight D. Eisenhower[7]

To be embarrassingly trite for a moment, a leader is simply someone whom people wish to follow. A good leader, however, also knows – and cares – where he or she is taking them.

But before I begin my description of what a good leader looks like, let me be completely clear: there is no absolutely right or wrong way to lead. There is no absolutely right or wrong leadership style, and even great leaders are human and will have their bad days.

However, a good leader must be able to do a few straightforward things.

A good leader is obsessed with the delivery of tangible business outcomes, not obsessing over details of the process that should have been followed or whether a particular project's action items have been completed. Effort is admirable but ultimately irrelevant. A good leader knows that delivery and results are paramount.

'Leadership is defined by results not attributes.'
Peter Drucker

They possess the ability to paint the big picture for their people, shareholders and customers. They give their people an aspiration to aim for. They are able to set a vision of the future that is both credible and captures their employees' imaginations. They are also capable of driving, inspiring, encouraging and enabling people to achieve that vision.

Good leaders care passionately about their company, their customers, their people and the future they are trying to achieve. They are not just in it for the money or the status.

A good leader appreciates that leadership is a privilege, not a birthright. A good leader appreciates that everyone in the organisation has placed their trust in them, and is fully aware of the responsibility that goes hand-in-hand with this.

A good leader realises that the company's customers are the number one reason that it exists. Employees come a very, very close second and shareholders third. Never, ever should this list be in any other order.

A good leader knows that if you deliver products and services that customers crave, and treat your people with the respect they deserve while empowering them to deliver in the way they believe is best for the customer, the results will come and the shareholders will be richly rewarded. Leaders who start with the shareholder in mind will be unable to think beyond the next month's figures and will be setting themselves up for a major clash with customers and staff – to the detriment of everyone, especially the shareholders they were trying so desperately to serve in the first place.

A good leader understands and empathises with their customers. They appreciate their needs and, of even higher importance, their wants, and they focus their company on meeting these expectations. A good leader puts the customer at the heart of the organisation and his people strive to ensure that every customer experience enhances the reputation of the company.

A good leader invites their people to find innovative solutions to problems and seek out new opportunities. They understand and empathise with their people, while simultaneously driving them to deliver outrageous results.

Good leaders command and receive a respect that is based on admiration rather than fear.

Good leaders understand that employees need to be emotionally committed to the organisation. Not only does every employee need to know what they personally need to do to deliver the strategy, but they need to be motivated to do so. While rational motivation is important (i.e. the logical reason for why each objective needs to be achieved), emotional motivation is the secret to success (i.e. when each employee has identified the personal benefit to them associated with delivery of the objective).

Good leaders give their people enough freedom to take decisions and make mistakes without fearing the consequences.

Good leaders aren't afraid to make decisions themselves, even when they don't have all the information to hand. And good leaders aren't afraid to make tough, even unpopular decisions. Good leaders also don't mind making mistakes, because they learn from them.

Good leaders are not afraid to show their weaknesses. In fact, they hire people to compensate for them. Good leaders hire people who are better than they are and have the confidence to get out of their way.

Good leaders invest in developing their people, understanding that they are the only genuine source of long-term competitive advantage.

Good leaders develop several people as their potential successors, because even those who don't get promoted will move on to bigger and better things outside of the organisation – and they will be motivated to deliver outstanding results in the meantime.

'I start with the premise that the function of leadership is to produce more leaders, not more followers.'

Ralph Nader[8]

Great leaders embrace stewardship, working to leave the organisation in a better state than they inherited from the leaders before them.

Great leaders are confident enough in their own abilities and secure enough in their own sense of self-worth to enable other people to develop their own leadership skills.

Great leaders also do one other thing exceptionally well. We all have an in-built insincerity sensor; we find it very easy to tell when someone is trying to pretend to be someone they're not.

So, above all, great leaders are not afraid to be themselves.

Chapter 32

Building Extraordinary Leadership Teams

While it is vitally important that your organisation's leaders are all doing the best jobs possible, most of the results in today's collegiate, meritocratic, open-plan business world are managed and performed by teams. So it is vitally important that you make sure you get the most out of your most important of crews: your organisation's leadership team.

Most employees look at their company's leadership team with a mixed air of awe and bemusement; awe at the confidence, wealth and status of the diners at the corporation's top table, and often a sense of bemusement as to how they got there and the lengths to which some of them will go to hold onto their seat.

Let's be honest with ourselves, behaviour among the top team doesn't always live up to expectations. Just two of many examples of this I could name include:

1. Differences of opinion almost caused fisticuffs during a Board meeting of one of the world's largest banks as the Group Marketing Director dared to disagree with the pronouncements forthcoming from the all-conquering head of the Investment Banking arm.

2. The Board of one of the world's leading global pharmaceutical companies was described by an insider as 'a pack of Alpha males trying to score points off one another.'

And family businesses can often be worse, as childhood pecking orders and ancient squabbles can come to the fore during times of stress, and family members are promoted over more competent employees.

Of course, the vast majority of leadership teams don't behave like this (or at least not all the time!), so what is it that makes these leadership teams effective? Or, better still, what makes a leadership team extraordinary?

Having been a member of numerous leadership teams and seen many dozens more in action across a variety of different industries over the last three decades, I have come to the conclusion that, in order to be extraordinary, leadership teams need to maximise their effectiveness, simultaneously, across three dimensions:

1. Individual effectiveness

2. Team effectiveness

3. Effectiveness as a leader.

A larger version of the following diagram is shown in Chapter 35 and a colour version of the image may be downloaded from www.changeandstrategy.com.

If you genuinely want to maximise the effectiveness of your leadership team, you cannot skimp on any one of these. Furthermore, you cannot be overweight in one of them in the hope that this will make up for a deficiency in another. Extraordinary leadership teams need all three dimensions – in equal balance.

Extraordinary leadership teams are made up of confident, effective leaders who respect and trust one another. They must respect one another's ability to deliver (individual effectiveness), ability to lead their respective departments (effectiveness as a leader) and ability to be a highly effective team member (team effectiveness).

Extraordinary leadership teams need to maximise their effectiveness across three key dimensions:

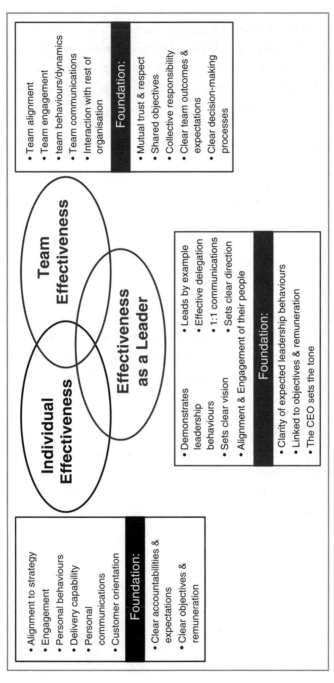

- Team alignment
- Team engagement
- team behaviours/dynamics
- Team communications
- Interaction with rest of organisation

Foundation:
- Mutual trust & respect
- Shared objectives
- Collective responsibility
- Clear team outcomes & expectations
- Clear decision-making processes

Team Effectiveness

Individual Effectiveness

Effectiveness as a Leader

- Demonstrates leadership behaviours
- Sets clear vision
- Alignment & Engagement of their people
- Leads by example
- Effective delegation
- 1:1 communications
- Sets clear direction

Foundation:
- Clarity of expected leadership behaviours
- Linked to objectives & remuneration
- The CEO sets the tone

- Alignment to strategy
- Engagement
- Personal behaviours
- Delivery capability
- Personal communications
- Customer orientation

Foundation:
- Clear accountabilities & expectations
- Clear objectives & remuneration

Source: www.changeandstrategy.com

Creating Extraordinary Leadership Teams

The main ingredients to building extraordinary leadership teams

Clarity

Clarity is essential; if the leadership team isn't genuinely clear about where the organisation is going, why, what needs to be done and who is accountable for delivering what, the rest of the organisation has no chance. The implications of the strategy need to be understood fully and there needs to be utter clarity regarding the expectations and accountabilities of each individual executive as well as the leadership team as a whole.

Alignment

A successful team needs to be aligned around this clear strategy. They need to ensure that everything they are doing both individually and collectively is working towards achieving the corporate goals.

Engagement

The team must be involved in defining the above, not just implementing it. Only when people have had a hand in the design will they be fully engaged in, and committed to, delivering the outcomes.

Clearly defined rules of engagement

A successful team defines what 'good' looks like in terms of team dynamics. How team members behave – how the team works – is just as important as what it needs to deliver. To be an extraordinary team, each team member needs to give the others permission to tell them when they are not displaying the agreed behaviours.

Shared objectives

A team can be genuinely effective only if all of its members are striving to achieve the same things. If every executive is focused on achieving their own individual objectives rather than the organisation's goals, they will never be a high-performing team.

Respect

Each team member needs to develop respect for the skills, experience and abilities that each of their colleagues brings to the table. Understanding one another's strengths and weaknesses is important, as a person's key strength is often also their key weakness. But let's keep some sense of perspective; this is a business, not a marriage.

A team of extraordinary leaders

Each member of the leadership team must be a leader in their own right. The team needs to define the leadership behaviours they are going to display, how they are going to ensure they live up to these expectations and how they are going continually to develop their leadership skills.

No magic pill

While a great deal can be achieved through specific interventions, this is a journey. Extraordinary teams evolve; they are not created overnight.

Chapter 33

Your People

Your people are the only ones who can deliver your strategy. Your people are the only ones who can bring about genuine, sustainable change.

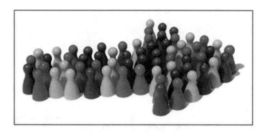

To deliver the change you require, your people need to be genuinely engaged and aligned to deliver. We have discussed ways and means of doing this throughout the book – clear two-way communications, genuine stakeholder engagement, strategy development, strategy execution...

In this chapter, I want to talk about your people; your talent. And I want to share two tools that I have found to be particularly useful. One is my take on an old HR staple for talent assessment and development, the 'Nine-Box Grid'. The other is a deceptively invaluable little tool for managing people, invented by a very good friend of mine, John McKee, CEO of an outstanding Northern Ireland consultancy, Linkubator (www.linkubator.com). It is called 'The Performance Choice Grid' and it maps attitude vs knowledge/competence. I believe it is one of the best people management tools I have come across.

The Nine-Box Grid

The Nine-Box Grid is a common tool used by HR departments and executive teams worldwide as a guide for talent assessment, talent development and succession planning. When used correctly, it can be a very useful guide to prompt and assist leadership teams to conduct valuable discussions about their most valuable asset.

But it requires effort, consistency, clear guidelines and persistence. A number of organisations don't embrace it fully or conflate it with their annual appraisal system. The former means its use fizzles out or becomes resented as 'yet another time-consuming piece of HR admin' (to paraphrase several managers across several organisations). The latter is a recipe for disaster as people fight with their managers and one another about their particular grid position rather than focusing on how to develop and improve performance.

The Nine-Box Grid should be used as a guide, as a prompt, as a starter for ten. It should be used to aid succession planning and to help tailor your people's development plans.

This grid is believed to have originated within McKinsey and was developed for GE in the late 1960s and 1970s to enable them to assess the potential of individuals. It is claimed that it is based on the Boston Consulting Group and their 'Boston Box' of business or product potential – but applied to individuals.

Having seen it in action across dozens of companies, the following figure shows the version I like the most. A larger version of this figure is shown in Chapter 35, and a colour version may be downloaded from www.changeandstrategy.com.

My recommendations on how to use it are as follows:

1. Be clear about why you are using it. The grid can be one or more of the following:

   a. A prompt for discussion and comparison of each employee of a similar level.

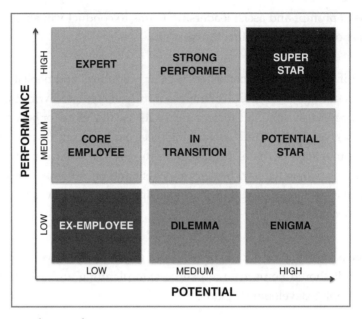

Source: www.changeandstrategy.com

The Nine-Box Grid

b. A guide for personal development. People within each box will have some development needs in common.

c. A guide for succession planning.

d. A guide for identifying talent gaps that recruitment may be able to fill.

e. A guide for remuneration package design. Where someone is on the grid should not affect their performance bonus, but there is an argument for tailoring remuneration packages differently for people within some of the boxes.

What is your primary reason for using it? What is/are your secondary reason/reasons?

2. Make sure you have the data to work with – that every 'evaluatee' has had an assessment form completed by their manager with input from other relevant parties, and that these forms are distributed well in advance.

3. Keep going – realise it is the beginning of a process not the end. Crack on with completing Personal Development Plans, Succession Plans and Retention Plans. Don't just stop at the grid.

Descriptions and implications of each box

The low performance row

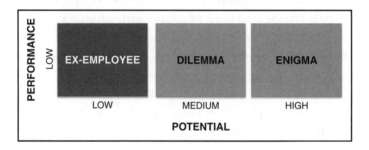

Box 1: Low potential/Low performance (Ex-Employee)   The people in this box of the grid have either left already or will need to be exited.

Box 2: Medium potential/Low performance (Dilemma)   What is the reason for their low performance? Is it their capability? Would specialist training help? Are they in the wrong job? Is their manager not doing his/her job properly? These people must move out of the box – preferably upwards.

Box 3: High potential/Low performance (Enigma)   If people are genuinely placed in this box, you need to look at their manager. They will either be reporting to the wrong person or in the wrong job.

The medium performance row

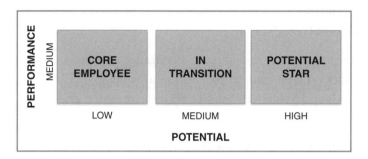

Box 4: Low potential/Medium performance (Core Employee)   These guys and girls are the backbone of your organisation. Depending upon your type of business, the majority of your people may be in this box – and there is nothing wrong with this whatsoever. Not everyone can be a superstar and not everyone is a superstar at every stage of their career. Look for ways to improve their performance but it doesn't matter if they never get out of this box. In fact, continue to develop their skills and productivity so that they remain 'effective employees' throughout their career. These people are the core target audience for the management development and personal development programmes offered by HR.

Box 5: Medium potential/Medium performance (In Transition)   Quite a few companies label this box 'core employees'. I think this can be a mistake as it can result in this box becoming over-crowded and almost meaningless. If you label it 'In Transition', it becomes useful. They are, in effect, 'Core Employees +'. My recommendation is to regard everyone in this box as needing to be placed elsewhere in the future – to the left and tagged as a 'Core Employee', to the right as their potential becomes more apparent, upwards as their performance increases or downwards if their performance takes a turn for the worst. The question to ask about each resident of this box is: what can you do to help them move right or up?

Box 6: High potential/Medium performance (Rising Star) Their performance is good but they have more to offer. It's not so much about training, these 'HiPoes' need a bigger challenge, a different opportunity, more responsibility. They should feature in your key projects and your succession plans.

The high performance row

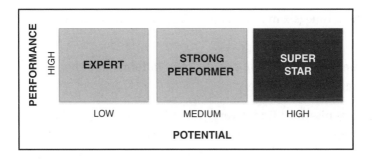

Box 7: Low potential/High performance (Expert) These folks may not be the best managers of people, but they are worth their weight in ostrich feathers and need to be rewarded accordingly. They don't (or shouldn't) have aspirations for dramatic career advancement but they are highly productive. They deliver. I recommend: (a) considering a different remuneration scheme for your 'Experts', one very closely tied to delivery; (b) using them as mentors for others in the organisation and (c) continually giving them recognition. You need to retain these people.

Box 8: Medium potential/High performance (Strong Performer) These guys deliver and have potential for future advancement. They are likely to be very good people managers while also having at least one eye on their own career. You need to keep them and to do that you will need to work with them to formulate a plan to help them get to Box 9.

Box 9: High potential/High performance (Super Star) By the time they have been assessed to belong in this box, they may have already been promoted. If not, the promotion will need to be soon or they may start to look outside your organisation or become despondent and slip down the matrix. One important thing to remember – when Box 9ers are promoted, they will no longer be in Box 9. They will then need to be assessed on the demands and requirements of their new role.

New employees/new to role

Give them time (six months?) before you place them on the grid.

Don't be afraid of scoring people 'low' in terms of either potential or performance

Some organisations find it very difficult, culturally, to label someone as low potential. Some organisations even find it difficult to label their people as low performance. This is especially so if your remuneration scheme is tied to people's position on the grid – so don't let this happen.

And lastly, embrace the grid

If done properly – if fully adopted – the Nine-Box Grid can be a highly useful tool to guide your identification and assessment of talent, the development of your people and succession planning. And all of this can only lead in one direction – enhanced performance for your organisation.

The Performance Choice Grid

What I love about Linkubator's deceptively simple tool is that it recognises the importance of attitude.

It doesn't matter how clever someone is, how qualified they may be or how much potential they may allegedly possess – if they don't have the right attitude, they will be next to useless. The good news is that helping people to identify when their attitude needs adjustment – and helping them make the adjustment – is one of the most rewarding and productive things that a manager can do. And we all have moments when our attitude needs a little adjustment.

John and I introduced the Performance Choice Grid (and the Strategy Execution Framework from Chapter 28) to the management team of one of the UK's largest pension providers a few years back. They have found it to be invaluable.

The following diagrams illustrating the Grid are also shown in Chapter 35's Change Toolbox and colour versions may be downloaded from www.changeandstrategy.com.

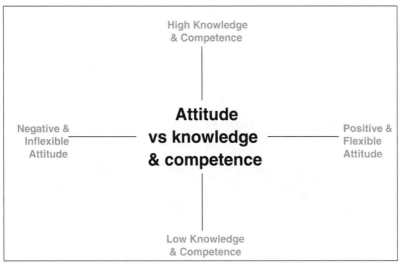

© **link**ubator

Source: www.changeandstrategy.com

Performance Choice Grid

It is simply a grid of attitude vs knowledge. But you will be surprised at the insight that can be obtained from simply plotting your people onto this grid. And, unlike the Nine-Box Grid, this time you will want your people to know where you have put them and why.

The grid can then be divided into four zones:

1. *The Owner Zone*: The high knowledge, good attitude zone which everyone should be striving to be in and move towards;

2. *The Learner Zone*: People with good attitude but low levels of knowledge;

3. *The Victim Zone*: Comprising people with high knowledge but poor attitude; and

4. *The End Zone*: Named as such because the combination of low knowledge and poor attitude cannot possibly be a recipe for success.

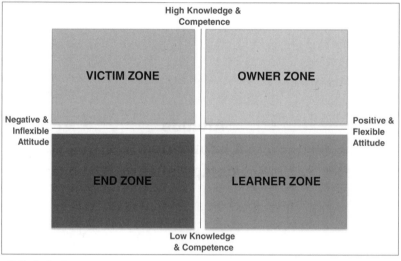

© **link**ubator

Source: www.changeandstrategy.com

Performance Choice Grid

Your people will need help moving from one zone to another.

The brilliant folks at Linkubator have gone to the trouble of describing different types of characters who reside on different parts of the grid – and each one is spectacularly accurate.

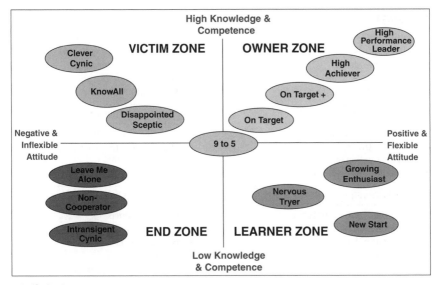

© linkubator

Source: www.changeandstrategy.com

Performance Choice Grid

These characters are incredibly useful to help us determine where we are on the Performance Choice Grid. Of even more value is asking others where they would place us – and why – and then contemplating any differences.

Linkubator's clients have found it to be a brilliant tool for managers to engage with their people on the thorny but crucial subject of attitude. First, managers explain the grid and the thinking behind it. Then they ask their people to place themselves on it and to discuss their rationale. Next, the manager reveals where on the grid he/she has placed the direct report – and why. Once the differences are discussed, they can, together, start planning actions to move the direct report towards the 'Owner Zone'.

Nearly every character possesses both positive and negative characteristics:

NEW START +	NEW START −
• Enthusiastic	• Poor project completion rate
• Keen to please and impress	• Inarticulate idea expression
• Full of new ideas	• Problems with priorities
• Flexible	• Takes on too many projects
• Potential growth to Owner Zone	• Needs attention

GROWING ENTHUSIAST +	GROWING ENTHUSIAST −
• Enthusiastic/exploring	• Questions, questions, questions
• Good for the team	• Makes frequent mistakes
• Brings new thinking	• Needs mentoring
• Heading for Owner Zone	

NERVOUS TRYER +	NERVOUS TRYER −
• Conservative, keen to learn	• Low confidence
• Supports the team	• Low self-esteem
• Has great potential	• Hesitant, fears failure
• Persistent	• Needs leadership

9 to 5 +	9 to 5 −
• Does the basic job well	• Could do better
• Quite loyal to the team	• Has low expectations
• Follows orders and instruction	• Needs monitoring
• Generally dependable	• Hard to shift to Owner Zone

DISAPPOINTED SCEPTIC +	DISAPPOINTED SCEPTIC −
• Knows the business	• Struggles with feedback
• Knows the politics	• Has taken a beating
• Knows what needs to be fixed	• May not listen
• Has potential if reinvigorated	• Potentially heading for End Zone

KNOW-ALL +	KNOW-ALL −
• High knowledge	• Won't listen or change
• High confidence	• Demonstrates knowledge
• Highly articulate	• Talks down to colleagues
• Effective when 'on-message'	• Highly risk-averse
	• Potentially heading for End Zone

CLEVER CYNIC +	CLEVER CYNIC −
• High knowledge	• Toxic towards the team
• High confidence	• Wittingly or unwittingly disloyal
• Highly articulate	• Won't listen or change
• Highly effective if he/she wants to be	• Knows who to blame
	• Potentially heading for End Zone

LEAVE ME ALONE +	LEAVE ME ALONE −
• Some potential for turning?	• Totally passive • Dead-weight • No value to the team • If not turned, needs firing

NON-CO-OPERATOR +	NON-CO-OPERATOR −
• Some potential for turning?	• Knows his/her rights • Kills team spirit • Negatively vocal • Won't change easily • If not turned, needs firing

INTRANSIGENT CYNIC +	INTRANSIGENT CYNIC −
• None	• Needs to be fired

ON TARGET +	ON TARGET −
• Well organised • Results orientated • Confident in own ability • Delivers against target	• Rarely over-delivers • Committed mainly to self • Can revert to '9 to 5' • Needs 'team-awareness'

ON TARGET + +	ON TARGET + −
• Very well organised • Strong results focus • Very confident • Delivers more than target	• Exceeds personal target – but stops • Can slip into 'BMW Syndrome' • Needs 'team-awareness'

HIGH ACHIEVER +	HIGH ACHIEVER −
• Sets 'rich' goals • Highly ambitious • Strong role model • Delivers well over target	• Often fails to delegate • Focus on self rather than team • Needs 'team-awareness'

LEADER +	LEADER −
• Owns 'rich' goals • Leads a strong team • Leads a learning team • Communicates continually	• Must react to situational change • Needs high ethics • Needs clear values • Needs rigorous consistency

How we used this tool in the management seminar I mentioned earlier was that we first asked every attendee to plot themselves on the grid. Then we asked them to explain their choice to the group, along with what they would need to move them into, or perhaps deeper into, the Owner Zone.

Then we asked them to think of one of their direct reports and repeat the process (without identifying the person to the group). Finally, we asked them where they thought the direct report in question would place themselves on the grid – and why.

This simple task was such a revelation that 90% of the attendees immediately started using the grid with their direct reports as soon as they got back to the office. It is a tool that enables detailed and even difficult discussions – but in a way that is proactive, for it ends with action.

And, as I said earlier, it also shines a spotlight onto the critical importance of attitude.

Chapter 34

Case Studies

This section contains a few select examples of real-life Change Catalysts and case studies of major change initiatives, some literally on a global scale. Each one has been chosen to illustrate one or more of the key points contained in the book.

1. Tim Wallace and the iPipeline team: Change Catalysts who are transforming the life insurance industry.

2. Michael Sheargold: a Change Catalyst who is transforming the Australian real estate industry.

3. Michael Gould: a Change Catalyst and Founder of the 'unicorn' Anaplan that is transforming the world of corporate planning and reporting.

4. Unlocking the value of HR.

5. Globalisation: a perfect example of how not to instigate change.

1. Tim Wallace and the iPipeline team: Transforming insurance

Tim Wallace and his team are dragging the vast life insurance industry kicking and screaming into the digital age.

The insurance industry, particularly in the US, has long been stuck in a bygone era. Until very recently, life insurance sales followed an entirely manual, cumbersome and paper-based process. Agents hand-wrote orders, printed policy documents, delivered them by mail and then waited – as if the last 20 years' technological revolution had simply never happened. The industry has been one of the last to reap the benefits of greater efficiency, enhanced productivity, improved customer service, higher profits and strong revenue growth that technology can provide.

Tim Wallace and iPipeline have changed all that.

'The technology has been available for a while,' says Tim. 'It was just this industry. Historically, it has been so far behind the rest of the world in the adoption and use of technology. It took a couple of innovative people internally in the industry and people from outside the industry like myself to come in and say, "Hey, there's a whole better way of doing this."'[9]

iPipeline's mission is 'to revolutionise the industry by bringing it fully and enthusiastically online and into the cloud'. And this is precisely what they have done.

With headquarters in Exton, Philadelphia and a further six offices worldwide (Cheltenham (UK), Fort Lauderdale, Hunterville, Philadelphia, Salt Lake City and Vancouver), iPipeline's technology is transforming every part of the insurance industry – insurers, distributors, producers and advisers alike – enabling them all to market, sell and process insurance faster and without errors.

Before the iPipeline revolution, the average insurance policy in the US was taking up to 55 days to process from application to adoption. With the iPipeline applications, this can all be done in a fraction of the time – from as little as an hour to a couple of weeks (for complex cases). The iPipeline process is not only efficient, effective and almost completely error-free, it almost completely eradicates lost sales due to client 'drop-out' – in the past too many customers simply lost patience with the seemingly never-ending manual process they were forced to endure.

To the garage born

Like so many other brilliant ideas and innovative companies, it all started in a garage. Back in 1995, iPipeline founder, Bill Atlee, was an insurance agent and, like all insurance salespeople, was drowning in a sea of paper. Every insurance carrier had their own application forms; every state had its own regulations. Keeping up to date with the plethora of products launched on the US life industry every week was an impossible task, especially as every company's underwriting rules

(continued)

were hidden behind cloaks of mystery and intrigue. How could he be sure that he was getting the best deal for his customers? The amount of time he wasted applying for policies that would take weeks, often only to be rejected, was infuriating and bad for everybody's business. There must be a better way.

So Bill reached for his coloured marker pens and a flip chart and started working with a small IT team to create a central online repository for the industry's application forms, underwriting guidelines and product information. 'Internet Pipeline' had been born.

'In the beginning, it was like trying to sell someone the first fax machine,' explained Bill. 'Until they could see it and use it, very few people could visualise what I was trying to create. I was in a classic Catch-22 situation. Without having the insurance carriers' forms online, I couldn't attract any distributors. Without the distributors, why would carriers bother to give me their forms? But we got there one carrier and one distributor at a time.'

In 2002, Larry Berran came on board to help get some discipline into the back-office of the company and to accelerate the sales and marketing efforts. 'I am an ideas guy and an insurance sales guy,' said Bill. 'I needed someone to help get the business organised and moving. With Larry on board, we clarified our product and service range, attracted $18 million of venture capital funding and the business grew to around 29 employees and $7 million annual turnover.'

Six years later, iPipeline attracted some further VC interest and Tim Wallace was hired to lead the company into the big time. 'I was very happy for Tim to come in as CEO,' said Berran. 'He had developed market-leading technology businesses before. He knew what needed to be done. He was someone I could learn from.'

'I'd known Tim for about three years and was very impressed,' said Mike DiPiano, who, as Managing Partner of New Spring Capital and an iPipeline Board member, was instrumental in hiring Tim Wallace to lead the company. 'He's very focused on the critical juice that a business needs. He does a terrific job of understanding his people and putting them in good places. He knows how to allocate resources, both capital and human. And he is very honest, which makes him a good leader. So we thought we'd give him a call and see if this was something he'd be interested in doing.'[9]

After doing his research, Tim Wallace went back to Mike DiPiano with his verdict: 'Mike, you have a hell of an opportunity here. You have a fragmented industry. Most of the software companies are lemonade stands, and they're servicing multibillion-dollar companies. These little companies are running mission-critical systems for the big guys. There's a huge opportunity here to grow a big software company.'[9] Which is precisely what he has done.

Under Wallace's leadership, iPipeline has exploded. Eight years after Tim's arrival, its annual revenues now exceed $110 million, and it employs 500 people in seven offices worldwide. It is now so much more than an online product library – it provides complete online quotes, illustrations, automatic underwriting, automated application, data services, e-delivery and fulfilment solutions for more than half a million insurance agents and advisers, 850 distributors and around 120 insurance carriers in the US alone. Its SaaS system integrates with more than 800 websites, including the industry's largest banks, wire houses, broker-dealers and insurance distributors. And, of course, it is the industry's one-stop repository for hundreds of thousands of insurance forms – which still differ by company, by state and, within each state, by a complex tangle of regulatory requirements.

iPipeline is one of the most exciting Software-as-a-Service (SaaS) businesses in the US and is the winner of a host of well-deserved and prestigious awards including the 2016 PTFS Best Technology Award, the Corporate LiveWire 2016 Innovation & Excellence Award, the 2015 PACT Enterprise Awards Technology Company of the Year, the 2014 Red Herring Global 100 Award (presented to the top 100 private

(continued)

companies across Europe, North America and Asia), the 2014 Marcum Innovator of the Year Award, the 2014 Digital Strategist of the Year Award, the 2014 BEA Insurance Solutions Firm of the Year Award; it is also a five-time finalist and winner in 2014 of SmartCEO's Philadelphia CEO of the Year.

In selecting its CEO of the Year, SmartCEO looks for CEOs who are true leaders among their peers. More than company revenues, profits and community popularity, SmartCEO's CEOs of the Year have proven track records of innovation and bringing value to the marketplace. They lead more than just companies; they lead industries in new directions.

A natural entrepreneur
Tim has always been an entrepreneur, starting from a pre-dawn paper round delivering the *Pittsburgh Post-Gazette* as a school kid. His work as a golf caddy, bar tender and apprentice chef at a local golf club funded his university tuition. To this day, he loves to cook for family and friends.

In 1983, Tim and his brother Tom launched The Waldec Group, one of the first computer resellers in Pittsburgh. 'This was when PCs were just coming out. Nobody knew what to do with them,' says Wallace. Waldec's clients eventually expanded to include U.S. Steel, Mellon Bank, PNC and the University of Pittsburgh Medical Center. 'After ten years, we sold our first company for a couple million dollars,' says Wallace. 'And we thought, "This sure beats working for somebody else."'[9]

He then co-founded XLConnect Solutions, which he sold to Xerox in 1998 for $420 million. He served for a time as CEO of the renamed XeroxConnect.

Prior to joining iPipeline in 2008, he became interim President and COO of MEDecision, a medical software company whose share price had fallen from $10 per share in 2006 to less than $2. Within a few months, Tim helped to stabilise the company and prepare it for sale to Chicago-based Health Care Service Corp for $121 million, or $7 per share.

The moment the MEDecision sale closed, Tim joined iPipeline and set about expanding the business. In 2012, he raised a further $71.4 million in venture capital, which placed iPipeline at No. 8 on a list of the nation's largest venture capital deals for the year. In 2015, $8 billion VC firm Thoma Bravo acquired 100% of iPipeline. 'iPipeline typifies what we look for in an investment opportunity,' said Holden Spaht, a Managing Partner at Thoma Bravo. 'The company is a market leader with a mission critical product offering and has a strong secular growth opportunity from the continued migration of life insurance applications from print to digital.'

Tim Wallace: Change Catalyst
Leading change comes naturally to Tim. As a matter of instinct, he incorporates virtually every ingredient for successful change that I have outlined in this book. He gives his people, his shareholders and his customers complete clarity of where the business is going and why. His businesses always start with the customers: iPipeline exists to improve the experience, economics and outcomes for insurance carriers, agents and the end consumers they all serve. He engages with people at all levels of the organisation. In fact, he had flash cards printed with every employee's name and photo so that he could memorise exactly who everyone was. He naturally finds the emotional triggers for everyone in the organisation – to make sure each and every employee is genuinely up for the change. He makes sure they anticipate as many of the implications of the change as possible. He has developed a strong, united and unwavering leadership team around him and he has worked with them to develop an open, honest and change-ready culture throughout the company.

Tim leads by example. 'I'll outwork anybody. I'm in the office most mornings by 6:30 and I love what I'm doing. If I didn't, I'd be doing something else.'[9]

(continued)

Tim is open and straightforward and he expects his people to be the same back to him. 'I tell you the unvarnished truth, whether people want to hear it or not. All too often you get into companies where the biggest elephant in the room is something nobody wants to talk about. I talk about anything.'[9]

He is never complacent: 'We can never stand still. We are always seeking to improve our offerings, our service, our reach, our customer relationships... To maintain our position as market leader, we need to stay hungry and alert – aware that our competitors are always looking to find a way to knock us off our perch.'

Tim is contagiously optimistic: 'I believe in trying to create really positive environments. The single best piece of advice I can give someone is to surround yourself with positive people. Negative people will disrupt and ruin the whole situation.'[9]

He also lives by the values of the company and expects everyone else to do the same. 'I take them through our core values and say, "If those values don't resonate with you, if you don't believe in this stuff, please leave, because you won't be happy here."'[9]

He hand-writes almost 500 thank-you notes a year for his staff when they go the extra mile. 'I can't tell you how much it means to people to get a hand-written thank-you note instead of an email.'[9]

And he builds his companies 'from the customer back'. 'If you're going to succeed, you've got to make them successful.'[9]

Tim Wallace has not 'merely' enabled the transformation of a company-with-a-good-idea into a market leader. He has, in conjunction with his iPipeline team, transformed an entire industry.

'We have only just begun,' said Tim. 'While we have made some excellent in-roads, the vast majority of life insurance policies still follow a costly, unwieldy, manual process. iPipeline has the potential to be three or four times its current size. Maybe even bigger.'

Considering that the company has grown 15-fold in the last 15 years, that is quite a prediction. But given the size of the market opportunity, the fact that the customer is firmly at the heart of this excellent company, their clarity of purpose, their clarity of strategy, their complete lack of complacency and with the skills of a renowned change leader at the helm – I fully expect their success to continue apace. And the entire life insurance industry will be far better off as a consequence.

2. Michael Sheargold: Real Estate Change Catalyst

Michael Sheargold is a force of nature.

He is eternally optimistic and permanently 'on' with boundless enthusiasm. He is also transforming the Australian real estate industry. And he's not even a real estate guy.

Michael is one of the most sought-after business coaches Downunder. An hour with him and you not only believe you can achieve more than you had ever hoped was possible, you can also see how to go about doing it. As he likes to say, 'The power of an idea is in its implementation.' Michael is all about results.

But Michael does so much more than harness the power of positive thinking. He helps his clients give themselves permission to succeed – and then he gives them the tools to make it happen.

Michael fell into real estate. He began his first entrepreneurial venture the moment he left school late in 1980. Rather than opting for university, he acquired *Queensland Motorcycle News* and transformed it into a going concern. He knew nothing about publishing but, as the State's youth motocross champion, he knew practically everything about motorcycles. He sold the magazine a few years later for a profit and switched his attention to learning how to sell, and the area he chose was the fledgling world of personal computers. His next

(continued)

step would change his life. He found a Canadian company producing innovative time management systems and obtained a franchise for Australia. Pretty soon, every second business person in the Sydney Central Business District could be seen striding around the city with their 'Priority Manager' folio tucked under their arm – and every one of them had been trained by Michael Sheargold.

One of these new Priority Management converts was a young realtor by the name of John McGrath, owner of a new and exciting agency in the east of the city. After turning all of his staff into 'Priority Managers', John asked Michael if he did sales training. Never one to miss an opportunity to say, 'yes', Michael's instantaneous reply was, 'Of course!' He was a great trainer and a great salesperson; of course he could do sales training!

The sales training was a great success. John embarked on a nationwide acquisition and growth programme – and each new principal and sales team was trained by Michael Sheargold. John McGrath swiftly grew his business into Australia's largest real estate network and, as John's network grew, so did Michael's repertoire. To sales training, he added negotiation, business development, practice management, managing people, leading people, motivating people... McGrath's principals and agents weren't just good salespeople; they were good business people. John then wrote a best-selling book about the experience in which he credited Michael for much of his success. Michael's business exploded as owners of real estate agencies across the country wanted a piece of the Sheargold magic.

Michael wanted to do more than teach realtors how to sell. He wanted to change the way they worked. He wanted to help them improve the way they managed their businesses. He wanted to turn them into better business people. He wanted to enable them to achieve their personal aspirations. He wanted to help them do the same for their people. He wanted to transform the industry.

Real estate agents have a reputation for helping people sell their properties; extracting as much money as possible from buyers – and moving on. That is not a sustainable business model as it shrinks an agent's market to a quarter of its potential. Today's sellers are tomorrow's buyers, and vice versa. The buyer who has paid too much will think twice about returning to the agent in question.

Successful businesses are based on repeat customers and word of mouth. In the real estate game, this means treating both seller and buyer well; building a reputation for fairness and service.

Furthermore, just because someone is a good salesperson does not mean they are a good business person. And, as is equally true in so many other industries, real estate principals are fundamentally salespeople at heart. Yet, when you are running your own business, you need to be more than your company's Sales Director. You also need to be Chief Executive Officer, Chief Marketing Officer, Chief Finance Officer, Chief Operations Officer, HR Director, Head Coach, People Manager and Leader.

Michael knew this from personal experience. He also knew that the industry was full of business owners who were crying out for help – and that the tools he had developed with McGrath were applicable to any and every agency in the country.

And so the Real Estate Results Network was born, with a vision to be 'the most dynamic network of forward-thinking estate agents who set a new benchmark in the real estate profession'.

For the last 20 years, Michael has been on a mission to transform the lives of real estate agents and their clients, or, as he puts it: 'To build the best business support system that creates for our members awesome results in their business and personal lives.'

RER Network ensures that each member's business has the right Strategy, the right Structure, the right Standards, the right Systems, the right Skills, the right Service and the right Support to stand out in their market in a positive and significant way.

The Real Estate Results Network has grown to encompass 70 offices from across Australia and New Zealand and 1400 Principals, Sales Managers, Agents and Property Managers. In any 12-month period,

(continued)

RER Network members win around 13 000 listings, sell 11 000 properties worth more than $9 billion and they manage in excess of 32 000 properties for their clients.

'One of the secrets of the network's success is its exclusivity,' explained Michael. 'Once we begin working with an agency, we do not work with any other agencies in their primary marketing area.'

'The second is that we support the independence and individuality of each of our members.'

'The third is the "network effect"; the fact that all of our members share insights and learn from one another. RER Network is a high-performing group of agencies that are dedicated to achieving outstanding results and helping one another to succeed.'

'The fourth is the quality, breadth and variety of the training and development we provide. This business is a people business. Developing people is the key to achieving a step-change in business performance – starting with leadership development and business planning. As I say to the Principals who work with us, "Your business will never outperform your leadership".'

The other core elements of the Network are Team Development, a broad and deep Knowledge Base, Systems and Resources, Brand and Marketing services and Recognition and Awards, and what Michael calls 'Products', encompassing a weekly 'Momentum' webcast, a weekly e-Tips newsletter and a library of high-quality video materials covering a wide variety of business-enhancing topics.

Recently, the RER Network offering has been expanded, with RER People, a specialist recruiting service, and RER Network Buying Power and Discounts.

Real Estate Results Network is a great business model, centred entirely on enabling its real estate clients to be more successful.

I asked RER Network's Managing Director, Shane McLucas, what the business could do to be even more successful. 'Clone Michael,' was his instant reply.

This is a common challenge for all successful consultancies – how to leverage the key Principal of the business. Global advisory firms have the same problem: the clients buy from the senior Partner with decades of experience but the work is actually delivered by others. Or, as Andersen Consulting clients used to describe it, 'The grown-up sells the business and then the school bus turns up to deliver.'

In order to get around the undeniable obstacle that there is only one Michael Sheargold, RER Network has created a programme – designed by Michael, developed by Michael, delivered by Michael, but one that leverages Michael's time as much as possible.

'The Internet allows Michael to be available on demand via pre-recorded videos, live webinars and, of course, our weekly Momentum and e-Tips products. He does a large number of group-based seminars and workshops and many of his one-to-one coaching sessions via video-conference. Of course, he is also available for in-person coaching, but that is priced at a premium,' explained Shane. 'Our clients buy a programme rather than Michael's time *per se*.'

And they love it. Here are just a few comments from RER Network's cadre of raving fans:

- 'I feel the best word to describe Michael as someone to work with is "genuine". Genuine interest in improving the industry. Genuine interest in improving the individual.' Chris Walsh, Newton Real Estate.

- 'My team and I have worked with Michael for nearly nine years and in my opinion, there is no other coach in the industry, in Australia or New Zealand. Michael is at the cutting edge and delivers upgrades and new initiatives with a clarity that gives us a strategic edge over our competitors.' Richard Young, Caporn Young Estate Agents.

(continued)

- 'He has been instrumental in our group's achievements and success – which has positioned Marshall White to where it is today. Michael has been coaching and mentoring all of us through the good times and the bad – he has empathy with each and every one within our organisation – his contribution has been invaluable and immeasurable to all of us. Michael's leadership, passion and dedication to the success of our people – and their standards of service – makes him not only an amazing real estate coach, but one of the most successful all-round coaches in Australia!' John Bongiorno, Marshall White.

Never complacent
But Michael and Shane aren't restricting their attention 'simply' to transforming the businesses and lives of a few thousand real estate agents, they are now taking aim at the entire industry – seeking to break the monopoly of the large listing portals that have a stranglehold on the industry. They are advisers and initial shareholders in 'Follow-It', a new mobile service that aims to reduce the cost of advertising a property from its current astronomical level and connecting buyers directly with agents.

Michael described Follow-It as being 'like Facebook for real estate. You can follow a house, a street, a neighbourhood, an agency or an agent and get real-time information pushed to your Follow-It app.'

Listing and marketing your house in Australia costs so much more than it should because of a duopoly between the two biggest listing sites, Domain.com.au and Realestate.com.au. Domain is owned by the Fairfax Media Group, publishers of *The Sydney Morning Herald*, *The Melbourne Age* and *The Australian Financial Review*. Realising that the web had the potential to decimate their classifieds business, they simply moved it lock, stock and barrel online. It has recently been valued at $1.3bn. Realestate.com.au is Murdoch's more dominant version of the same thing. It is listed on the Australian Stock Exchange with a market cap of $6.9bn.

The Follow-It minnows will have a battle on their hands! Fairfax and News Corp are formidable and fearsome opponents who will do anything to preserve their pricing structures and market dominance. This is why the Follow-It team has positioned its service as complementary to the big portals. But whether the Follow-It technology service ends up being copied by the big boys, acquired by them or actually achieves the seemingly impossible and creates a genuine alternative for agents and home owners – odds on they will have made a big difference to the industry.

And 'making a difference and supporting the transformation of people's lives' is the driving force that motivates Michael Sheargold each and every day.

This is what makes him a Change Catalyst.

3. Michael Gould and Anaplan: The UK's newest unicorn

Anaplan is one of Britain's newest unicorns – i.e. a technology company with a valuation in excess of $1 billion.

Ten years ago, the company was one man: its founder, York-based computer scientist, Michael Gould. He spent the first two and a half years designing the technical architecture and coding the calculation engine before he hired his first handful of additional programmers. The first customer came on board in 2010. The likes of McAfee, HP, Pandora, Kimberley Clark and Aviva swiftly followed suit.

Today the company has more than 700 employees with plans to expand to 800 by the end of the year, 17 offices worldwide, including a global HQ in Silicon Valley, 600+ global customers, more than 100 000 people using its software and a revenue run-rate in excess of $100 million per annum. It has secured more than $240 million in venture

(continued)

capital funding and was recently named by *Forbes* magazine one of the world's best 100 cloud companies.

Anaplan has exploded. Why?

Because it is transforming the way that business decisions are made. It is that simple and that profound.

Anaplan gives business leaders the ability to do something that they had previously only dreamed of; it enables them fully to understand and accurately forecast the consequences of their new change initiative, strategy, M&A... before they pull the trigger.

'Understanding the implications of decisions is critical to good decision making,' says Michael Gould, echoing the sentiments in Chapters 3 and 13 of this book perfectly. 'And yet for large multinational organisations, this has traditionally been virtually impossible due to the jumbled architecture of disconnected legacy systems through which they have to try to navigate. Anaplan's core calculation engine is designed to enable business leaders to model highly sophisticated "what ifs" across a very large and multifaceted data set at lightning speed. It can process tens of billions of data cells while giving the user a sub-second response.'

The business planning cycle of multinational corporations can take months. For a large number of organisations, most of the year is taken up with planning for the next one. This was the exact problem that HP turned to Anaplan to solve. Its sales quote planning process started three months before the year end and the sales teams often wouldn't receive their compensation letters until the end of Q1. The process of setting top-down sales targets across geographies, territories and markets; receiving bottom-up feedback from the sales teams and cross-referencing it all with the manufacturing and logistics would take five to six months. Inevitably, due to the fact that the whole process was performed using hundreds of disconnected spreadsheets, it was awfully difficult to know if the data were accurate; too many letters would contain errors and could take weeks and months to be finalised.

After half-year revisions and a summer break, it was then time to start the whole thing over again. There had to be a better way.

HP signed its contract with Anaplan in February 2013. The new Quota Planning System was live five months later. The salespeople received their quote and remuneration letters at the start of the year. 'I have been at HP eight years and I have never seen a start to the year like this thanks to Anaplan,' said Sue Barsamian, Senior VP of Indirect Sales at HP. But it was not just the ability to set sales quotas efficiently, productively and accurately which attracted HP to Anaplan, it was also the ease with which the system allowed them to adjust on the fly when circumstances changed – which they always do. Salespeople come and go, currencies fluctuate, product release dates change... sales quotas have to change. 'Anaplan makes this eminently easier to manage and control,' declared Sue. But one of the biggest and unexpected benefits to HP was the ability to use Anaplan's analytics capability to get insight from the data in the Anaplan system. 'Anaplan helped us to find out what was working and, more interesting, what was not working in our sales model and allowed us to make changes that we never would have discovered or uncovered without the insights we can get from the Anaplan engine,' said Sue.

The leadership of Legal & General decided to reorganise the company from six business units to seven. The Chief Financial Officer was tasked with modelling the change in terms of costs and FTEs (full-time equivalents). He, in turn, briefed his financial controller to come back to him with a range of solutions for how this could be done. He expected the task to take a week to accomplish. Half an hour later, the financial controller marched into the CFO's office with much more than one answer – he was armed with a complete organisation model that enabled them both to process any number of 'what if' scenarios to help the leadership understand the implications of a variety of options so that they could make the right decisions. The financial controller was using Anaplan.

(continued)

Hundreds of similar stories can be found at www.anaplan.com.

'Customers first use Anaplan to solve specific problems; to create point solutions,' explained Michael. 'HP and McAfee's first priority was sales quote planning. For Barclays and Morgan Stanley it was workforce planning. For Kellogg's it was their entire financial budgeting process. For P&G it was managing their trade promotions programme. For Unilever it was supply chain planning. The key thing that each assignment had in common was that a plethora of spreadsheets were being used throughout the decision-making process – to prise data out of a variety of legacy systems, to consolidate data from different teams up through the chain of command and then distribute the information down again for revisions. It was time consuming and fraught with errors. We solve all of that and give control to the business people at the same time.'

'Now some of our clients are starting to look across their entire business – not just solve point problems but using Anaplan to connect all of their departments into one organisation-wide planning system.'

Anaplan calls itself 'The Smart Business Platform: Democratising advanced decision-making power across an entire business.'

The nightmare that is planning with spreadsheets

Large corporations have many hundreds of spreadsheets acting as sticking plasters (or 'Band-Aids' if you hail from the US or Australia) trying to make sense of their jumble of systems. Many of these spreadsheets are doing tasks for which Excel was not really designed. The whole process is inefficient, unproductive, wastes countless billions of dollars a year, is incapable of dealing with large volumes of data, suffers from the inevitable problem of 'garbage-in, garbage-out' and results in poor management and poor planning. How can a leadership team manage a company to the best of their ability with inadequate and untimely information? How can a leadership team plan properly without insight to help them make decisions? The answer: they can't and they struggle. This is a worldwide problem.

Furthermore, the accelerating pace of change in the world of business is only making matters worse. Long gone are the days when a company could set its five-year strategy and sit back to focus on the implementation. The business world moves far too fast for that. These days, strategies must be dynamic, fluid and tightly coupled with execution. (As we have discussed several times throughout this book: *'Strategy without execution is a daydream; execution without strategy is a nightmare.'*) The problem is that fluid, real-time analysis of information and dynamic insight-based decision-making are virtually impossible if we have to rely on a disconnected jumble of traditional IT systems.

The Anaplan technology
Anaplan's technology can crudely be divided into the following components:

- A calculation engine, the HyperBlock™, capable of managing billions of cells in a single model and recalculating in less than a second, with the ability to calculate outcomes from 'what if' scenarios in real time, combined with the power of predictive analytics.

- A data hub which sits between the client's systems and the Anaplan calculation engine.

- Connectors to industry standard ETL platforms like Informatica for data integration.

- The Living Blueprint user interface which places control of the system firmly in the hands of business people rather than IT departments; giving users the ability to define, manage and modify business rules – i.e. define the data they access, control how it is displayed and decide what they do with it.

(continued)

- An AppHub for developers to provide users with new and proven apps for the Anaplan platform.

The secret of Anaplan's success

I asked Michael what was the secret of Anaplan's success. He named four things:

Technology that works
That solves a major market need
Investment in the growth of the business
Building a great team.

But after spending some time with him, I believe there are three additional reasons for Anaplan's stellar growth:

Michael's determination to hire people who are better than he is
His relentless focus on delivering tangible and genuine results for their clients
His and Anaplan's ability to prioritise/'stick to their knitting'/focus on what they are best at.

And, as we have seen in the preceding chapters, these are key traits of a successful Change Catalyst.

In terms of the fifth key to success listed above, Michael not only hired a CEO, marketeers, salespeople, HR and finance experts but he has also hired experts in his areas of speciality – systems architecture and programming. I asked him how it felt to hand his baby over to other people and his reply was very matter-of-fact, 'I found people who were better than me in both of these areas, so I hired them. My role is now mainly focused on the customer engagement side – helping customers design their overall solution.'

With regard to the sixth reason for success, it can be easy for tech companies to blind their business clients with pseudo-science and baffle them with tech jargon rather than focusing on making sure the business client is reaping the benefits of genuine and tangible improvements. 'It is one thing to sell the big vision, but it must be anchored in reality,' explained Michael. 'We have to deliver real benefits for real customers. A key question we must make sure we answer in every engagement is "what's in it for me?". Every user of the system must experience a benefit, not just the leadership.'

And when it comes to the seventh key to success, Anaplan realised its core value lay in its systems architecture and calculation engine and that it would make much more sense to partner with renowned integration specialists rather than build their own. It also realised that it was never going to compete in the consulting arena (strategy consulting, process re-engineering...), so it works with the world's largest system integrators and has partnered with the world's leading consulting firms.

Several years ago, I came across a consulting firm with a very rudimentary version of the Anaplan system. It was a piece of software that extracted data from standard enterprise management systems and fed the information into a dashboard to help organisations manage 'strategy execution'. Several major companies were using it but the technology was in desperate need of re-engineering and revamping to turn it into a stand-alone SaaS-based software business. I proposed spinning off the fledgling and mainly part-time IT department into a separate entity and, with VC funding, transforming this prototype system into a global strategy execution platform. After all, SaaS-based businesses are valued at ten times more than consulting firms. After a year of discussions, the owner eventually decided against it – and another potential unicorn disappeared in a puff of lost opportunity.

But Anaplan appears to be the real thing.

Just read what some of its customers have to say:

(continued)

'I don't think Anaplan actually has any true competitors. There is nothing that actually has the level of detailed reporting power without running calculation scripts and other things. The big ERP solutions are part of a stack and Anaplan isn't – it's the platform you can do almost anything with.' Jeff Brobst, VP, FP&A, Intel Security

'Through using Anaplan, we have a more agile and efficient planning process.' Aviva

'Our set-up pre-Anaplan was classic spreadsheet nightmare.' Eat. The Food Company

'We have taken our FP&A team from spending 80% off their time processing numbers through Excel with a hope and a prayer that the numbers were right to now spending 80% of their time providing analytics to the business.' Service Source

'We are far more productive; able to reduce the time it takes to do sales forecasting.' Excelitas

The Anaplan story is not just a case study of how to turn a good idea into a highly successful and valuable global enterprise; of the merits of hard work, dedication, vision, determination, focusing on making a tangible difference, being aware of one's own limitations and knowing where your genuine value-add lies.

It is one of the ultimate Change Catalyst stories. Michael Gould and Anaplan provide leaders with the tools they need to change their businesses successfully; to make fully and genuinely informed decisions based on an understanding of the implications before they press 'go'. What's more, the Anaplan team are not 'just' transforming one industry – they are setting out to transform every industry.

And as their stellar trajectory attests, through unique technology that genuinely delivers, a high-achieving team-based ethos and a worldwide network of offices and global partners, they appear to be doing precisely that.

4. Unlocking the value of HR

For the first couple of decades of my working life, my philosophy when it came to the 'Human Remains' department was to avoid it at all costs. Receiving a call from HR was akin to getting a call from the Tax Department or a surprise visit from the police. Even if you are absolutely innocent of all possible wrongdoing, for a fleeting instant you find yourself thinking that you must be guilty of something. Maybe they've found those rude post-it notes and the handwriting analysis has just come through from forensics.

As a management consultant, I found that HR rarely had the budget, the decision-making authority or even the influence that they professed to enjoy. HR was rarely on the Board and if it was, it was rarely on equal terms with those useful departments that actually sold stuff, dealt with customers or counted the beans. This obviously has changed significantly over the years.

As an employee, HR's purpose in life seemed to be to make recruitment far more difficult that it needed to be, to pronounce edicts as a panicked reaction to the latest change in employment law, launch an avalanche of last-minute job cuts as soon as the market hiccupped, continually re-write the parking policy, to inform you of the derisory nature of your pay rise or to notify you that you were 'hereby at risk of redundancy'. HR seemed to rival Internal Audit as the department vying for the title of 'Best Business Prevention Department' and was

(continued)

a lay down misère when it came to the 'Best Department to Lay Low and Avoid' category.

However, each one of my preconceptions was to be turned on its head the day I was offered, and even more surprisingly, accepted, the job of HR Director. One day I was a worry-free management consultant, all care but no real responsibility; the next, with no history, qualifications or training in the profession, I was HR Director of a £300M, 1000-person subsidiary of a FTSE 250 company, wondering, 'How the hell did that happen?'

Half of the HR Department thought that appointing a 'business' person to lead HR presented an exciting opportunity for them and the department as a whole; the other half regarded my appointment as the gravest possible insult to their profession and the most ridiculous decision that the CEO had ever made. My wife tended to agree with the latter group.

What no one told me was that HR is tough! It has to do all the horrible, dirty jobs that no one else throughout the rest of the business wants to do, or, to be honest, is all that capable of doing. It is responsible for the thankless and Herculean task of 'right-sizing' the organisation – and instructed to do it quickly, cheaply, impossibly error-free and in a manner that doesn't result in any of the Directors attending an employment law tribunal. It is responsible for performance management of underperforming employees – because, let's face it, very few of the 'business' managers have any real competence in it or appetite for it. It is responsible for the equally impossible task of ensuring that the annual pay rise and bonus processes are fair and run smoothly. Every time an employee leaves (mostly, as has been proven in countless surveys, due to the poor quality of their immediate manager), HR is expected to fill the vacancy in the blink of an eye, and is blamed for any and every delay in the process. They have to counsel grieving employees and hear complaints against incompetent managers. They have to investigate claims of sexual harassment, of discrimination on the grounds of gender, religious belief, sexual orientation or disability. They have to promote diversity in the workplace, yet still make sure that all roles are filled with the best possible candidates. They have to ensure the company and its Directors comply with employment law and best practice without preventing the company from hitting its numbers. They have employees bursting into tears one day, and senior managers berating them for 'not putting the company first' the next. It's tough, thankless, underrated and underpaid. So what sort of masochist goes into HR?

Well, women mostly. The first thing to hit me as I walked into the foyer of my very first HR industry conference in 2004 was that the place was wall-to-wall women. The few men in attendance were shy, retiring wallflowers or outrageously superficial or on stage presenting. Why does the profession attract so many women and so few men? Are women more ruthless than men? Are women more emotionally intelligent? Are women more caring than men? The answer to all these questions may well be in the affirmative, but it still doesn't fully explain the imbalance. I think it's a combination of bad press and long, widely held prejudices about the profession. But perhaps, as in most things in life, women are just better at it.

Sesame's HR experiment

When Sesame and its parent, Misys (the UK's largest software company at the time), asked me to be HR Director, I thought it was some kind of elaborate prank. 'HR? That's the one thing not on my CV!' I blurted out as my mouth decided not to wait for my brain to engage. 'We think you'll be great. Bring a fresh perspective to HR,' was the response. Well, flattery will get you everywhere. So I agreed. I learnt more in those four years as HR Director than in almost any period of my career. As it turned out, appointing an 'enthusiastic amateur' to the role definitely had its advantages.

(continued)

As I had never been in HR before, I had full rein to ask every single dumb question that entered my head. Adam Morgan, author of the highly successful business book, amusingly entitled *Eating The Big Fish* calls it 'intelligent naivety'; the ability to ask the dumb questions which others are too afraid to ask. I'm not sure how many of my questions rated too highly on the intelligence scale, but I sure had the naive bit down pat! The whole department knew I was new to the profession; I had no way of hiding it, so I was free to ask all the dumb questions I liked.

The great thing about being completely new to a profession is that you don't know enough to jump into the detail. Your ignorance forces you to stay high level, paint pictures of what you want the future to look like and engage your team in working out how to get there – for the simple reason that you don't actually know the answers, or know where the pot holes are – and in HR they seem to be everywhere! In short, it forces you to lead, before your ingrained urge to micro-manage can take hold.

It also gives you carte blanche to pose the sorts of questions that would seem much too shallow, too frothy or too 'consultanty' if you had decades of experience in the profession. Questions like, 'What is the department trying to achieve?', 'How do we want the depart-ment to be regarded in three years' time', 'What do we want our HR people to be doing five years from now?', 'What's the purpose of the HR department?', 'What sort of HR department do you want to be a member of?'... all those sorts of slightly cringeworthy queries that most hardened professionals tend to avoid. When you are on the field in the heat of the battle, you are too busy or too embarrassed to ask these things, but someone coming in from the outside can seize this opportunity.

This is important because even in the most cynical British organisa-tion, these are the questions that the people in the department desper-ately want to know the answers to.

Key learnings from my stint as HR Director

I learnt an enormous amount from my four-year stint in HR. Some surprises; some blinding glimpses of the obvious. Here are the main ones:

1. **The people at the so-called bottom of the corporate hierarchy know a great deal more about how to make things better than those at the top.** Give them a vision of the future that they personally find compelling, the belief that this vision is not only possible to achieve but that the future of the company depends upon it, and empower them with the ability to work out how to make it happen – and they will deliver. In fact, they will surprise you with results that are considerably better than you could possibly have achieved on your own.

2. **Specialist departments such as HR need to think, speak and act as if they were at the sharp end of the business (but they also need to be capable of being at the sharp end of the business).** Otherwise, they become alienated, irrelevant and at best considered a necessary evil. For example, they need the rest of the organisation to understand that the appraisal/objectives system is not just a form to keep Head Office happy; it's not just something you have to fill in before your team can get their bonuses; it's not just a paper-trail exercise in case staff 'go postal' and start firing off discrimination claims against managers – it is a vital tool that actually enables the company to achieve its targets.

   HR needs to demonstrate that they understand the business and, even more important, how they can make a tangible difference.

3. **Get the basics right first.** An HR department can't even start to think of transforming itself into a 'business partner' on equal terms with other parts of the organisation if it can't get its of-

(continued)

fer letters out on time or keep everyone's personal details up to date. They have to prove they are relevant; they have to prove they are competent before they can hope to become change drivers.

4. **Preconceptions run deep.** If the rest of the organisation thinks that the team is incompetent and irrelevant, this attitude is not going to shift overnight. Your reputation will lag well behind your new-found confidence, professionalism and aptitude. Every mistake, however rare, will be seen as evidence that nothing has really changed. Swallow your pride, stick to your game plan and ride with the punches. It may take a while, but the rest of the organisation will come around eventually, usually when new recruits start to compare you favourably to the HR department of their previous employer.

5. **Recruit on attitude rather than knowledge.** Give me someone with a desire to work as part of a team, the desire to deliver real outcomes, the desire to share information and the ability to think 'out of the box' to use a hackneyed phrase, and I will employ them every time over someone who wears their years of experience as a badge of honour.

6. **Succession planning may be laborious, but it is important.** Too many leaders purposefully ignore succession planning to avoid the chance that they will be replaced prematurely by the successor that they have diligently developed. Confident leaders in companies with progressive cultures actively develop successors because their shareholders demand it. To do this, you have to be transparent and public in the fact that certain people are being developed as potential successors to the top jobs. Then those currently in the top jobs need to become mentors to their potential successors. When embraced by the leadership, succession planning not only mitigates the risk of a senior person leaving the company; it also prevents the current executives from

becoming complacent while motivating the successors to deliver outstanding results.

7. **If you can't change the people, you will have to change the people.** Shocking cliché, but, like most shocking clichés, true. You will always find people, especially in any specialist function such as HR, who cling onto information like a drowning man clings onto a life raft. They believe (they know) that information is power and they are genetically incapable of using their knowledge for the good of the company. They prefer to sit back and patronisingly criticise managers for the way they try to manage their staff, rather than using their knowledge to enable and assist their fellow people managers to improve the way they do their jobs. This attitude probably stems from their mistaken belief that they need to be perceived by the rest of the organisation as the flawless experts. If you put yourself on a pedestal in such a manner, it is much safer to stay on your perch and lob criticism at those below than climb down and show the world that you're only human yourself. Some people won't change, so they need to be replaced.

8. **Invest in management development.** The number one driver of company performance is the ability of the managers to motivate and enable their people to deliver. Every enlightened leader knows this instinctively, but it was proven beyond any shadow of a doubt by the Corporate Executive Council's 'Driving Performance and Retention Through Employee Engagement', as discussed earlier. The bottom line of the study was that the ability of managers to manage people is the key to a company's performance.

The company I walked into as the newly crowned HR Director proudly displayed its 'Investors in People' plaque in reception. However, every employee who accidentally noticed it

(continued)

either laughed or rolled their eyes skyward. The company may have invested in filling out all the forms required to get the award but not in developing its people. So we designed an intensive and practical Management Development Programme to give managers the tools, the desire and the permission to deliver great results through their people. We aimed this programme at the engine room of the company – junior and middle management – for the simple reason that this was going to have the greatest impact on company performance. It did. We put every single manager through this programme and they loved it. Morale soared, team performance soared and staff loyalty grew.

When it comes to management development, most companies start with the senior leadership team, which can be the wrong way around – and besides, it was my experience that the senior managers were too proud, too long-in-the-tooth or too scared to embrace such a programme... until their people started to come to them with people management issues and ideas; until they saw their managers and team leaders grow in confidence and use techniques that the senior managers either didn't know or had never been taught. Eventually, the senior managers started to complain that they weren't getting any development. Then we knew it was time to announce the next step – The Leadership Development Programme.

After only a year of such management development programmes, new starters were citing the fact that they heard we invested in people development, and existing employees were citing the development they received as being one of the key reasons for recommending their friends to join the company. Word gets around. Apart from enhanced recruiting, improved morale and better performance stemming directly from better people management, I can't think of one reason why anyone would want to waste money on people development.

9. **The roles that are pivotal to a company's success are not always the most senior ones.** Ask many companies to list their pivotal roles and they will simply download the org chart and start from the top, which is either lazy or sycophantic, or both. I recommend defining a 'pivotal role' as one which has a significant direct impact on a company's performance, and being harsh with selection. Start with a small handful of roles. To help with the selection and deselection process, you may wish to add two extra criteria that must be met for a role to be considered truly pivotal:

   a. If Superman or Homer Simpson was in the role, would they make a significant difference one way or the other?

   b. Could this role be a source of tangible competitive advantage?

   You may then discover that the Sales Director is not a pivotal role, but the Major Accounts Manager is (and the star performer in the role needs to be looked after at all costs); you may find that the Finance Director may not be pivotal, but the Customer Service Director is; that the Governance Director may not be pivotal but the Head of Compliance is. You may find that the second or third tiers of the company possess a gold mine of pivotal roles – and often a gold mine of unexploited talent, too, but that's a different subject entirely. In this process we are playing the ball not the man; it is the role we are assessing for its 'pivotal-ness', not the person in it. The latter is talent management and it is too easy to get the two things confused.

   So, you've identified your pivotal roles, but what do you do with them? Make sure you have put your top people in these roles, make sure that they perform and make sure you have a

(continued)

string of highly credible successors for each of these roles, for they are the jobs upon which the company's future depends.

10. **Take talent management and development seriously.** Most companies have 'talent development programmes' that involve endless form filling, biannual day-long talent assessment meetings and a pseudo-scientific form of corporate Suduko known as The Nine-Box Grid. If used properly, it can add a great deal of value. If not, well... actually, just use it properly (see Chapter 33 Your People).

11. **It's the outcome that is important, not the process.** I'd rather have a manager scribble out clear, measurable objectives on the back of a toilet roll than have them waste agonising hours trying to get their head around HR's latest SMART form. Not everyone will like your forms or your process, but who cares; what's the outcome they are looking to achieve?

12. **The CEO holds the key.** For an HR Department to make the quantum leap necessary to live up to its full potential requires a CEO who is 100% committed to the retention and development of their people. It requires a CEO who doesn't treat humans as resources to be found on a balance sheet (I knew a CEO who actually said in a speech to his troops, 'the biggest costs in this business walk in and out of this building every day', and then wondered why morale was low...). It requires a CEO who 'gets it'; a CEO who understands that people are his key source of competitive advantage and is therefore willing to grant the HR Department the power it needs to help them turbo-charge the company.

13. **Trust your people.** We had a great time turning the Sesame HR Department around from a fragmented, humbled, accident-prone, ineffective, reclusive and disrespected department into one that was competent, vibrant, knowledgeable, enabling and, most importantly of all, a leader of change. And we did this by

unearthing some outstanding talent that already existed in the department and with only one new senior hire. Together the team of Lisa Winnard (who later became HR Director), Helen Jones (who went on to be HR Director of a spin-off subsidiary which was then acquired by iPipeline as fate would have it), Claire Duffy, Deborah Godbold (outstanding Management Development trainer) and their teams did all the work. I just pointed into the distance, stood at the white board and waved my arms around a lot, and made sure the rest of the Board gave us their full support. Their work was well rewarded when the team won an industry award for 'Outstanding Leadership in HR'.

Don't you just love happy endings?

5. Globalisation

One of the most dramatic economic forces of the last half century has been globalisation. One could argue that globalisation began many centuries ago when the British, French, Dutch, Spanish and Portuguese merchant ships explored the world and expanded their trade horizons. However, the globalisation I am talking about is the most recent acceleration of this trend – fuelled by the lowering of trade barriers and then the Internet.

How the West has coped with globalisation is one of the best examples of how *not* to instigate change.

Lowering of trade barriers around the world, spurred on by the rapid ubiquity of the web, has produced a global market for goods and services. The increasingly free flow of capital across borders has created vast economic benefits on a global scale – and has lifted millions of people out of poverty.

(continued)

The world is now far more interconnected than ever before, enabling flows of information and increasing political transparency, even within some of the most despotic and undemocratic governments. I say 'increased' transparency because many countries across Asia, Africa and the Middle East still have a long way to go as regimes restrict access to the Internet, afraid of the dissenting views that transparency inevitably brings. But globalisation, the rise of the middle classes within the developing world, the ubiquity of the Internet and cheap airfares have all served to increase transparency and the flow of information.

Prices of electronic and hi-tech manufactured goods have plummeted over the last few decades while at the same time their quality has risen dramatically. Televisions, smartphones, PCs, laptops, tablets, solar technology, white goods… we can now enjoy incredible quality at prices that were unimaginable only a few years ago. Advancements in pharmaceuticals and medical treatments are the direct result of global competition and massive R&D spending. Thanks to the Internet, research is cheaper and quicker than it has ever been, we can order goods from anywhere around the word, communicate with anyone on the planet, publish from our homes, book flights to anywhere, pay bills, bank, invest… all without leaving our houses. Globalisation has made our lives more exciting, more interconnected and full of increasing wonder.

Solar energy is now one of the cheapest energy sources thanks to the continual improvement of Chinese manufacturing. China can now produce photo-voltaic cells at a fraction of the price of Germany at the same or better quality. In 2015, Dubai went out to tender for a solar farm. By the time the contract was awarded, they were able to double the number of solar panels for the same price. In 2016, they are doubling up again. India is planning the world's biggest solar farm and the world's first 100% solar-powered airport. We will witness a proliferation of solar energy in the coming years – not because of the Paris Climate Change Accord, but because solar power is cheaper than coal-produced power. And this situation is not a blip; it is set to continue.

Globalisation has disrupted entire industries and entire new industries have been forged. In 2015, the performance of just four companies was equivalent to the entire gains of the S&P 500 – Facebook, Amazon, Netflix and Google. Every one of these was a humble start-up 20 years ago. Two of them have disrupted existing industries; Netflix (along with its imitators in Amazon Prime and Apple TV) has destroyed Blockbuster and an entire video industry and Amazon has changed the entire landscape of retailing across the Western world as all but the best prime-location shopping malls and department stores are struggling to be successful commercially.

Globalisation has indeed changed the world.

However, common to many change initiatives, the leaders responsible for driving globalisation (mainly Western corporations, governments and global institutions) seem to have forgotten to consider the dreaded 'I' word – implications. No one seems to have planned ahead.

While globalisation could indeed be said to have lifted more than a billion people out of poverty across Asia, South America and central and eastern Europe, it has also created a new underclass in the West as millions of lower-skilled jobs have been exported to lower-cost countries. This has decimated communities and created generations of hopeless people across the developed world. The dwindling demand for unskilled or semi-skilled labour in the West has put even further downward pressure on wages. Forty-two per cent of Americans now earn less than $15 an hour, a level deemed to be the minimum level for a 'living wage' in the US. (And to illustrate the inherent discrimination of American society, 48% of women earn less than $15 an hour, 54% of African Americans and 62% of Latinos earn less than this 'living wage'.)[10]

At the same time, globalisation has created immense wealth and vast global corporations – to the benefit of investors, pension fund shareholders, executives and successful entrepreneurs. While it has

(continued)

created scores of new 'hi-tech' jobs and careers which did not exist a generation ago, many millions of lower-wage, under-skilled workers in developed countries have been left behind.

Dangerously high inequality

The gap between rich and poor has expanded rapidly over the last few decades to the point where 1% of the world's population now owns as much wealth as the bottom 50%.

In the US, *income inequality* has expanded exponentially these past few decades. Someone in the top 10% now earns nine times the annual average income of the other 90%. Nine times sounds like a big difference; it isn't. Let's narrow our vision by a factor of ten and take a look at the top 1% of income earners in the US. Someone in the top 1% earns *38* times the average wage of the 'bottom' 90%. 38 times! But just hold on to your hat... the top 0.1% of earners enjoy average incomes that are a staggering 184 times the average earnings of the 'bottom' 90% of the working population.[11] One hundred and eighty-four times. The US CEO-to-worker compensation ratio was 20:1 in 1965. Today it is 300:1.[12] Roughly speaking, the average CEO is paid as much in a day as their average employee earns in a year. And, of course, unemployed people usually earn even less.

But *wealth inequality* in the world's largest economy is even more staggering. According to the Fed's most recent Survey of Consumer Finances, the bottom fifth of American households had a median net worth of just $6400 in 2013. (Reports from earlier years have this figure as negative.) The next fifth had a median net worth of $27 900. Let's be blunt; that's not much. If we move to the top of the food chain, the median net worth of the top 10% was $3.3m. The wealth of the top 10% is more than 500 times that of the bottom 10%. But that is nothing. $3.3m may seem like a lot of money, but it is 'chump change' to those at the very top of the tree (to use an Americanism that was designed perfectly for just such an occasion). The individuals listed in the 2015 Forbes 400 Rich List are worth, on average, $5.8 billion. Each.

The gap between the Haves and the Have-Nots has become obscenely large. And the Have-Nots know it.

The 2008 'Great Recession' advertised the fact that our political and economic systems are geared to help the rich get richer – while the average man in the street gets poorer.

The greed, dishonesty, hubris and downright fraudulent practices of Western banks and their co-conspirator rating agencies were laid bare in 2008 after the collapse of the benignly named 'sub-prime' mortgage market, which resulted in the disappearance of Bear Stearns and Lehman Brothers, the merger of several other investment banks and the bail-out of Fannie Mae, Freddie Mac and publicly listed banks and insurers across America and Europe. And who provided the funds to bail out the so-called Masters of the Universe? The taxpayers, of course. The same taxpayers who lost their jobs, had their houses repossessed and soon found their pay packets unable to keep pace with inflation. To add insult to injury, the man on the street could only watch as governments started printing virtual money in the form of 'Quantitative Easing', enabling the same bankers who had caused the devastation to earn bonuses anew through selling this cheap finance to one another.

In the eight years since the global financial crisis, average wages in the US and Europe have stagnated. In fact, a 2016 report by McKinseys declared that incomes from wages and capital were flat or fell for two-thirds of households in 25 advanced economies between 2005 and 2014. Only 2% of households suffered the same fate during the previous decade. To further exacerbate the problem, welfare has been cut and the cost of living has continued to rise. At least two-thirds of households in advanced economies have gone backwards during this last decade.

(continued)

Meanwhile, the FTSE and S&P 500 stock market indices have doubled, corporate profits have risen and multinational corporations have been assiduously avoiding tax.

Corporations lining their own pockets

Globalisation has also enabled corporations to use international inconsistencies and legal loopholes to minimise their tax. Many multinationals artificially shift their profits, on paper, to low-tax havens where they do little or no real business. A US group called 'Citizens for Tax Justice' reviewed the accounts of 288 of the Fortune 500 companies and found that, on average, over a five-year period (2008–2012), the companies paid 19.4% tax – far less than the official 35% corporate tax rate. Twenty-six companies paid no tax at all during this five-year period, while a third paid no tax in at least one of those years.

Microsoft, Apple, Google, Amazon and Starbucks have all been accused of avoiding UK corporate tax on a massive scale. In 2012 it was revealed that Microsoft paid no UK tax on $1.7bn of software sales by channelling revenues through Luxembourg. Apple paid less than 2% tax on its UK earnings during 2011. Google generated around £2.5 billion in UK sales that same year but paid just £6m in corporation tax. Global CEO, Eric Schmidt, told Bloomberg in 2012 that he was 'proud' of his company's tax minimisation strategies, adding that 'It's called capitalism.' 'We are proudly capitalistic. I'm not confused about this.' That year, Google halved its global tax bill by funnelling $10bn of sales revenue through Bermuda.

One would have hoped that all of this highly successful tax avoidance would at least enable and encourage companies to invest this cash in plant, equipment and building the business – with the resultant knock-on effect of boosting the whole economy. Sadly not. European corporate investment has actually decreased since The Great Recession of 2007/2008. Throughout the EU, the investment rate of non-financial corporations has fallen from a high of 23% in 2007/2008 to 19% today.[13]

In the US, corporate investment reduced by 20% in the two years immediately following the recession and has increased slowly ever since, so that now it is actually 10% higher than it was eight years ago. But this is the worst recovery the US has ever seen in terms of business investment. Eight years after previous recessions, business investment had rebounded to be 20%, 30%, 50%, even 70% higher than the level of investment going into the recession.[14] Not this time.

Corporations are hoarding cash. According to Standard & Poors, the top 2000 US non-financial companies held $1.82 trillion in cash and investments as of year-end 2014. Moody's put the figure at $1.65 trillion – a quarter of which was held by Apple, Microsoft, Google, Cisco Systems and Oracle. UK corporates hold approximately £500bn in cash, according to figures published in the UK National Accounts. Imagine the productive, economy-boosting uses all this cash could be used for if it was invested.

Even worse, rather than using their cash mountain for productive purposes, companies have been buying back their own shares – artificially inflating share prices even further. According to Standard & Poors, US companies spent $2.5 trillion buying their own shares in the five years from 2011 to 2015. While the 'right' reason for share buy-back schemes may be to provide some protection from hostile take-overs (although companies also say it is another way to return capital to shareholders – an argument that doesn't quite make sense to me), the 'real' reason I strongly suspect may be linked to the corporate executives' share-based incentive plans.

Compounding the situation even further, companies have been taking advantage of the cheap credit available due to government reaction to the 2008 Great Recession and have been borrowing vast sums. According to Bloomberg, US corporate debt reached $29 trillion by the end of January 2016. Global corporate debt has now reached a multiple of three times gross profit (or EBITDA – Earnings Before Interest, Tax, Depreciation and Amortisation).

(continued)

Thus we have ended up with the unholy trinity of vast corporate debt, immense unproductive cash mountains and inflated share prices. What could possibly go wrong with this picture?

A friend of mine regularly updates a chart of the spread between the non-financial sector net debt vs its net equity for the last 60 years. These two lines were far apart during the 80s recession, the dotcom crash of 2001 and the Great Recession of 2007/8. The gap is widening again.

All of these statistics, when combined with burgeoning government debt across the world and sick economies on every continent, serve to increase expectations of a forthcoming recession – which could easily develop into a crisis for the simple reasons that the world has not recovered from the last one and central banks are out of ammunition, having sent interest rates to below zero and printed eye-watering sums of virtual money. Of course, as happened in the last recession, it will again be the middle and working classes that end up paying the price.

The political and corporate elite know there is a problem

With a heavy dose of irony, 'inequality' was one of the key buzzwords at the latest Davos World Economic Forum.

Lady Lynn Forrester de Rothschild established the Coalition for Inclusive Capitalism several years ago as a 'global effort to engage leaders across business, government and civil society in the movement to make capitalism more equitable, sustainable and inclusive'.[15] The organisation's aim is, through changes in the way businesses operate and invest, 'to extend the opportunities and benefits of our economic system to everyone'. Members of the Coalition include many of the world's most prominent politicians, royals and business leaders.

Lady de Rothschild, CEO and Founder of the Coalition, accurately describes the problem:

'Since the financial crisis of 2008, capitalism has been attacked as a system that has failed to create broad-based prosperity. Because of this, and growing income inequality and uncertainty, there is a marked withering of public trust in business. Businesses, many of which saw their responsibility limited only to shareholder value, must work to restore trust from all members of society.'

The Executive Director of the Henry Jackson Society (HJS), a British think tank that was used to arrange one of the Coalition's all-star London conferences, described the problem in slightly more apocalyptic terms'... we felt that such was public disgust with the system, there was a very real danger that politicians could seek to remedy the situation by legislating capitalism out of business'.[16] This could be straight out of a scene from Ayn Rand's right-wing masterpiece *Atlas Shrugged*.[17]

Lady de Rothschild firmly believes, and is supported by an increasing amount of academic research, that companies that follow inclusive and sustainable standards perform better for their shareholders than those that do not. I applaud her initiative. Of course, the $300 trillion[18] question is how to transform these admirable aims and vital sentiments into real action. Given the political upheaval that 2016 brought upon so many parts of the world, the critical importance of this is now self-evident.

The massive popularity of Donald Trump and Bernie Sanders during the 2016 US Presidential Election was, in a rather large part, the direct result of a genuine and understandable adverse reaction to globalisation by the new American underclass. As was the 2015 election of Jeremy Corbyn, a far-left politician, to the Leader of the Opposition in the UK and the receipt of 4 million votes in the last general election by the UK Independence Party. The British Labour Party is now the biggest political party in Europe in terms of membership. The UK Independence Party is the UK's largest political party in the European Parliament. Across Europe, far-left and far-right parties are gaining

(continued)

popularity and seriously threatening the status quo. A large number of Britons who voted to leave the EU did it as a protest vote against immigration and globalisation; many of them telling reporters that 'they had nothing to lose'. The peasants are indeed revolting.

This was all inevitable and predictable – perhaps even manageable
Globalisation is an ideal illustration of poorly managed change; of a failure of those driving the change to bother to consider the implications of the change. Very little of substance has been done to help or look after those who were always going to be left behind. The fact that low-skilled Western jobs would move to developing countries was indeed an inevitable consequence of globalisation. This was self-evident decades ago. But virtually no planning was done to assist the people who were inexorably going to lose out. Globalisation meant that Western economies would have to adapt – while they would lose low-skilled manufacturing jobs, they would need to create more high-end manufacturing jobs, more hi-tech skills, more service businesses. While that may be logical, not everyone is capable of making the transition – and we neglected to look after those who were simply not able to do it.

When I say 'look after', I don't just mean 'hand-outs'. I also mean 'leg-ups'. Those displaced by globalisation don't only need financial assistance; they also need re-training and re-skilling. The June 2016 report of the National Federation of Independent Business (NFIB), America's small business association, announced that 44% of small businesses struggled to find qualified candidates to fill their vacant positions. Companies are finding it difficult to find qualified candidates for a growing number of higher-skilled jobs while a significant rump of unskilled and semi-skilled people are left floundering.

Like any change, globalisation comes at a cost. The cost needn't be civil unrest. It could just be money. If a small proportion of the immense wealth and vast corporate profits generated by globalisation were to be reinvested in the creation of a decent safety net and proper re-training and repatriation programmes – the numbers of displaced people could be minimised. All of this should have happened many years ago.

It is important that this is addressed, because the impact of the new wave of artificial intelligence and enhanced robotics will make globalisation look like a hiccup. A generation ago, China's factories were manned by thousands of people. The latest plants require a handful of people and hundreds of robots. Many workers across almost every industry will be replaced by advanced computers. This, too, is inevitable. So, unless governments wish to establish a police state that arms the few Haves against the multitude of Have-Nots, we had better start searching for solutions to look after those who are – and will be – displaced.

A glimmer of hope?

Two things happened on 13 July 2016 that gave me a glimmer of hope that, possibly, leaders may be starting to think about this. One was the maiden speech by the UK's new Prime Minister, Theresa May. She chose to eschew traditional Conservative Party rhetoric regarding the importance of business and tax reduction. Instead, she chose to focus on issues of social injustice. She spoke of fighting against:

> '. . . the burning injustice that if you're born poor you will die, on average, nine years earlier than others. If you're black you are treated more harshly by the criminal justice system than if you're white. If you're a white working class boy you're less likely than anybody else in Britain to go to university. If you're at a state school you're less likely to reach the top professions than if you're educated privately. If you're a woman you will earn less than a man. If you suffer from mental health problems, there's

(continued)

not enough help to hand. If you're young you will find it harder than ever before to own your own home.

But the mission to make Britain a country that works for everyone means more than fighting these injustices. If you're from an ordinary working class family, life is much harder than many people in Westminster realise. The Government I lead will be driven, not by the interests of the privileged few, but by yours. We will do everything we can to give you more control over your lives. When it comes to taxes we will prioritise not the wealthy, but you. When it comes to opportunity we won't entrench the advantages of the fortunate few, we will do everything we can to help anybody, whatever your background, to go as far as your talents will take you.'

Perhaps Theresa 'gets it'. Let's hope so. The proof, as they say, will be in the pudding.

The second thing that happened on that same day was Senator Bernie Sanders's endorsement of Hillary Clinton as the Democratic Presidential Candidate. Thanks to Senator Sanders's highly popular campaign in the Democratic Primaries, Hillary was forced publicly to embrace several of Bernie's policies. She pledged to *make the biggest investment in new good-paying jobs since World War II'* and to raise the minimum wage. She pledged to invest in a *'clean energy economy'.* She pledged to *'make college debt-free for all'.* She pledged to *'defend and strengthen the tough reforms President Obama put in place on the financial industry'* and *'to make sure Wall Street corporations and the super-rich pay their fair share of taxes'.* She also announced her intention to *'expand Social Security to match today's realities, not cut or privatize it'.*

But then she lost. Even with these pledges, the American victims of globalisation rejected her and voted for Donald Trump instead – not because they didn't like the things she was saying above, but because they didn't believe she would deliver them. Unfortunately, neither will Trump or the Republican-controlled Congress.

Universal Basic Income
Of course, some European countries (Finland, Holland…) are already several steps ahead and toying with the idea of a 'Universal Basic Income' – the payment of a fixed sum by the government to every adult over a certain age in the nation, irrespective of their income, whether they are in work or not. A UBI would most likely have to be funded by increases in corporation taxes and the highest income tax rates. Now, before my Republican-leaning friends start foaming at the mouth and hollering 'socialism!' it is not such a daft idea. If large enough, a UBI would replace virtually all other forms of welfare and remove the current disincentive for welfare recipients to return to work – as currently such people lose so many benefits that it is often not worth their while. Whether a UBI is part of the solution or not, we need to do something; we need to find innovative solutions to the impact that globalisation has had on large swathes of our population and we will need to find solutions to the widespread decimation of jobs that AI and advanced robotics will inevitably cause in the future.

Half a millennium ago, Sir Isaac Newton showed the world that 'for every action there is an equal and opposite reaction'. The wonderful irony is that in the US, the reaction of many of those displaced by globalisation has been to vote for a billionaire standing for the right-wing Republican Party. But let's be clear: the 2016 Presidential Election is only the beginning of this equal and opposite reaction. It is the start of the US's 'Arab Spring'. The displaced have awoken; they have found their voice; they have become angry and while they may be venting their anger at Muslims and Chinese and Mexicans, the real targets

(continued)

for their anger are establishment politicians and multinational corporations. They are unlikely to retreat into relative silence after the election
for the simple reason that, as we saw with Brexit, they have very little
to lose.

Change always comes at a cost. When helping clients instigate
change, I advise them that they must choose whether to *'pay now or
pay later – and it always costs much more if you decide to pay later'.*
This mantra is just as relevant when it comes to globalisation. I am
afraid we will now have to pay more.

The lack of change leadership when it comes to globalisation – the
lack of appreciation of the implications of the change – is now coming
home to roost. In *Atlas Shrugged*, the elite ran away to a hidden valley
to start afresh, leaving the unions and bureaucrats to drive the rest of
the world into the ground. Back in the real world, the displaced are still
with us – and due to the prolonged inaction of generations of Western
leaders, there are a lot of them.

And they're not happy.

Chapter 35

The Change Toolbox

This chapter contains a hand-picked selection of some tools, methodologies and models that I have found useful over the years. This chapter could have been hundreds of pages of its own accord, but in the interests of your sanity, I have only included a few of the ones that have really stood out for me as being particularly novel and/or particularly valuable:

- Strategy Framework

- Strategy Execution

- Organisation Design

- Creating Effective Leadership Teams

- What Does a Successful Leadership Team Look Like?

- The Nine-Box Grid

- The Performance Choice Grid

- Stakeholder Analysis.

Full-size colour versions of all the figures presented in this chapter may be downloaded from www.changeandstrategy.com.

A winning strategy …

- is anchored in reality
- is customer-centric
- is aspirational yet achievable

- is based on an honest appraisal of capability and risks
- is compelling and clear
- includes all of the components below – including execution

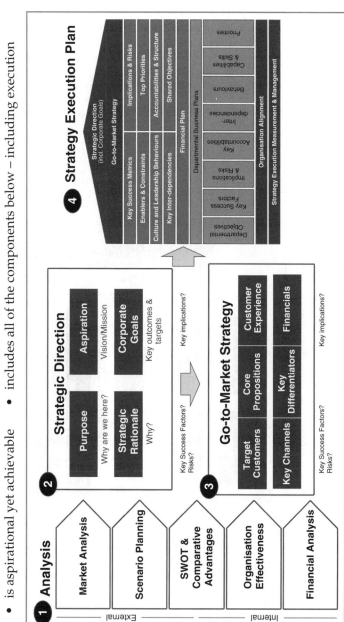

Source: www.changeandstrategy.com

Strategy Framework

A winning strategy ...

- is anchored in reality
- is customer-centric
- is aspirational yet achievable
- is based on an honest appraisal of capability and risks
- is compelling and clear
- includes all of the components below – including execution

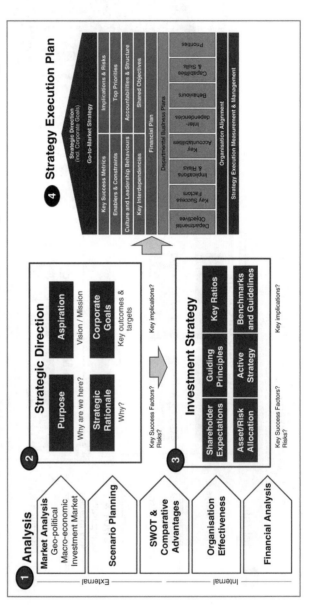

Source: www.changeandstrategy.com

Strategy Framework – for an institutional investor

A robust **strategy execution plan** is critical to enable every department to work together to deliver the outcomes that the business requires.

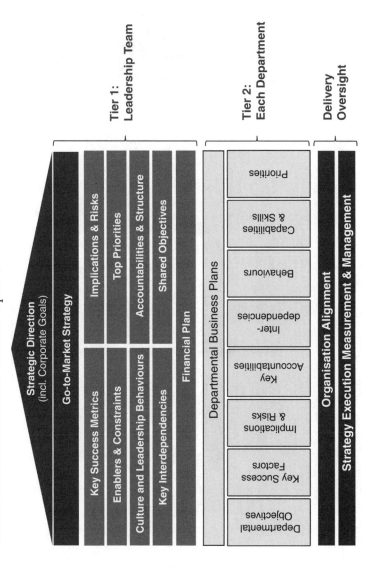

Source: www.changeandstrategy.com

Strategy Execution

Organisation Design is much more than structure. It involves clarifying the organisation's strategy and the implications of the strategic direction then designing every aspect of the organisation to make sure it is capable of delivering the required results.

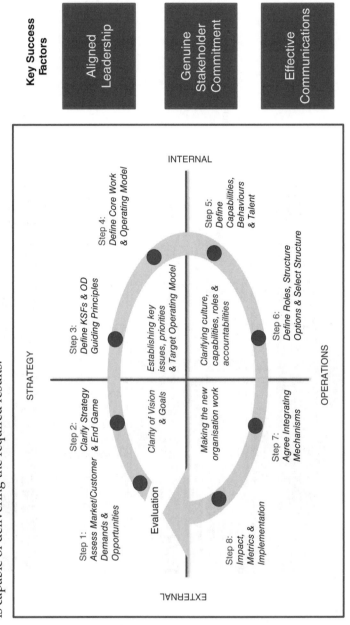

Source: www.changeandstrategy.com

Organisation Design

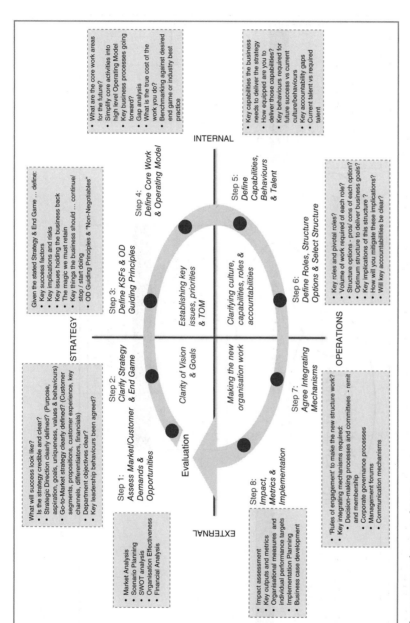

Source: www.changeandstrategy.com

Key questions for each stage

Extraordinary leadership teams need to maximise their effectiveness across three key dimensions:

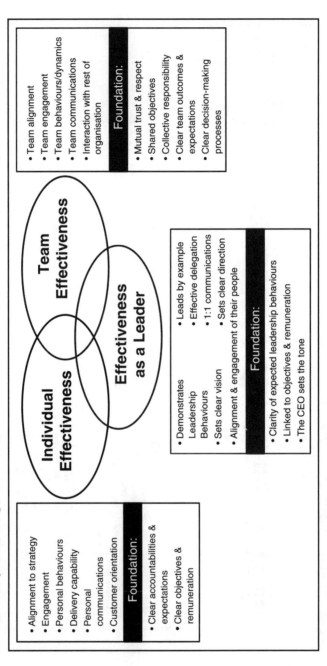

- Team alignment
- Team engagement
- Team behaviours/dynamics
- Team communications
- Interaction with rest of organisation

Foundation:

- Mutual trust & respect
- Shared objectives
- Collective responsibility
- Clear team outcomes & expectations
- Clear decision-making processes

Team Effectiveness

Individual Effectiveness

Effectiveness as a Leader

- Demonstrates Leadership Behaviours
- Sets clear vision
- Alignment & engagement of their people
- Leads by example
- Effective delegation
- 1:1 communications
- Sets clear direction

Foundation:

- Clarity of expected leadership behaviours
- Linked to objectives & remuneration
- The CEO sets the tone

- Alignment to strategy
- Engagement
- Personal behaviours
- Delivery capability
- Personal communications
- Customer orientation

Foundation:

- Clear accountabilities & expectations
- Clear objectives & remuneration

Source: www.changeandstrategy.com

Creating Extraordinary Leadership Teams

A leadership team <u>not just a team of leaders</u>

Based upon a foundation of:

- Alignment around a clearly defined strategy
- Clear expectations
- Clear rules of engagement
- Mutual trust & respect
- Shared objectives
- Collective/cabinet responsibility
- Clear decision-making processes

Behaviours of a Successful Leadership Team

Collective ownership of issues

Individual responsibility

Cabinet responsibility

Supportive of one another

Open to constructive criticism

Open to changing structures, reporting lines and responsibilities

Bring solutions as well as problems

Able to cope with ambiguity

Able to cope with matrix management

Focused on delivering business outcomes . . . together

Source: www.changeandstrategy.com

What Does a Successful Leadership Team Look Like?

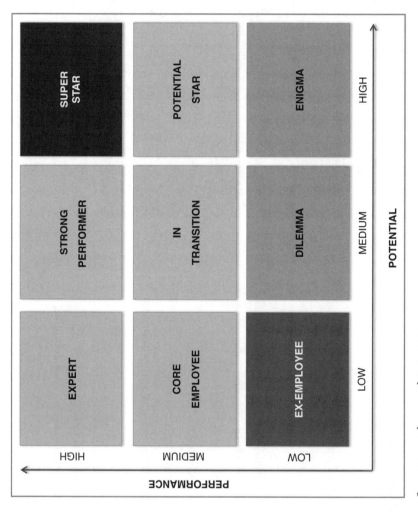

Source: www.changeandstrategy.com

The Nine-Box Grid

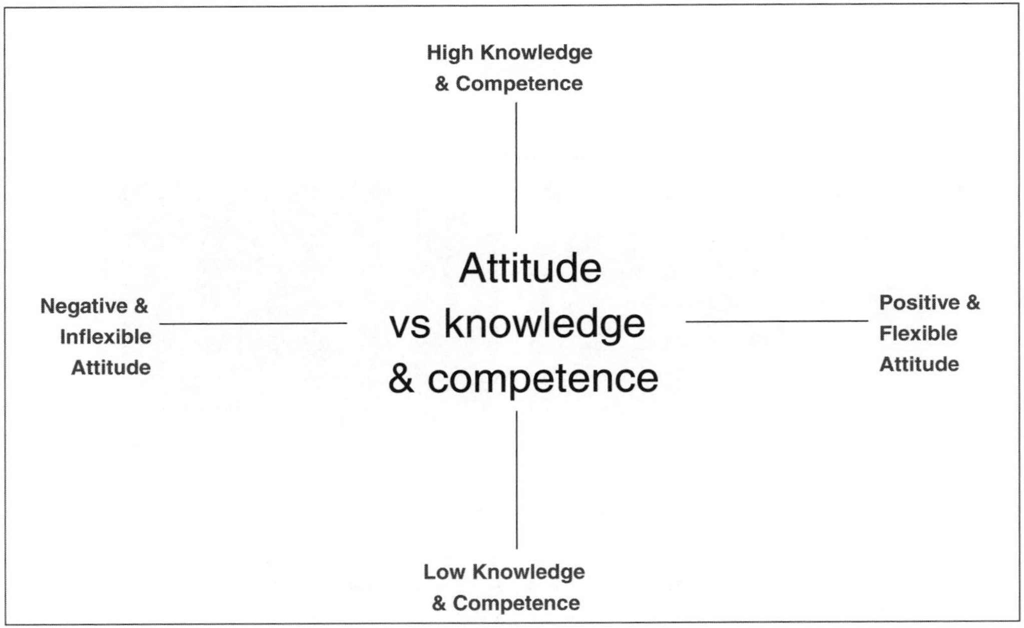

High Knowledge
& Competence

Attitude
vs knowledge
& competence

Positive &
Flexible
Attitude

Negative &
Inflexible
Attitude

Low Knowledge
& Competence

© linkubator

Source: www.changeandstrategy.com

Performance Choice Grid

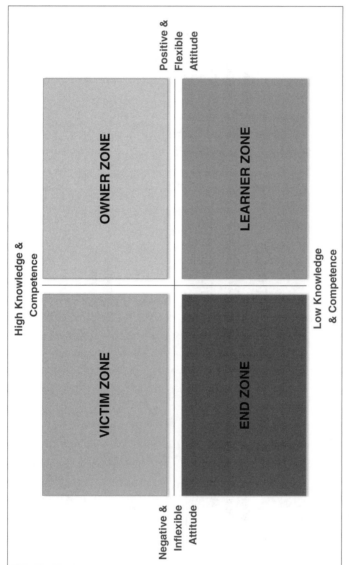

© **link**ubator

Source: www.changeandstrategy.com

Performance Choice Grid

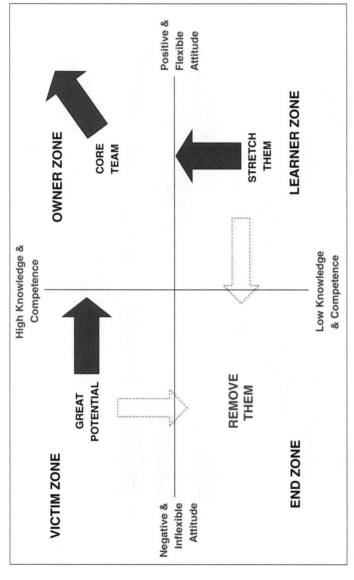

© *linkubator*

Source: www.changeandstrategy.com

Performance Choice Grid

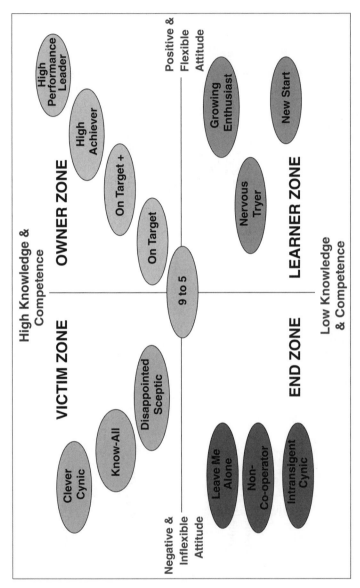

© *linkubator*

Source: www.changeandstrategy.com

Performance Choice Grid

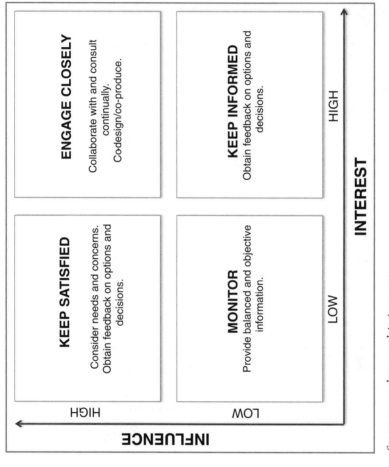

Source: www.changeandstrategy.com
Stakeholder Impact & Engagement

	Advocates *For the change and influential*	Acceptors *Likely to go along with the change*	Neutrals	Sceptics *Able to be persuaded*	Resistors *Against the change*	Saboteurs *Against the change and influential*
Names						
Default actions						

Source: www.changeandstrategy.com

Stakeholder Segmentation

Stakeholder name	Category	Impact of the change on them (Low, Medium, High)	Impact on the project	Influence on the project (Low, Medium, High)	What is important to the stakeholder?	How could the stakeholder contribute to the project?	How could the stakeholder block the project?	Strategy for engaging the stakeholder

Source: www.changeandstrategy.com

Stakeholder Analysis Matrix

Notes

1. Courtesy of www.skills2lead.com, as were a number of the examples above.
2. French mathematician, physicist, inventor, writer and philosopher (1623–1662).
3. Courtesy of Richard Rumelt 'Good Strategy Bad Strategy'. Seminar on US National Security Strategy, Washington DC, 2007.
4. Direct plagiarisation of Bill Clinton's internal campaign strategy, 'The economy, Stupid', during his successful 1992 Presidential election campaign.
5. Founder and CEO of Intel Corporation (1936–2016).
6. Hayden Christensen (1997) *The Innovator's Dilemma*, 1st edition, Harvard Business Review Press.
7. American politician and general who served as the 34th President of the United States from 1953 until 1961.
8. An American political activist, author, lecturer and attorney (1934–).
9. Quote given to SmartCEO's Marjorie Preston and published in her excellent 2014 article 'How Tim Wallace and iPipeline are Revolutionizing the Insurance Industry'. www.smartceo.com.
10. http://fortune.com/2015/04/13/who-makes-15-per-hour/
11. Courtesy of inequality.org
12. Courtesy of an Economic Policy Unit report by Alyssa Davis and Lawrence Mishel, 12 June, 2014.
13. The gross investment rate of non-financial corporations is defined as gross fixed capital formation divided by gross value added. This ratio relates the investment of non-financial businesses in fixed assets (buildings, machinery etc.) to the value added during the production process.
14. 'Why Business Investment Is Slumping in Five Charts' by Andrew Van Dan and Eric Morath, *Wall Street Journal*, 1 December, 2015.
15. http://www.inc-cap.com/about-us/
16. Courtesy of *The Guardian*, 28 May 2014.
17. Random House, 1957. Rand's fourth, last and longest novel about a dystopian United States, wherein many of society's most prominent and successful industrialists abandon their fortunes and the nation itself.
18. Total size of global financial assets according to www.marketwatch.com

Part Five

And Finally, Tell 'em What You Told 'em

It's a wrap

And so, with the dulcet tones and sage advice of my old Churchill-inspired Air Force Writing Skills instructor ringing in my ears, let me do my best to summarise the last 35 chapters.

Eighty-eight per cent of change initiatives fail. A similar proportion of mergers and acquisitions fail. A similar proportion of corporate strategies fail. A similar proportion of large IT projects fail.

If you actually pause for a second and think about this figure, it is quite staggering. Change has an 88% failure rate. No leader who embarks upon an exciting new adventure sets out to fail, obviously. Yet, seven out of eight times, they do.

The two questions that naturally follow on from this alarming statistic are:

1. Why?

2. How can I make sure that my next change initiative/M&A/strategy/IT project is among the one in eight that succeeds?

Why?

The top ten reasons why the vast majority of change initiatives fail to deliver their anticipated outcomes are listed in the left-hand box of the figure, starting with the main over-riding reason – that people simply don't like change.

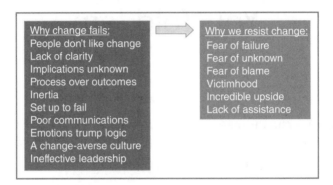

Why change fails:
People don't like change
Lack of clarity
Implications unknown
Process over outcomes
Inertia
Set up to fail
Poor communications
Emotions trump logic
A change-averse culture
Ineffective leadership

Why we resist change:
Fear of failure
Fear of unknown
Fear of blame
Victimhood
Incredible upside
Lack of assistance

Why people resist change, outlined in the right-hand box, is often due to a combination of three big fears (the fear of failure, the fear of the unknown and the fear of being blamed). The lure of victimhood is another powerful and paralysing force for inaction. To help people escape the cold comfort of victimhood, we must help them to take ownership of the situation in which they find themselves. A distrust of the leadership's mantra that the upside will be worth the effort, and a lack of support to make the change make up the list of the forces of resistance that we must help our people overcome if we wish our new initiative to succeed.

The other nine reasons why the vast majority of change initiatives fail include a lack of clarity about what we were trying to achieve and why; implications not being fully understood; an obsession with process over outcomes; initial or mid-term inertia; inadequate project set-up and governance; poor communications and stakeholder engagement; we simply forget that emotions trump logic every time; the existence of a change-averse culture; and/or a leadership that doesn't stay the course.

Emotions rule our decisions, no matter how logical and analytical we think we may be. Instinctively, we know this to be true, and our instincts are fully supported by the research of Portuguese neuroscientist, Antonio Damasio, who conducted a study of people with damage in the part of the brain where emotions are generated. He found that these people behaved quite normally, apart from one key impairment – they were not able to feel emotions. A surprising consequence of this also came to light – they also couldn't make decisions. They could describe what they should be doing in logical terms, yet they found it very difficult to make even simple decisions.

How can I make sure that my next change initiative/M&A/strategy/IT project is among the one in eight that succeeds?

The top ten necessary ingredients for successful change are displayed here. The most important of which is the appointment of a Change Catalyst to drive delivery; someone to guide the organisation to deliver the outcomes the business needs.

A Change Catalyst is a business person, not a project manager. A Change Catalyst is aligned to your shareholders, not just the stakeholders. A Change Catalyst understands the business: the drivers of profitability, the drivers of shareholder value, the drivers of customer satisfaction, the drivers of employee satisfaction. A Change Catalyst understands the market: the short-, medium- and long-term trends facing the industry and how successful competitors could

Successful change requires:

A 'Change Catalyst'

Clarity of what and why

Implications understood

Outcomes focus

Pause for reflection

Governance and planning

Genuine engagement

Emotional triggers

Strong leadership

A change-ready culture

take advantage of them. A Change Catalyst is regarded as a peer by the 'business end' of the organisation.

A Change Catalyst also possesses an 'EQ' to match their IQ. They are able to empathise with, and be respected by, people at all levels of the organisation. They are able to gain the trust of the company's leaders, managers and employees alike. A Change Catalyst makes every group feel safe and confident to discuss their concerns and suggestions openly without fear of adverse consequences.

The nomination of a Change Catalyst is the ingredient that is most often overlooked, and this common omission is one of the key reasons why 88% of change initiatives fail.

The other nine essential ingredients for successful change are completely aligned with the reasons for failure in Part One – complete clarity about what we are trying to achieve and why; detailed understanding of the implications of the change; a laser-like focus on the outcomes; a change process that includes a 'pause for reflection'; clear governance and thorough planning; genuine engagement of people at all levels of the organisation; finding the emotional triggers; a strong, committed, aligned and unwavering leadership team; and the establishment of a change-ready culture.

Culture looms large as both an enabler and an obstacle, which is why a whole part of the book was dedicated to corporate culture and the art of culture change. Your culture will determine your success. It is that important.

Corporate culture is the lingering effect of every interaction between the leadership, the management and the employees. It manifests itself in every interaction between the employees and the customer.

Culture change fails when it is de-coupled from strategy. Culture is not the remit of HR; it is the remit of the CEO and the entire leadership team. To change your organisation's culture, I recommend you treat it as a programme of work like any other. A culture change checklist was outlined in Chapter 24.

To help you lead change in any large organisation, the relatively new concept of 'Cultural Intelligence' is well worth understanding and developing. 'Cultural Intelligence' is a person's ability to adapt as he/she interacts with others from different cultures. The inventors and proponents of the term firmly believe that we can develop strategies and skills to improve our 'Cultural Intelligence', which will help us to distinguish behaviours that are driven by someone's background from those that are specific to them as individuals.

And while it is important to observe how people from other cultures tend to behave, it is arguably even more important to observe our own default behavioural settings.

Successful change starts with strategy, which is why the first three chapters of Part Four were all about this important topic – setting a Vision, Mission and/or Purpose; understanding values and exploring what a good strategy looks like.

Every strategy needs an anchor and a North Star. Something to ground it in reality and a neat set of words or phrases that capture what it is we are trying to achieve, why and how. Whether your organisation is a Vision company or a Mission company will be determined by your culture – by how your leaders and people respond to such things. Whether you proceed down the Vision path, the Mission path or a combination of the two, I do recommend developing a good Purpose Statement: a clear and concise statement of what we do and, more importantly, *why* the organisation exists. I love Purpose Statements for the simple reason that a good one brings clarity to an organisation.

However, no matter which set of words you choose to adopt, remember that their purpose is to set the direction and guidelines for your strategy.

As long as they are aspirational, credible, achievable, clear and help guide your people to deliver the strategy, they will have done their job.

When it comes to 'Values', I posit that every company has both 'real' values and 'right' values. The 'real' ones are the ones your employees believe accurately reflect your *actual* corporate culture. The 'right' ones are the aspirational ones you plaster on your walls and Annual Reports.

In fact, companies possess three categories of values:

1. What their customers think their *brand values* are;

2. What their employees believe their *corporate values* to be; and

3. The *aspirational values* that the leadership has determined to be critical to deliver the strategy.

Every company should identify all three and label them accordingly.

The Strategy Framework previewed in Chapter 27 is designed to help you engage your leadership team in the development of a holistic strategy – one that you will all own together. But, of course, even the most expensive and innovative strategy will be a complete waste of time if it can't be executed. The Strategy Execution Framework outlined in Chapter 28 has been designed to help identify the key elements required for successful delivery.

And successful strategy execution will also require attending to what some people incorrectly term the 'softer side' of business. Which is why we explored how to conduct Organisation Design in a way that results in an organisation that delivers – and how 'OD' is so much more than structure. We talked about the challenge of overcoming complacency, a condition prevalent within established market leaders. We discussed what a good leader looks like, how to build extraordinary leadership teams and spent a chapter talking about 'Your People', exploring a couple of models including the brilliant 'Performance Choice Grid' – one of the best people management tools I have ever seen.

After reviewing some case studies in detail, the key tools and models that were discussed throughout the book were then laid out in Chapter 35. Please feel free to download them from www.changeandstrategy .com, copy them or tailor them to meet your specific needs. They are living documents. They need to be improved and enhanced continually. And please let me know how you get on. Share your experiences at www .thechangecatalyst.co.uk and join in the conversation.

Change is indeed the only constant, and the pace of change isn't slowing down. Change is not something we can ignore or avoid. It is part of our lives: our personal lives and our business lives. As change leaders, we must embrace change personally and help our people to do the same – if we want our next change initiative/M&A/strategy/IT project to be among the one in eight that succeeds.

And to give you the greatest chance of success – appoint a Change Catalyst.

'It is not the strongest of the species that survive, nor the most intelligent, but the one most responsive to change.'

Charles Darwin

English naturalist, father of the science of evolution and author of *On the Origin of Species* (1809–1882).

INDEX

Join the conversation

Share your experiences in instigating change.

Tell us about the outstanding Change Catalysts you have met.

Do you disagree with some of the statements and opinions in the book? Perhaps you think certain areas of the book could have been covered in more detail. Perhaps there are elements I have missed completely...

Visit **www.thechangecatalyst.co.uk** and join the conversation.

---

change | strategy
www.changeandstrategy.com

To download the tools and models featured in the book or to explore the many ways that Campbell has helped organisations to instigate successful and sustainable change, go to **www.changeandstrategy.com**.

To discuss potential solutions to your change and strategy needs, email **campbell@changeandstrategy.com**.

Change is inevitable. Successful change isn't.